the Japanese Kitchen

the Japanese Kitchen

A book of essential ingredients with 200 authentic recipes

Kimiko Barber

Photography by Martin Brigdale

kyle books

This edition published in 2007 by Kyle Books
An imprint of Kyle Cathie Limited
general.enquiries@kyle-cathie.com
www.kylecathie.com

Distributed by National Book Network
4501 Forbes Blvd., Suite 200
Lanham, MD 20706
Phone: (301) 459 3366   Fax: (301) 429 5746

ISBN 978 1 90492 066 3

10 9 8 7 6 5 4 3 2 1

Text © 2004 by Kimiko Barber
Photographs © 2004 by Martin Brigdale
See other acknowledgements on page 240

Kimiko Barber is hereby identified as the author of this work in accordance with Section 77 of the Copyright, Designs and Patents Act 1988.

Project editor **Sarah Epton**
Designer **Megan Smith**
Copy editor **Robina Pelham Burn**
Editorial Assistant **Vicki Murrell**
Proofreader **Stephanie Horner**
Food stylist **Linda Tubby**
Props stylist **Helen Trent**
Production by **Sha Huxtable** and **Alice Holloway**

The Library of Congress Cataloguing-in-Publication Data is available on file.

Colour reproduction by Sang Choy, Singapore
Printed and bound in China by C & C Offset Printing Company Ltd.

Author's acknowledgements

Where do I start? I have worked with so many wonderful people on this book. But first, I would like to thank Jacqueline Korn, my agent, whom I regard more like my headmistress and who put me in touch with the equally formidable Kyle Cathie, my publisher.

The book would never have been made without the most professional and warmest help from my editor, Sarah Epton and the rest of the team: Robina Pelham Burn, Stephanie Horner, Megan Smith, Helen Trent, Vicki Murrell, Sha Huxtable, and Alice Holloway. And not forgetting Linda Tubby, who is the most artistic and reliable food stylist. I also thank Martin Brigdale and his gorgeous young assistants for taking such beautiful photographs and providing good music during the shoots.

I would like to extend my most sincere gratitude to Mr and Mrs Makazaemon Nakano and the senior management group at Mitsukan Corporation for their extremely generous help and guidance in my research.

Thanks to my three sons, Maxi, Frederick and Dominic, for putting up with a very busy 'mummy', who wasn't able to attend their rugby and cricket matches as often as she would have liked.

Last but not least, I would like to thank my husband, Stephen, for everything; his encouragement, support, IT help and, above all, his unqualified understanding towards my work.

Page 2: A Japanese housewife preparing rice offerings; Page 5 (l–r): A Shinto ceremony; Rice seedlings in Omachi; A young mother and daughter in traditional dress; A wheatfield; A detail from a rice paper float in the Napata Matsuri festival; An early twentieth-century family mealtime; Page 24: Walking single file through a rice paddy on the way to a family picnic; Page 40: Making noodles the traditional way; Page 58: Digging for bamboo shoots; Page 96: Japanese women collecting wild mushrooms; Page 108: Kaiseki lunch served overlooking a traditional Japanese garden; Page 118: A nori seaweed farm; Page 130: Gathering shellfish at Kabira Bay; Page 162: A fisherman searching for sea urchins: Page 172: Men carry a giant chicken float in the Karatsu Okanchi festival; Page 180: A Maiko in a corner shop; Page 190: Twins search for the juiciest tangerine in the box; Page 200: A woodblock print of Japanese women in Heian-period costume collecting medicinal herbs; Page 214: A factory worker inspects giant vats of fermenting soy sauce: Page 228: The backbreaking task of hand-picking tea leaves.

Contents

In the beginning When did it all begin? It is, of course, impossible to give a precise date when the first Japanese appeared. Archaeological evidence suggests that Pithecanthropus Man already inhabited the eastern part of the Asian continent, an area that later became Japan, some 70,000 years ago. About 10,000 years ago, after the Ice Age, the Japanese archipelago became separated from the Asian continental landmass and the inhabitants became stranded on the islands of Japan. The discovery in 1966 of some 18,000-year-old human skeletons on the southern island of Okinawa strongly supports the theory that my early Japanese ancestors came from southern Mongolia and interbred with the original inhabitants. These Stone Age men were nomadic hunters and gatherers. They ate what nature offered each season, consuming a wide range of fruits, nuts, grains, fish, shellfish, wild animals, and birds.

By some 12,000 years ago, those early hunters and gatherers were beginning to settle down and had started making pottery, though they were still dependent on hunting and gathering. This is called the Jomon period, named after the characteristic rope-imprint decorations on their pots.

Introduction

Rice: the soul of Japan

As a small child growing up in Japan, I never thought it strange that *gohan*, the word for 'cooked rice,' also meant 'a meal.' The two words are synonymous. For the Japanese, a bowl of rice is a meal in itself. It is the staple food, but its significance goes far beyond that. It is bound up with Japanese history, politics, economy, culture, and national identity; rice is the soul of Japan. From the earliest times, he who grew the most rice and managed the land on which rice was cultivated had political power. Rice was the alternative currency and was the most important source of tax revenue. Until the Meiji Restoration in the late nineteenth century, every feudal lord's wealth was measured in terms of rice revenue. Rice features in almost every religious ceremony and seasonal festival in Japan. It is the mother of many Japanese foods and drinks, including sushi and saké. It is central to Japanese cuisine: everything else developed around it.

The very nature of rice cultivation defined Japanese social structure and the behavioral habits of the nation.

Recent carbon dating indicates that rice was introduced in the thirteenth century BC (five hundred years earlier than previously believed), and brought to southwest Japan from China, possibly via the Korean peninsula. It was the single most important event in the whole of Japanese history and, of course, its food culture. Rice cultivation rapidly spread eastwards to the rest of the country, except to the northern island of Hokkaido, and laid the foundations for Japan as a nation. Former hunters and gatherers became farmers and began to settle on more permanent sites that became villages.

As time passed, the villages that were located on sites favorable for rice cultivation grew better fed and wealthier; they acquired more land and became more powerful. Amaterasu Ohmikami, the mythical deity and founder of Japan, is said to have ranked rice above all other grains, such as millet and barley. The first nation of Yamato was formed near Nara in the third century AD by a large agricultural clan, who were later to become Japan's imperial family. Even to this day, the Japanese emperor has a small rice paddy he attends himself inside the imperial palace grounds. Every year, in front of a group of rapt press photographers, the emperor of Japan puts on his waterproof boots and plants rice seedlings in the paddy field.

Rice cultivation is very labor-intensive and time-consuming. There is an intriguing explanation as to how the Chinese character for rice (米) was formed. The ideogram resembles the number 88 in Chinese (八八) and it was said that a farmer had to attend the plant 88 times to get one grain of rice. In becoming Japan's staple food, rice made Japan into an industrious nation. Its production cannot be carried out by a single farmer but requires a community effort—at each key stage of rice growing, villagers form a production line and cooperate with one another. The nation was founded as a village farming society. Social unity and cohesion, so essential for rice cultivation, are highly valued in Japan and are evident even in today's modern industrialized society.

Rice is a high maintenance crop that requires skilled land management. Japan is a mountainous country with very few plains suitable for rice cultivation, so rice has always been in short supply. It was not until as late as the 1960s that Japan's rice production finally exceeded its consumption. This long history of relative scarcity shaped the Japanese attitude towards rice and explains why the Japanese regarded it as a sacred food for the rich and powerful. Rice stores well, which is another reason why it became the major alternative currency in early societies.

By the early seventh century, the imperial court had established itself in Nara. Rice had become the staple food of the ruling upper class, while the majority of the population subsisted on poorer food such as millet or barley. One of the earliest records, dating from 720 in the Nara period, lists the various products—silk, cotton, preserved fish, seafood, and cooking oil—that were used as tax payments, but these are dwarfed by rice. The growing importance and popularity of rice led to the development of other foods, drinks, and seasoning ingredients to accompany and complement it. The early Japanese knew instinctively that rice is acidic and needed to be neutralized by alkaline food—and that is where salt comes in.

A nineteenth-century woodblock print of rice planting.

A child eating a typical packed lunch—a box of boiled rice.

The story of salt: the taste of Japan

In the beginning there was salt. The four original civilizations—Egypt, Mesopotamia, India, and China—all had major indigenous sources of salt, and salt was integral to each civilization. Salt is essential for human life and in the Japanese kitchen salt is the single most important seasoning ingredient. The country is surrounded by sea but it was not until the twentieth century, after a man spent twenty-six years traveling the country looking for a salt mine, that the nation finally concluded that the sea was their only source of salt. Salt is regarded as a 'purifying' agent and it features not only in almost all Japanese cooking, but is one of the most prominent features in Japan's myriad sacred ceremonies.

Archaeological findings suggest that as early as 3,000 years ago Japanese people were extracting salt from the sea by heating sand or burning seaweed. By the sixth century, with the development of rice farming, methods of salt extraction were more refined. Techniques for extracting salt from the sea included drying and burning seaweed, then mixing the ash with seawater; the ash and seawater mixture was then boiled or the seawater was left simply to evaporate. These early methods were neither easy nor efficient and, what's more, early forms of salt did not keep well and were very difficult to transport. It is no wonder that salt was so

highly prized. In the seventh-century imperial court of Nara, as in ancient Rome, salt formed a part of the salary paid to high-ranking courtiers. It was also an important tax-in-kind from coastal regions, and salt was donated to temples and shrines as a sacred offering. In fact, salt was worth twice as much as rice in the Nara period. The salt industry was highly valued and protected from very early on in Japanese history, and in the nineteenth century the industry was nationalized and the distribution of salt was controlled by the state. It was not until 1997, when the state monopoly ended, that the salt industry was liberalized.

It is impossible to separate the development of salt and rice. Prehistoric Japanese hunters and gatherers received enough salt in their daily diet by eating animal intestines, but when rice farming was introduced and rice was established as the staple food of the nation, an additional intake of salt was crucial: the early Japanese seem to have had an instinctive understanding of the neutralizing benefits of salt and the need for it in their diet. Salt served not only as an important seasoning ingredient but also as an effective antiseptic and preservative— vital in the days before freezers and refrigerators.

It was because of its scarcity and poor storage qualities that early Japanese people mixed salt with other ingredients, such as grains, beans, vegetables,

seaweeds, meat, and fish, to make *hishio*. This practice was almost certainly introduced at the same time as rice cultivation. *Hishio*, in all its forms, whether as a nutritious, fermented, preserved food or as a seasoning, became one of the most important elements in the evolution of the Japanese kitchen. There were four types of *hishio*; grain *hishio* (salt mixed with rice, beans, and barley, or other types of grain, such as millet, and left to ferment, the forerunner of the nation's favorite seasonings: soy sauce and miso); grass *hishio* (salt mixed with vegetables and seaweeds—the origin of all Japanese pickles); meat and fish *hishio* (salt mixed with meat, animal intestines, or fish and left to ferment

naturally, which later became *shiokara* and, later still, sushi); and fish *hishio* (which developed into *shottsuru*, a pungent fish sauce and regional seasoning ingredient still found in coastal parts of northeast Japan). The pungent fish sauce widely found in Thailand, Vietnam, and other Asian countries is closely related to fish *hishio*.

The ancient knowledge and technique of fermentation was further developed and led to the discovery of the most popular alcoholic drink; saké.

▲ *Gradation fields along the beautiful Japanese coastline.*
◀ *Salt harvesters raking salt into piles.*
◀ *Wrestlers throw salt to purify the fighting ring at a Sumo match.*

The introduction of Buddhism

The introduction of Buddhism from China around the middle of the sixth century and its subsequent adoption by some of the more powerful clans and later by the imperial family was one of the most important events in the history of Japan. With it came the second most fundamental change to the nation's diet (the introduction of rice being the first). It is against Buddhist belief to slaughter animals and birds for food, so to become a devout Buddhist one has to adopt a vegetarian diet. By the seventh century, during the imperial court of Nara, Buddhism had become firmly established among the ruling upper class. Religion and political power became inextricably linked, and emperors and aristocrats erected many temples to symbolize their power over the rest of the population.

While ordinary people of sixth-, seventh- and eighth-century Japan still enjoyed a varied diet, the upper class and the priestly caste were beginning to adopt a vegetarian diet. In 730, the first imperial decree banning the slaughter of horses, cattle, monkeys, and chickens for food was passed, in accordance with Buddhist belief that killing is sinful. It is doubtful, however, whether the decree had the desired effect—further decrees with a wider range of banned items, including fish and wild birds, were to follow later. Buddhist worship reached feverish heights in 752 at the ceremony of the Opening of the Eyes of the Great Buddha at Todaiji Temple in Nara. The killing of any creature was forbidden for the whole year—strangely enough, pork (for pigs had already been introduced from China as domestic animals) was the only exception—and fishermen had to be compensated with rice for their loss of earnings. It is curious that dairy farming never became widespread in Japan, even though it was flourishing within the confines of the imperial palace, where milk, butter, and cheese were produced. By the time Zen Buddhism had become established in the thirteenth century, dairy farming had disappeared completely.

▸ *A bronze statue of the Buddha.*

▴ *A mother and her children wash their hands before praying.*

Heian period: the age of refinement

From the beginning, Japan had been strongly under the influence of neighboring China and Korea. Between 630 and 894 over ten envoys were sent to the Tang dynasty court, bringing back a whole spectrum of political institutions and cultural and religious practices. But as the Tang dynasty went into decline, these costly and often hazardous missions were finally stopped, putting an end to over two and a half centuries of cultural import. In 794 the imperial court moved to Kyoto, marking the beginning of nearly four centuries of rarified, aristocratic society. It was during this period that Japan began to move away from the direct influence of China and to develop and refine its own cultural identity. Food was no exception.

By the early tenth century, regency politics conducted by the powerful Fujiwara family had begun to reduce the political function of the imperial court, leaving it with a symbolic, ceremonial role. The numerous seasonal ceremonies performed at the imperial court became increasingly formalized, as did the food and drink used in the ceremonies. This ritualization of food, and indeed of meals themselves, made the presentation and esthetic aspect of a dish more important than its nutritional value. For the upper classes the food was to be 'eaten with eyes' and was appreciated for its elegant presentation. Hearty appreciation of food was frowned upon and strict dining etiquette was observed during the meal. The most traditional Japanese cuisine of *honzen ryori* has its origin in this period. Meat had disappeared completely from the upper-class table and only a small amount of poultry was tolerated. Fish was allowed and much prized but since Kyoto was a landbound city with no easy access to the sea, it had to be eaten in small quantities and in preserved forms. Tables and chairs disappeared and, in contrast with the preceding Nara period, the diners sat directly on the floor in front of small individual tables or trays on legs. Spoons also disappeared and *hashi* (chopsticks) became the main eating utensil.

While the aristocracy sought esthetic refinement in all aspects of their life, including the food they ate, commoners were still relatively unconstrained by Buddhism and enjoyed a wide variety of food. In the capital, Kyoto, there were two regular markets: one in the east, which was open during the first half of each month, and the other in the west, open in the second half of the month. There were over fifty different products on sale as well as eleven regulated items, including rice, salt, hishio, seaweed, and fish. Many other towns and cities also had regular market days.

It was around the ninth century that saké brewing technique was refined to increase output and improve quality, as demanded by the aristocracy and imperial court.

The decorative roof of a Heian shrine in Kyoto.
Saké jug and bowl with cherry blossom.

Saké: the nectar of rice

Saké, Japan's famous alcoholic drink, was almost certainly discovered accidentally rather than invented. Instead of drinking, the early Japanese used to eat a form of alcoholic chewing gum called *kuchikami no saké,* meaning 'chewed in the mouth saké.' As the unsavory name suggests, this early saké was made by chewing cooked rice, chestnuts or millet, then spitting it out into a vessel and leaving it to ferment for a few days. We understand today that enzymes in saliva will turn the starch in rice into glucose, which will in turn be converted into alcohol as airborne yeast lands and grows on the chewed mash. This ancient brewing method was one of the religious rituals performed in the Shinto festivals and was still practiced until quite recently in some Ainu (indigenous) villages in the northern island of Hokkaido and in rural parts of the southern island of Okinawa, where only young virgins (who were thought to be mediums of the gods) were allowed to chew the rice.

The first milestone in Japan's long history of saké came with the establishment of a special brewing department within the imperial palace during the Nara period. A group of skilled artisans, who had probably come originally from China on trading missions, were appointed to make saké. (There were many different departments in the palace—silk production, weaving, carpentry, bookbinding etc—producing the wide range of products essential to palace life.) But in Kyoto during the Heian period, from the end of the eighth century, saké started to be drunk socially as well as being the most important oblation in religious ceremonies. While commoners were still feasting on versions not much better than moldy mash, the emperors and palace courtiers were drinking several different varieties of saké. In fact, records show that these craftsmen and women were producing at least fifteen varieties of saké for religious rituals, ceremonies and seasonal festivals, with a wide range of flavors and colors. Some were sweet, some were darker in color and some were brewed specifically for their high potency.

Outside the imperial palace walls, there were about 180 independent brewers in Kyoto alone. With the development and growing elegance of Japanese cuisine, saké had become an important element of the Japanese dining scene. Although the earlier craftsmen had come from China, the brewing techniques they subsequently developed were different than those practiced in China during the same period. For example, Chinese saké (*lao jiu*) used a glutinous rice and was brewed in sealed containers, while the Japanese used a less glutinous rice and left the mash to ferment in open-top casks.

The transfer of political control from the imperial court of Kyoto to the first samurai government in Kamakura took the saké industry outside the palace walls. Saké breweries began to flourish in the grounds of temples and shrines, using their plentiful rice supply, and enjoying their religious protection and the labor of their industrious monks. Fushimi (near Kyoto) established itself as the major saké producing area. As the country entered the civil war period (1467–1560), the fortunes of the saké industry rose and fell accordingly, but the technology of saké brewing continued to develop; pasteurization—its discovery based more on observation and experience than scientific experiments—began to be practiced. Texts from 1599 show that the three-stage saké brewing process used today had already been developed. And when polished rice replaced brown rice, all the key elements of saké-making as we know it were in place.

After a century of civil war, the new and powerful Tokugawa regime that was to last two hundred and sixty years was established in Edo (present-day Tokyo) in 1603. All aspects of the domestic economy grew and the saké industry was no exception. Osaka became the huge collection center for rice tax and the saké industry grew in and around Osaka. But it was the invention of *taru kaisen,* or 'cask ships' (specially designed seafaring ships for transporting casks of saké to Edo), combined with the discovery of high-quality water, that made Nada a new major saké-brewing center, which it remains today. Many saké-brewing families became wealthy and expanded their business activities to include money lending, rice broking, and the manufacturing of other ingredients, such as soy sauce and rice vinegar. Ordinary people drank lesser-quality, opaque saké while high-ranking samurai, who had lost their original military roles but had become members of the urban bureaucracy and great consumers, enjoyed the higher-quality, clear saké. By the mid seventeenth century, Edo had a population of over one million and was the largest city in the world.

In 1871, four years after the Meiji Restoration that reinstated the emperor as the central figure of the new government, the restrictive licensing system that kept out new entrants was replaced with one that allowed anyone who had the resources to make saké. This was aimed at drumming up much needed tax revenue for the new and impoverished government coffers. One year later more than 30,000 new breweries had joined the industry and halved the market share of the old established makers in Nada and Fushimi. The new government was interested in the saké industry primarily as a good source of tax revenue and kept raising tax every year until many smaller brewers were forced out of business. The larger manaufacturers rode the storm and steadily regained their lead. It was during this period that the present structure of the industry was established: the breweries of Nara and Fushimi produce 'national brands' that are available throughout Japan, while smaller, local breweries produce *jizake* (local saké) for regional markets.

The industry, meanwhile, continued to modernize itself and improve its production techniques. The tax department of the Treasury Ministry established a saké research institute in 1904 and three years later it sponsored the first state-funded tasting competition, a major industry event that still continues today. However,

the Second World War dealt a crushing blow and the whole industry came under direct government control. There was rationing and diminished production until the end of the war and in 1943, 3,340 of the 6,919 brewing facilities were commandeered for munitions factories, reducing the total output by a third. The quality of saké was also to suffer: the addition of pure alcohol to a fermenting saké mash, a practice that began in the eighteenth century but was banned in the late nineteenth century, was revived and legalized in order to overcome the wartime shortage of rice. In 1941, completely synthetic rice-free saké was invented—a shocking development for a drink that is meant to be the pure essence of rice! Although the practice of adding small amounts of alcohol during fermentation was later proved to give some benefit to the flavor and aroma, the purists argue that it comes at a price.

Slowly the saké industry clawed its way back to its pre-war production level, but post-war Western influence meant that saké was no longer the nation's favorite drink. In 1965, consumption of beer surpassed that of saké for the first time. Perhaps it was the threat of competition, but the industry began to focus on quality not quantity and introduced a clearer, more user-friendly labeling system. It is a far cry from the French *appellation contrôlée* system, but today consumers have a better idea of what they are buying and if non-rice adjuncts or flavoring are used, the label says so. The industry has also tried to update its image and is winning popularity among the young, especially women. Today, saké is making a comeback in the fashionable jazz coffee shops or slick bars in Tokyo.

▼ *Brightly decorated saké barrels.*

The Middle Ages

The power struggles between different factions of the ruling Fujiwara clan eventually led to the end of aristocratic regency politics and the emergence of the martial element, personified by the samurai (once employed by the aristocracy as lowly palace guards), as the new ruling class. In 1192 the emperor granted Minamoto Yoritomo the right to set up a new military government at Kamakura, west of present-day Tokyo. The Kamakura period was to last for just over a hundred years and was followed by a further two hundred years of political instability, punctuated by civil war, until 1603 when Tokugawa Ieyasu set up a new military regime in Edo, present-day Tokyo. The Tokugawas ruled in the name of the emperor, who was confined in seclusion in the imperial capital, Kyoto. This was one of the most turbulent periods in terms of food, too, and many fundamental changes occurred in Japanese cuisine.

The introduction of Zen Buddhism

The austere Buddhist sect of Zen arrived from China in the late twelfth century and with it came the strict vegan cooking of *shojin ryori*. The Zen monks, who are believed to have introduced the technique of tofu-making, originally practiced *shojin ryori* as part of their harsh training of self-denial. It was a simple meal consisting of a bowl of rice, soup, and one or two side dishes of vegetables. The expression 'one soup and two vegetables' still exists today and it sums up the basic structure of the Japanese meal. The three tenets of *shojin ryori* were that cooking must be done with sincerity, cleanliness, and good presentation to bring out the best in the ingredients and maximize appreciation of the meal. This doctrine survives in the modern Japanese kitchen and is the fundamental principle of Japan's cuisine.

Zen became popular among the ruling samurai class perhaps because of its austerity and the harsh training, which resonated with the military mind. However, it is interesting that although Zen Buddhism was quickly accepted by the samurai class and enjoyed their political patronage, the pragmatic samurai never adopted the strict vegan cooking of *shojin ryori* in their kitchen. The samurai class continued eating a variety of meat and fish and took plenty of outdoor exercise. *Shojin ryori* was confined to inside the white clay walls of the Zen temple.

The introduction of the tea ceremony

With the advent of Zen Buddhism came many new developments. One was the Chinese *ten jin* (snacks eaten between meals) and the introduction of new cooking techniques, notably frying with oil. Another was the reintroduction of tea. Although tea had been brought to Japan much earlier, possibly in the sixth century, it was regarded as medicinal, and had not caught on among the upper classes as an everyday drink. It was a Zen Buddhist monk called Eisai who brought back some *Camellia sinensis* seeds in 1191 and popularized tea drinking in Japan. There is an apocryphal story that Eisai, instead of saying a prayer for a shogun who was suffering from a bad hangover, offered the ruler a bowl of tea. By the fourteenth century, tea had become the most important nonalcoholic drink. The upper classes held tea parties, which were sometimes riotous affairs where guests bet on the variety of tea they were drinking, and which often ended in bouts of saké drinking.

During the turbulent civil war period between the fifteenth and sixteenth centuries, the samurai class came to appreciate tea drinking for the momentary peace and tranquility it brought; a distraction from the brutal reality of war. One of the most famous teahouses of Ginkaku Ji Temple (the Silver Temple) in Kyoto was built during this period. A prominent monk called Junko Murata laid the foundations of the tea ceremony—*chado* or *sado* which literally means 'way of tea'—and incorporated the Zen philosophy of *wabi* (serenity) and *sabi* (rustic simplicity) into the ceremony. If the Chinese and English are to be credited for making the consumption of tea into a way of life, it was the Japanese who elevated tea drinking to its highest level and created the sublime art of *cha-no yu*. Today's tea ceremony owes most to the famous tea master, Sen-no Rikyu, who put the Zen philosophy of tea drinking into practice and laid down rules governing every aspect of *cha-no yu*. The essence of *cha-no yu* is in its approach to life and appreciation of nature through the simple act of serving a single bowl of tea. *Cha-no yu*, led by Sen-no Rikyu, became such a highly respected social and intellectual activity among the ruling samurai and wealthy merchant classes that Sen-no Rikyu was appointed tea master by two consecutive samurai rulers of the era, Oda Nobunaga and Toyotomi Hideyoshi. In the world of *cha-no yu*, the role of tea master is not merely to serve tea but also to act as mentor and confidant, so it is tragic but not surprising that

▲ *Women at a* nodate *outdoor tea ceremony.*

▲ *A sunken hearth at a tea ceremony.*

▸ *A spectacular setting for a Shinto ceremony at Itsukushima shrine.*

Rikyu eventually became too influential for Hideyoshi's liking, and was ordered to commit ritual suicide.

Today, Rikyu's teaching of *cha-no yu* lives on through three schools: Ura-Senke, Omote-Senke, and Mushanokoji Senke, founded by his three grandsons. It is impossible to overstate the profound effect that the tea ceremony has on the entire spectrum of Japanese culture. The ceremony is the distillation of Japanese culture, incorporating as it does all aspects of the classical arts, such as calligraphy, scroll painting, ceramics, flower arrangement, architecture, and gardening. In terms of food, the tea ceremony led to the birth of *kaiseki ryori* and also *wagashi*, the traditional Japanese confectionery that became an important accessory to the tea ceremony from the middle of the sixteenth century.

The birth of *kaiseki ryori*

The rise of the tea party led to the development of *cha kaiseki*, a simple vegetarian meal served before the tea ceremony, which has its origin in the *shojin ryori*, the frugal vegetarian diet eaten by Zen Buddhist monks. The meal was served before the tea ceremony so as not interfere with one's appreciation of the tea.

In Japanese, *kaiseki* is written in two different ways: 懐石 and 会席. The first spelling means 'a stone held in the bosom' (Zen monks would hold a heated stone against their bodies to overcome the pain of hunger and cold during the long hours of meditation). Originally it was meant to be a humble meal consisting of a bowl of rice, soup, and one, two or at most three accompanying vegetable dishes. Although *kaiseki ryori* evolved from *shojin ryori*, it is different as it includes meat and fish. Today, however, *kaiseki ryori* is served outside the tea ceremony and this first spelling is often wrongly used to represent the elaborate Japanese meal that is far divorced from its origin. The other spelling of *kaiseki*—会席— literally means 'party place.' Though the meal comprised nine courses, it represented the simplified banquet that developed among the ruling samurai class in the fifteenth century. In modern times, it refers to a formal, elaborate party meal that is served with saké. Today the two spellings are often confused and used interchangeably to describe elaborate, traditional-style Japanese cooking.

The arrival of Christianity

In 1543 a Chinese boat with some Portuguese on board was shipwrecked off the southern coast of Kyushu, thus beginning 96 years of trading with Portugal, Spain, Holland, and England. These countries were grouped together and disparagingly called *nanban*, or southern barbarians, because they arrived in Japan from the south via India and China, and, to Japanese eyes, were clumsily large and rather hairy. Six years later a Portuguese Jesuit missionary landed in Kagoshima with the aim of spreading Christianity in earnest. Disenchanted local warlords were quick to 'convert' in order to profit from trading with the Portuguese and acquire newly imported guns and firearms. To this day Japan's Christian minority is concentrated in the southern island of Kyushu. The political and cultural impact of Christianity on Japanese society was devastating: it shook the institution of Buddhism to its foundations. As far as Japanese cuisine was concerned, Christianity, which allowed man to slaughter other living creatures for food, could not have been more diametrically opposed to the teachings of Buddhism. Meat eating was reintroduced and became popular among the newly converted warlords.

Nanban trading brought many new vegetables, fruits, drinks, and other foodstuffs, including sugar cane, potatoes, sweet potatoes, sweetcorn, spinach, chiles, peanuts, pumpkins, figs, bananas, watermelons, grapes, tomatoes, bread, biscuits, sponge cakes, and wine. Perhaps the most famous of all new imports was tempura. There are a number of intriguing theories as to the derivation of the word; in both Latin and Spanish *tempora*, means Friday, when the Catholics abstained from eating meat and ate fish instead. Some say that it came from the Portuguese word *tempero*, which describes a method of cooking. The origin of the word aside, tempura is one of the most popular dishes in Japanese cuisine and it is a good example of how the Japanese take something new and transform it to suit their own taste.

Lush, green tea fields with the snow-capped Mt. Fuji in the distance.

The Edo period: the age of feudal society

After some hundred years of civil war and political upheaval, Tokugawa Ieyasu emerged as the eventual victor to unify Japan. In 1603 he established the powerful new shogunate government in Edo, ushering in 260 years of the feudal Edo era.

The preceding period of civil war saw the collapse of society to a point at which family lineage or ranking meant little. In order to reestablish the social order, the government first divided the whole country according to rice productivity and carefully gave each feudal lord, or *daimyo*, his own territory. Those feudal lords who had been on the side of the opposition before unification were placed next or near to the feudal lords who were supporters or relatives of the Tokugawa clan, so the former enemies of Tokugawa were watched over by loyal *daimyo*. All feudal lords were made to present their wives and children as hostages who were forced to take up permanent residence in Edo. Furthermore, each feudal lord had to live in the capital every other year. This practice was called *sankinkotai* and was imposed to keep the feudal lords in check both economically and strategically. It had the added benefit of stimulating the development of the road system, which in turn encouraged wider distribution of food and gave rise to regional specialities.

To bring order to the population, the new government laid down a strict class system based on occupation. The samurai warriors were naturally at the apex, followed by farmers in the second rank, manufacturers and craftsmen in the third, and merchants at the bottom, as they posed potential economic threats. Farmers, who accounted for nearly 90 percent of the population, were given a relatively high social status in order to increase agricultural production, especially rice.

We have already seen that rice was the major alternative currency in Japan during the Edo period: each feudal lord's worth was measured in terms of rice production. At the end of the seventeenth century total rice production was approximately 25 million koku (1 koku equals 180 liters of rice). The farmers paid tax in rice and were effectively excluded from the currency system. The authorities collected up to 60 percent of farmers' annual

The ultimate balancing act: a delivery boy attempts to get through the doorway of a soba noodle shop.

rice crop and they used the rest to 'buy' other essentials, such as salt and oil. The government laid down detailed laws about how the farmers should live, what they should wear (they were prohibited from wearing silk, for example), and even what they should eat. They were forbidden to sell farmland and the farming of cash crops such as tobacco, cotton, and rapeseed was regulated. In order to ensure there was enough rice to feed the samurai class, ordinary farmers were not allowed to eat the rice they grew. They had to eat lower-quality grains such as millet, barley, and buckwheat for most of their lives.

The noodle culture

It was the country's dependency on rice, and rice alone, that gave rise to noodles becoming the major alternative food. Wheat and buckwheat were grown firstly, to supplement the farmers' meager diet after they had given up half the rice harvest and bartered away the remainder and secondly, to exchange for other goods. Both the central government and local feudal lords encouraged the development of new farmland and gave tax incentives to encourage farmers to grow a second crop after the rice harvest. Buckwheat was the perfect choice for a second crop. It can be harvested 75 days after sowing and can be

grown on hilly sites with poor quality soil. With the evolution of milling techniques, soba noodles made from buckwheat flour became not only the major supplementary food for farmers but also one of the most popular street snacks in Edo; in the Tokugawa stronghold alone there were some 3,000 soba noodle stands. Soba noodles gained favor in Edo, while in the other great cities of Kyoto and Osaka, somen and udon noodles, made from wheat flour, were the most popular.

The impact of isolation

Since the arrival of a lone Portuguese Jesuit missionary in 1549, Christianity had spread steadily in Japan, especially in the southern island of Kyushu. *Nanban* trading also proved to be highly profitable for the feudal lords of the region. This, however, caused serious military and economic concerns for the Tokugawa government. In 1616, in the interests of regulating foreign trade, the central government limited foreign trading to the port towns of Nagasaki and Hirado. In 1624, Spanish traders were banned altogether and Japanese trading ships were prevented from going abroad. But it was the revolt of Christian converts and local farmers who rose against their local feudal lord at Shimabara in the southern part of Kyushu in 1637 that finally provoked the government into taking the drastic measure of closing the nation to the rest of the world for the next 200 years. The stubbornness of the rebels—it took nearly two years of fierce fighting and heavy causalities on the government side to subdue them—shook the Tokugawa regime and stirred up the latent discontent of farmers in the rest of the country. In 1641 Nagasaki became the sole trading post and all foreign traders, except Dutch, Chinese, and

Korean ones, and all missionaries, were expelled. Christianity was prohibited and foreign trade became tightly controlled. The persecution of Christians was stepped up and Buddhist temples and Shinto shrines throughout the country were ordered to watch over the nation.

In terms of food, Japan's self-imposed isolation and the banning of Christianity reinforced the Buddhist vegetarian diet and made it the backbone of Japanese cooking as we understand it today. The country enjoyed an era of relative peace and prosperity without foreign influence, during which agriculture, fishing, and other industries developed. The merchants of large cities like Edo and Osaka led the growth in the domestic economy, becoming very affluent and developing their own urban culture. The lengthy isolation meant that Japanese cuisine had time to consider newly introduced ingredients and cooking methods and to develop its unique character and identity. It was a period of maturity for Japanese cooking. The expansion of agricultural productivity meant not only that there was more food but also that a number of drinks and seasoning ingredients, such as saké, soy sauce, and rice vinegar, became more widely available. The production of soy sauce and rice vinegar led to the development of *nigiri zushi* and *Edo mae zushi* (see p.21) in Edo.

▸ *Businessmen slurp steaming noodles at a ramen shop.*

▴ *A typical Japanese street food stall.*

◤ *Sushi chefs at the Fukuzushi restaurant in Tokyo.*

Sushi: the national favorite

Sushi is the generic term for a rice-based dish. There are more varieties of sushi than any other type of Japanese food and it is the undisputed national favorite. Its origin goes as far back as the mid sixth century when Buddhism was introduced from China. Sushi began life as a way of preserving fish. Fish was first salt-cured, then packed in cooked rice in a wooden barrel with more salt and left to ferment naturally for almost a year. As the rice ferments, the starch produces lactic acid which, together with salt, works as a natural preservative. Initially the fermented rice mash was discarded and only the fish was eaten.

This oldest form of sushi, called *nare zushi*, still survives as a regional speciality of the area around Lake Biwa, the largest freshwater lake in Japan. There are many historical records to show that *nare zushi* was brought to the old imperial capital of Nara and Kyoto as a form of tax payment. Both cities were landbound and, in the days of poor transport, fish, highly appreciated as a source of protein, had to be preserved.

It was not until the late seventeenth century, when increased rice production led to the wider availability of rice vinegar, that vinegar was added to cooked rice to give it its characteristic acidic flavor. The addition of the vinegar transformed sushi and led to the invention of many different varieties of sushi, many of them still to be found as regional specialities. The majority of sushi was still being made with wooden molds to press the vinegared rice into shapes—*nigiri zushi,* or hand-formed sushi, had yet to be invented. A sushi chef called simply Yohei (only the samurai class was allowed family surnames; the rest of the population in the Edo period had just a first name) is credited as the inventor of *nigiri zushi* in the 1830s. Instead of using a wooden mold, Yohei formed a rice ball by hand, smeared wasabi paste on it (the antiseptic quality of wasabi was already known) and added a topping of fish or shellfish. In the days of no refrigeration and poor transport, the fish topping was not truly raw but was marinated, salted, or cooked to stop it from spoiling.

Yohei's newly invented quick sushi gained almost instant popularity in the Edo area and soon many sushi chefs were copying his idea. *Nigiri zushi* is often called *Edo mae nigiri* or *Edo mae zushi*. The literal translation of *Edo mae* is 'in front of Edo,' which meant Tokyo Bay, where fish and shellfish were once in plentiful supply.

Although *nigiri zushi* is the most popular form of sushi today, both inside and outside Japan, it was not until the end of World War II in 1945 that it overtook all other forms of sushi. During the post-war food rationing period, the Allied Occupation authorities (GHQ) issued a directive allowing the exchange of one cup of uncooked rice for ten pieces of *nigiri zushi* and a sushi roll. There was no mention of other types of sushi, so in order to stay in business, the sushi chef had to serve Tokyo-style *nigiri zushi* regardless of whether he was in Osaka or Kyoto.

It was about the same time that street sushi stalls began to disappear completely, to be replaced by shops. Until then sushi shops served take-away customers during the day—mainly women, who were not supposed to be seen eating in public—and stalls, meanwhile, were a familiar feature on Tokyo street corners at night. There were over 6,000 sushi stalls, or twice the number of soba noodle stalls, in Tokyo alone. These stalls were hauled into their allotted position, which was strategically placed to catch hungry men on their way back from public bathhouses. Customers stood while eating, sharing communal bowls of soy dipping sauce and pickled ginger, and wiping their hands on a short cotton curtain hanging behind them. A sure sign of a popular sushi stall was a filthy curtain, which showed that many customers had eaten there.

Sushi has come a long way from its beginnings as a method of preserving fish. Today, sushi is gaining international popularity as the world's healthiest fast food. Sushi epitomizes the essence of Japanese cuisine: the careful selection of the freshest seasonal ingredients, clean and skilful preparation, and simple yet exquisite presentation.

The Meiji Restoration: the age of modernization

In 1867, the last shogun, Tokugawa Yoshinobu, returned the helm to the emperor, drawing a curtain over 260 years of feudal isolation. The new government was centered on the Emperor Meiji, who renamed Edo 'Tokyo' (Eastern Kyoto), and for the first time in over 1,000 years the emperor left Kyoto, moving to the new capital, Tokyo. The Meiji government feared that Japan was next in line to be colonized, possibly by the British, who had taken control of Hong Kong after their victory over China in the First Opium War (1840–2). The new government, dominated by former samurai from the west of Japan, was anxious to catch up with the West and encouraged the whole nation to learn and modernize as fast as possible. The old feudal class system was quickly abolished: farmers, craftsmen and merchants became equals and were allowed to adopt family names. They were no longer restricted in their choice of profession and became free to move around the country. In 1873 the ban on Christianity was lifted.

The modernization movement also extended to the Japanese kitchen and changed the nation's diet once again. To lead the way, the emperor adopted a Western hairstyle, wore Western clothes and served French cuisine at state banquets. At the New Year celebration in 1872, the Emperor Meiji set an astonishing example to the nation by eating beef: it was the first time in 1,200 years an emperor had eaten meat. Intentionally or not, the emperor determined fashion: to be *haikara* (modern) in the Meiji period was to wear Western clothes with a Western hairstyle, while holding a book translated from the Dutch in one hand and eating *gyunabe* (a Japanese interpretation of beef stew) with the other. A new culinary term, *yoshoku*, was invented to represent a whole range of Western cuisine as opposed to *washoku* (Japanese cooking). The most notable dishes to emerge from the period are *sukiyaki* (see p.56) and *tonkatsu* (see p.177)—all of them Japanese interpretations of Western meat dishes.

The emperor's gallant efforts to imbue the nation with Western culture were aided by an unfortunate medical incident in the army. The new government had set up a special regiment under the direct command of the emperor. The regiment was largely made up of poor, lower-ranking samurai, who were unaccustomed to eating rice on a daily basis. When they were served polished rice, which was a particularly prized food, they quickly developed severe rickets. The authorities had no idea how to deal with the situation and simply left the malnourished soldiers in the hands of equally baffled Chinese and German doctors. The soldiers in the German hospital were put on the hospital diet of bread and milk while the doctors tried to prescribe the appropriate treatment. In fact, there was no need for special treatment, as the vitamins contained in bread and milk were enough to cure them of their rickets and the group made a full recovery. In sharp contrast, the soldiers in the care of the Chinese doctors were given yet more rice and all eventually died. After this event, the Japanese army embraced a vitamin-rich diet of bread and milk for their soldiers. However, the rest of the nation's palate was much slower to become westernized and there remained a yawning gulf between the diet of the urban and rural populations.

The Meiji era brought many changes but perhaps the most significant was the end of starvation as a cause of death, as cheaper imported rice became available. Contrary to the common perception that the Japanese have eaten rice ever since it was first cultivated more than 3,000 years ago, until the late 1960s, Japan had never produced enough rice to feed the whole nation. While foreign trade was forbidden, the Japanese had made up for the deficit by eating other grains—such as wheat, millet, barley, and soya beans—and their by-products. The opening of the nation's kitchen to imports resulted in the introduction of many new ingredients, among them cabbage, asparagus, onions, tomatoes, peaches, grapes, tangerines, and apples. The brewing of beer from hops was officially promoted by bureaucrats and military officials in order to economize on rice, but it took time to spread throughout the nation. Meat consumption, especially beef, also took off. The records show that in 1867 there were just 7,000 cattle in the whole country, while ten years later the number had grown to over 20,000. Average meat consumption per capita was to increase more than tenfold during the next 60 years.

▲ *A caricature of a Meiji-period bureaucrat, sprawled drunk, wearing newly fashionable Western clothes—including stripey socks.*

The modern Japanese kitchen— some food for thought

The speed of modernization during the early part of the Meiji era was astonishing and for a while it looked as if Japanese tradition was going to disappear completely. Fortunately, as the nation became more prosperous and gained confidence, the newly introduced Western culture settled into a place of its own alongside traditional Japanese culture. The same coexistence can be seen in the modern Japanese kitchen. It is quite normal to find both Japanese and Western dishes served side by side at an ordinary family meal. During its first phase, this desperate rush towards modernization led to expansionism: first the Sino–Japanese war in 1894, quickly followed by the Japan–Russia war in 1904 and the First World War between 1914 and 1918. It was not until Japan's defeat in the Second World War that this dangerous, nationalistic expansionism finally ended.

Thanks to Japan's post-war economic success, it is often forgotten that the country was facing a nationwide famine immediately after the end of World War II. Had it not been for the food relief program organized by the General Headquarters of the American Occupied Force,

a large proportion of the nation would most certainly have starved to death (a fact not publicized or included in Japanese history textbooks). By 1955 the Japanese economy had made a remarkable recovery, helped by Allied economic aid and the special war demand made by the USA during the Korean War. The economic white paper published in 1956 declared that the country's economy was 'no longer post-war.' If the Meiji period saw the first phase of the modernization of the Japanese kitchen, the second phase came in the unprecedented economic boom between 1955 and 1973, when annual growth topped 10 percent and Japan's GNP was second only to that of the USA. It is now at that stage of maturity when food is no longer in short supply and the quality and composition of the nation's diet is being reviewed.

▲ *Modern-day Tokyo at night.*
▼ *A nineteenth-century woodblock print depicting sophisticated outdoor dining along the river bank in Kyoto.*

It is impossible to imagine Japanese cuisine without rice. Rice was introduced to Japan either directly from China or via the Korean peninsula during the prehistoric era, as long ago as the thirteenth century BC. By the sixth century AD, rice, a rich vegetable protein and carbohydrate, had become firmly established as a staple food of Japan and remains so to this day. Rice is the second most important grain crop in the world after wheat and today approximately a third of the world's population depends on this annual plant. Curiously, Japan only achieved total self-sufficiency in rice in the late 1960s, when its consumption began to fall as a result of the steady westernization of the nation's palate. Beans have always played an important role in Japanese cuisine as a major source of protein—particularly when strict Buddhist vegetarianism was observed—and the Japanese have developed numerous ways of using them.

1 Rice & beans

米 Kome [RICE]

The influence of rice on Japanese society and culture is described in the Introduction (see p.8). It is impossible to over-emphasize the importance of rice and the effect its cultivation had on Japan and its people. Rice is more than the staple food; it is the soul of the nation and the whole of Japanese cuisine developed around it.

How it grows One popular method of classifying different types of rice is to group them as either Indica rice or Japonica rice, a method first devised by a Japanese botanist in the 1920s. This classification is not entirely satisfactory, however, since there is a group of rice that falls between the two categories, called Java rice. Classifying according to the stickiness and the shape of the rice grain is practical and is therefore the most popular approach.

In Japan, it is Japonica rice, rather than the long-grain Indica or Java rice, that is grown, developed and refined to suit the tastes and climate of the country.

Today, there are over 300 different types of Japonica rice—more commonly known as short-grain rice—grown in Japan. Such varieties are highly labor-intensive and are not suited to large-scale, mechanized farming methods.

In Japan, young seedlings are first raised in nursery beds until they are large enough to be transplanted into water-filled paddy fields during the rainy month of June. The rice needs a long, hot growing season, but just when the young grains are forming in September, Japan often experiences fierce typhoons that can have devastating consequences. Rice also needs a warm, dry maturing period before the harvest in autumn. In general, the plant requires high maintenance, skilled land management, and good luck with the weather—it is no wonder that Japan never managed to satisfy its own demand until relatively recently.

Appearance and taste In Japan, three major groups of Japonica rice are grown: *uruchi mai*, *genmai,* and *mochi gome.*

Uruchi mai (Japanese-style short-grain rice) This term covers most of the short-grain rice that is grown and eaten in Japan, unless otherwise stated. The most popular brands include names such as Koshihikari and Sasanishiki. The grains are removed from their husks and polished. When cooked they become tender and moist but retain an al dente texture; they are also slightly sticky, so it is possible to pick up a mouthful with chopsticks. Plain boiled rice is almost pure white with a silver shimmer and a gentle hint of sweetness. Most of the Japanese-style rice sold outside Japan is grown in California on dry fields, but some products come from Spain and more recently from China. Although they tend to be slightly harder and occasionally brittle when cooked, the general appearance and taste compares very well to Japanese-grown rice.

Genmai (brown rice) There are different degrees of polishing and genmai/kuro gome (meaning black or brown rice) is the least polished type. Traditionally all rice was eaten unpolished, with only the outer husk

▸ *From top to bottom—uruchi mai, genmai, and mochi gome.*

removed. High in fiber, brown rice is the most nutritious, retaining more vitamins and minerals, but is not always popular with the Japanese. As the name implies, this kind of rice is light brown in color, and it feels harder than other rice, even in its uncooked state. It requires much longer cooking compared to the polished uruchi mai and is chewier but nuttier in taste. Today, although the polished white uruchi mai is the most popular type of rice in Japan, genmai is regaining popularity because of its health benefits.

Mochi gome Mochi gome, though grown in much the same way as uruchi mai, is whiter, rounder, and plumper in appearance. It is much stickier than its sister and is used to make mochi (rice cakes, see p.31), senbei (Japanese rice crackers) and mirin (sweet cooking saké, see p.224).

Buying and storing Although it is now possible to buy Japanese-grown rice outside the country, most of the so-called Japanese-style rice sold in the West come from California, Spain, and China. The taste of newly harvested rice in late autumn is considered to be the best, but one of the reasons for rice's popularity is the fact that it keeps so well, especially if it is stored with the husk on and unpolished. In Japan, especially in rural areas, it is still possible to buy rice in loose form: a housewife can choose from several varieties of rice and have it freshly polished and delivered. Polished rice should be stored in an airtight container in a cool, dark, and dry place and eaten as soon as possible.

Health benefits Polished rice comprises 75 percent carbohydrate and 8 percent vegetable protein, which is the highest protein content of all grains. However, much of the vitamins A and B is lost in the polishing stage. Today in Japan, some polished rice is sold with added vitamins or cooked with small portions of unpolished genmai.

Culinary uses In this section, the term 'rice' refers mainly to uruchi mai and to a lesser extent to genmai; the culinary uses for mochi gome are described later (see p.30).

It has already been mentioned that the Japanese word for cooked rice (*meshi*) is the same as the word for a meal. Rice is the staple food of Japan and is eaten in some form or other at every meal. Plain boiling is the classic way to cook rice, and it is traditionally served in an individual bowl with a separate bowl of miso soup. This is the simplest Japanese meal and other dishes, however elaborate they may be, are mere accompaniments to the rice.

One of the most important aspects of Japanese cuisine is that it follows the growing seasons: seasonal vegetables—young bamboo shoots in spring, tender peas in summer, earthy wild mushrooms or sweet chestnuts in autumn—are boiled with rice to give distinctive dishes according to the time of year.

A big bowl of plain boiled rice can be served with different toppings and sauces as a one-bowl meal, often for lunch. Those big-bowl dishes are called *donburi mono*, whatever their toppings. Among the favorite toppings are: chicken and egg (called *oyako donburi*, meaning, not surprisingly, 'parent and child bowl'), tempura of fish and

▲ *Gradation rice fields after the rice harvest.*

◀ *Young rice plants.*

vegetables (called *ten don*), pork cutlet (*katsu don*) and sautéed beef (*gyu don*). *Una don* (broiled, seasoned eels on a bowl of rice) is the nation's favorite dish on the Day of the Cow, which falls in the middle of August—the Japanese believe that it keeps them healthy for the rest of the year and about 1,000 tons of freshwater eels are eaten on that day.

Sushi is the nation's favorite rice dish all year round. A mixture of rice vinegar, sugar, and salt is added to boiled rice that is then tossed and fanned to cool it down. Good sushi begins with good sushi rice and top sushi chefs spend years during the first part of their long apprenticeship perfecting the art of making sushi rice. It is no wonder that top sushi restaurants in Japan carefully select their own blends of rice, while some even specify where and how the rice is grown.

In Japan, the glutinous cooking broth from rice is the first 'solid food' babies are given when they are weaned. *Kayu* is best described as rice porridge and is given to babies, the elderly, the sick, and pregnant women. To make it, rice is cooked with more water than usual (the amount of water varies according to how soft and liquid you want the porridge). It used to be the traditional breakfast of the upper classes and to this day it is associated with delicacy and refinement. Although traditional New Year celebrations are growing less common, the ancient tradition of cooking *nanakusa-gayu* (Seven Herbs rice congee) on 7 January still lives on. Later, on 15 January, the Coming of Age Day is celebrated with *adzuki gayu*, or rice porridge with adzuki beans.

When leftover plain boiled rice—hot or cold—is added to soup it is called *zosui* (雑炊) but in the old days, it was written (増水), which meant literally 'added water.' The distinction between *kayu* and *zosui* is not entirely clear: some cookery books say that *kayu* is made from uncooked rice while *zosui* is made from cooked rice. Another difference is that

kayu is not seasoned with salt. But one clear difference between the two is their image and applications: *zosui* has a robust and practical image and is often served as an emergency relief food. Indeed, during the severe food shortages of World War II and its immediate aftermath, there were many public and private *zosui* kitchens to be found in large cities.

Kani zosui

[RICE PORRIDGE WITH CRABMEAT AND SPROUTING BROCCOLI]

Zosui or 'mixed cooking' is a delicious and economical way of using up cooked rice with whatever vegetables you may find in your refrigerator. The key is to add more liquid to make the ingredients go a long way. It makes a comforting one-pot meal that is easy to digest.

Serves 4
4 oz. (½ cup) sprouting broccoli, trimmed
14 oz. (6½ cups) cooked rice
1 pint (2 cups) dashi broth (see p.169)
2 teaspoons salt
1 tablespoon light soy sauce
4 tablespoons saké
7 oz. (1½ cups) cooked white crabmeat
2 eggs, lightly beaten
1 tablespoon rice vinegar

Wash and trim the broccoli and cut it into bite-size pieces. Blanch and set aside. Put the rice in a large sieve and rinse under hot water to separate the grains. Put the rice, dashi broth, salt, soy sauce, and saké in a saucepan, cover, and place over a medium heat. When it has come to a boil, remove the lid and reduce the heat.

Add the crabmeat and broccoli, stir and cook for 3 minutes more. Pour in the beaten egg, mix, then turn off the heat and put the lid back on to let it steam for another 3 minutes. Add the vinegar (it brings out each ingredient's flavor and brightens the green of the broccoli) just before serving.

⌐ *A housewife prepares the family's packed lunch boxes of rice.*

▸ *Rice porridge with crabmeat and sprouting broccoli.*

Ninniku staki yaki-meshi

[FRIED RICE WITH BEEF AND GARLIC]

This robust fried rice dish uses the cooking juice from the beef and garlic.

Serves 4

2 tablespoons vegetable oil
2 garlic cloves, peeled and crushed
1 medium 7 oz. sirloin steak, diced
1 teaspoon freshly ground pepper
2 tablespoons saké
1 lb. 12 oz. (12¾ cups) cooked rice
2 teaspoons salt
2 tablespoons soy sauce
2 scallions, chopped

Heat the oil in a wok over medium heat and quickly sauté the garlic and meat. Season it with ground pepper and saké.

Add the cooked rice and stir well, making sure the rice is coated with the cooking juice from the meat. Adjust the seasoning with salt and more pepper if you like.

Drizzle soy sauce down the side of the wok and turn off the heat. Add the chopped scallion and stir. Divide into 4 equal portions and serve.

餅 Mochi gome & Mochi [GLUTINOUS RICE & RICE CAKES]

Mochi deserve a separate entry. While ordinary *uruchi mai* is an everyday staple in Japan, mochi gome, though grown in the same way, is regarded as something of a luxury and eaten on special occasions. It is ground to make rice flour, which is used for *senbei* (Japanese rice crackers). Newly made mochi (rice cakes) are soft and sticky but they dry quickly to almost brick-like hardness. In Japan, small bite-size mochi are cooked in a special New Year soup (every family has its own recipe which is passed down from mother to daughter), as it is believed that eating mochi brings a long life and wealth. The classic New Year decoration is two mochi—a large one on the bottom and a slightly smaller one on top—which are displayed until January 11th, then eaten in soup. This custom dates back to the eighth century and the two mochi, called *kagami mochi*, meaning 'mirror rice cakes,' are a symbol of the sun and moon, darkness and light, and men and women. Although mochi can be made at any time they are mostly consumed during the New Year period.

History It is widely believed that the first rice introduced to Japan was red mochi gome, a glutinous rice variety —historical records certainly confirm that mochi gome was grown. By the eighth century, the round mochi that we know today were being used for New Year celebrations.

Appearance and taste White and smooth in appearance, mochi come in varying sized discs. Compared to its brother, a grain of mochi gome is whiter, larger, and rounder. It contains more sugar and when it is steamed (mochi gome is more often steamed than boiled) it becomes very sticky and tastes sweeter. Its taste is not dissimilar to that of plain boiled rice, but the main difference is in its very sticky and chewy texture.

Culinary uses Mochi gome is steamed with adzuki beans to make *sekihan* or red rice (see p.39) for special celebrations such as birthdays and weddings. I am very fond of it: it looks very pretty—a glossy pink speckled with the deep red of adzuki beans—and it tastes sweeter than normal plain boiled rice, but above all, it brings back memories of many happy parties.

Manufacture Making mochi is quite an occasion: it normally takes place some time towards the end of December. To make mochi, steamed mochi gome is pounded with a wooden mallet in a giant mortar until sticky and smooth, then shaped into discs of varying sizes. Pounding steamed rice is an exhausting business and is considered a man's job, one often performed by the head of the household. I remember the year when my young uncle first took over the job from my grandfather and there seemed more chatter than usual among my grandparents and young unmarried aunts; it was the following year that he got married.

Buying and storing Mochi gome should be bought and stored in the same way as normal uruchi mai (Japanese short-grain rice). Making mochi traditionally with a mortar and mallet is a dying art, especially in Japan's large cities. Although the invention of an electric mochi-making machine (the Japanese equivalent of a bread-making machine) slowed down the inevitable trend, most Japanese housewives today buy ready-made, vacuum-packed mochi, which keep perfectly well for many months.

↘ *Broiled rice-cake sandwich with melted cheese.*
↖ *A rice planting ceremony.*
↘ *A traditional senbei (rice crackers) shop.*

Age mochi to yaki miso

[DEEP-FRIED RICE CAKE WITH SWEET MISO CANAPÉ]

By the middle of January every year, mochi to the Japanese become rather like Christmas cake to many Westerners—we are bored with them but sentiment prevents us from throwing them out. This was the case in our family until one year my grandmother came up with the idea of deep-frying the mochi and serving them as snacks. Sweet yaki miso paste is my contribution.

Serves 4
Vegetable oil, for deep-frying
4 ready-made, vacuum-packed mochi,
   cut into bite-size cubes
For the yaki miso
4 tablespoons miso (preferably light colored)
1 egg yolk
1 tablespoon sake
1 tablespoon mirin
1 tablespoon granulated sugar
1 teaspoon yuzu (or lime) juice

Heat the oil over a medium heat and deep-fry the cubes of mochi until they are golden. Drain them on kitchen paper towels and keep them warm.

Put all the ingredients for the yaki miso, except the yuzu juice, in a non-stick skillet. Over a medium heat, dry fry until the mixture becomes the consistency of cream cheese. Add the yuzu juice and stir well.

Dab a small mound of the yaki miso paste on each deep-fried mochi cube and serve.

Broiled rice-cake sandwich with melted cheese

Makes 4
4 thin slices of the cheese of your choice
4 ready-made, vacuum-packed mochi
4 strips of nori (dried seaweed)
A small amount of soy sauce for dipping

Cut the cheese slices smaller than the mochi. With a sharp knife, make a horizontal slit at the side of each mochi and insert a slice of cheese. Broil the mochi sandwich under a medium heat for 3–4 minutes on each side or until it turns golden brown.

Cut a nori strip 1 inch wide and long enough to go around the mochi. Wrap the nori strips around the mochi and serve while hot with a little soy sauce for dipping.

米製品 Komeko [RICE PRODUCTS]

Japanese cuisine generally favors grain over flour, and this applies to rice, which tends to be eaten in grain form rather than milled into flour, which is used to make bread and noodles. However, since rice is the staple food of Japan and Japanese cuisine has developed around rice, it is not surprising to find a variety of products made from rice. Komeko, literally meaning rice powder or flour, is a generic term covering a number of different varieties of rice flour and its products.

Shiratama This is made from ground mochi gome (glutinous rice) and is also called *kan zarashi ko*, which means 'cold blanched powder,' giving a clue to how it's made. During the coldest part of winter, the flour is washed and rinsed in cold, clean water. It is then soaked in more cold water, to blanch it, for between three and ten days. The wet mash is poured into a very fine cheesecloth bag, then hung in the cold air to dry naturally. The result is a very fine grade rice starch with a subtle taste and a silky texture, and it is used to make Japanese dessert cakes and sweets. In the ordinary domestic kitchen it is often mixed with water

and rolled into small dumplings which are eaten with sugar as a simple snack, or added to sweet adzuki porridge, and served as a sweet snack or a dessert. The dumplings are sometimes floated in clear soup on account of their pure white, elegant appearance and pleasing silky texture.

Domyoji This is an abbreviation of *Domyoji hoshii*, which is a form of dried preserved food. Buddhist nuns originally made it as an offering at Domyoji Temple in south Osaka, where it gained popularity among the temple's congregation, who believed it cured illnesses. Mochi gome (glutinous rice) is first soaked in water, then steamed and dried. The dried rice grains are coarsely ground, to make a flour that can be easily reconstituted with water—its convenience and the fact that it kept well made it a useful field ration for the armed forces. Today, it is used to make Japanese cakes and desserts. The nutritious element is much the same as plain boiled rice.

▲ *From left to right: shiratama-ko, domyoji, and nuka.*

Nuka (Rice bran) In a country where rice is regarded as almost sacred, no part of the plant is wasted, including the husks. Bran is the generic term for the byproduct obtained from polishing grains such as rice, wheat, barley, and millet. In Japan, however, rice bran dominates in terms of quantity and usage, and in the context of the Japanese kitchen, 'bran' most often refers to rice bran. Rice bran is much higher in nutritious value than polished rice: it contains carbohydrate, fat, protein, vitamins, and minerals such as phosphorus. It is used for animal feed and in some health and beauty products. But the main, most traditional, and singularly unique, use of rice bran is for pickling vegetables and fish.

Rice bran is first lightly toasted to bring out the aroma, before being mixed with salt and water and left to ferment to provide a unique pickling bed. Although my grandmothers kept their own pickling barrels, my maternal grandmother was a champion pickle-maker. As tradition requires, she gave some of her precious rice bran to my mother when my mother married and left home. She kept several barrels in the well hut and tended them every day, turning the bran over to keep the pickling bacteria live and healthy.

As I recall, she pickled almost every spare vegetable from my grandfather's vegetable garden, ranging from winter cabbages to eggplants and cucumbers in the summer. I could always tell—in fact, smell—whenever she had been near the pickling barrels: the smell of a pickling bed is distinctive and very powerful. The strong flavor of the fermented rice bran seeps through to the vegetables, making them soft but with a fresh crunchiness, and adding a distinctive taste. The simplest Japanese meal of rice and a bowl of miso soup is not complete without a few slices of pickled vegetables.

Furutsu shiratama

[FRUIT SALAD WITH RICE DROPS]

There is no tradition of ending a meal in Japan with desserts. Instead, seasonal fruits are served. This is an example of how the Japanese adopted what is essentially a Western fruit salad and transformed it into something of their own.

Serves 4
7 oz. mixed fruit salad of your choice
For the syrup
2 oz. (¼ cup) soft brown sugar
3 fl oz. (⅓ cup) just-boiled water
Juice of 1 lemon
2 tablespoons honey
For the rice drops
4 oz. (1⅓ cups) shiratama-ko
3–4 tablespoons water

First make up your fruit salad or use a ready prepared mixture. Make the syrup by dissolving the sugar in the hot water and stirring in the lemon and honey, then set aside to cool. Add the fruit salad to soak in the syrup.

Put the shiratama-ko in a bowl and add the water gradually. Mix well to make a smooth dough. Divide the dough into small balls the size of the tip of your thumb.

Gently squash the balls between your index finger and thumb to make an indentation in the center. (This is to ensure that every part of the balls cooks through at the same speed.) Bring a saucepan of water to a boil and drop in a few balls at a time, scooping them out as they float to the surface. Cool the cooked balls in a bowl of cold water. Mix the fruit salad with the balls and serve.

大豆 Daizu [SOYBEAN]

grown soy is preferred by Japanese food manufacturers because it has a higher protein and fat content.

History It is believed that the soybean originated somewhere in the northwestern part of China where it has been cultivated for over 5,000 years. It was first introduced to Japan from China about 3,000 years ago.

Appearance and taste Soybeans can be grouped into three basic types: yellow (the most common), black, and green. In Japanese the soybean is called daizu, meaning 'big bean,' as opposed to the adzuki bean, which translates as 'small bean.' The yellow variety varies in size: the smaller ones are preferred for eating while larger ones are processed to make oil and other products. Like many other pulses, the soybean has very little taste of its own but what it has is peanut-like.

Culinary uses Although the soybean is the most important variety of bean, it does not take center stage in Japanese cooking but plays a vital supporting role. Dried soybean is simmered in broth with other vegetables, while black soybean is appreciated for its glossy appearance and is one of the key dishes at New Year. On the eve of *setsubun* (the beginning of spring), Japanese children throw toasted yellow soybeans at the demons (most often their fathers wearing masks) who are trying to enter their house, and chant 'demon out, happiness in.' It is the tradition to eat the same number of beans as one's age to keep healthy. Roasted soybeans are pounded to a powder to produce aromatic yellow *kinako*, which is used to make Japanese confectionery.

Buying and storing Soybean is most commonly sold in dried form, which keeps almost indefinitely if stored in a cool, dark, airy place. Outside Japan, dried soybean is sold in health stores or in larger supermarkets.

Health benefits Soybean is highly nutritious. It has a high percentage of vegetable protein (35 percent, compared to 8 percent in rice and 10 percent in wheat), is 20 percent fat and is rich in various vitamins, especially vitamins B1, B2, and E. It contains a variety of minerals, including calcium and iron. It is no wonder that soybean is called 'beef of the field.' Soybean's high level of amino acid is known to reduce cholesterol and lower

The soybean is the most important variety of bean not only in Japan but in the world. It is one of the five most important agricultural crops, alongside wheat, barley, maize, and rice. Current world production amounts to over 180 million tons. The USA is the largest producer, followed by Brazil, Argentina and China. Japan imports 5 million tons, of which 4 million tons are used to make cooking oil and the rest is eaten in a variety of forms, such as tofu, miso, and natto (fermented soybean), or used to make Japan's famous soy sauce. Although fewer than 300,000 tons are produced domestically, home-

blood pressure, and is believed to be anti-carcinogenic. Studies show that consumption of soy can also delay the female menopause.

Gomoku-mame

[SIMMERED SOYBEANS]

This is real home cooking: a dish of simmered beans was served at almost every meal when I was a young child. Soybeans are sold dried, so soak them overnight to ensure that they are nice and soft when cooked. Do not add salt until the end.

Serves 4–6
1 lb. (2⅓ cups) dry soybeans
3 oz. (½ cup) lotus root
3 oz. (½ cup) gobo (burdock) root
3 oz. (½ cup) carrot
½ sheet konbu (dried kelp), roughly chopped
4 oz. (½ cup) sugar
4 tablespoons soy sauce
1 teaspoon salt

Start by soaking the beans overnight in a saucepan containing three times their own volume of water.

Drain the beans, cover with fresh water, put the saucepan over a medium heat and bring to a boil. Add a cup of water as it begins to boil, reduce the heat and bring back to a boil. Simmer for 30–60 minutes or until the beans feel soft to the touch.

Meanwhile peel and chop the vegetables into fingertip-size pieces and soak them. Add the vegetables and konbu to the beans once the beans are cooked through, add 2 tablespoons of the sugar and cook further. Stir occasionally to ensure all the ingredients are coated with the juices.

When the vegetables are cooked, add the rest of the sugar and seasoning and stir well. Cook until almost all the liquid has gone. This can be served hot or at room temperature and will keep for a few days in the refrigerator.

▾ *A traditional tofu shop.*

納豆 Natto [FERMENTED SOY BEANS]

My husband considered himself a bit of a connoisseur of Japanese food until he first came across natto. If there were a list of the ten strangest foods of Japan, natto would most certainly be on it. But it is one of the healthiest and cheapest sources of soybean protein and, given time and encouragement, natto may well become a mainstream ingredient like its cousin, tofu.

History There are two varieties—more traditional *shiokara natto* and the more popular *ito-hiki natto*. *Shiokara natto* is widely believed to have originated in China and was introduced to Japan some time in the eighth century. According to legend, natto acquired its name because it was first made in the kitchen of a Buddhist temple called Nassho. There are no historical records, however, to tell us when *ito-hiki natto* was first 'discovered.'

How it is made The soybeans are first soaked and cooked. Friendly starter bacteria are then added and the soybeans are allowed to develop for 24–36 hours under warm and damp conditions.

Appearance and taste To unaccustomed eyes, the appearance of natto must seem very strange: small soybeans clustered together and covered with whitish slime. Natto becomes very sticky when stirred or mixed and has a strong, pungent smell of fermentation. The taste is best described as like that of a very mature Camembert cheese with a slimy texture. In short, natto is an acquired taste.

Health benefits Despite its strange appearance and taste, natto is highly nutritious: it is high in protein, fat, and fiber and it is also rich in various vitamins, especially vitamin B2, which ensures healthy skin, hair, and nails. It removes excess fat from the blood, so helps to prevent hardening of the arteries. Natto is easily digestible and good for a healthy intestine.

Buying and storing In the West, natto is most likely to be sold frozen in small polyurethane packs with little sachets of seasonings such as soy sauce, dashi broth or mustard. Keep refrigerated and once defrosted, eat within five days.

Culinary uses The most popular use for natto is as part of the traditional Japanese breakfast. It can be served in miso soup, mixed with fresh vegetables, or used as a topping ingredient.

Oroshi natto

[NATTO WITH GRATED DAIKON]

This is one of my favorite breakfasts. A refreshing mixture of natto and shredded daikon is put on hot boiled rice—a power breakfast in one bowl.

Serves 4
2 packets natto
7 oz. (1 cup) daikon, peeled and shredded
1 tablespoon soy sauce
2 umeboshi (pickled plum), pitted and mashed

Empty the natto into a bowl and with a pair of chopsticks or a fork mix it well until it develops a sticky consistency.

Add the shredded daikon, soy sauce, and mashed umeboshi and mix well again. Divide the mixture between 4 small serving dishes or serve on hot boiled rice.

▸ Packets of dried beans for sale—the variety is wide-ranging.

小豆 Azuki [ADZUKI BEAN]

The adzuki bean is the second most important dried pulse in the Japanese kitchen and probably the best known in the West. It has been cultivated for nearly 3,000 years, since prehistoric times, and has long been regarded as an auspicious food.

Appearance and taste Adzuki beans come in four forms; the most commonly known deep red, and also green, yellow, and white. The smallest variety is a similar size to the mung bean while the largest variety, which is highly prized, can be twice as big. Uncooked beans are very hard and almost indigestible but once cooked they have a faint, sweet aroma and a sweet, chestnut-like taste.

Culinary use The adzuki bean and glutinous rice are an inseparable pair—they are always cooked together. The Japanese associate red and white with joyous occasions and so they serve the pretty pale-pink and red *sekihan* (steamed glutinous rice with adzuki beans) at birthdays, weddings, and the many seasonal festivals. The adzuki bean is more commonly made into *an*, a sweet adzuki bean paste which is used as fillings for Japanese cakes.

Buying and storing The adzuki bean is easily found in supermarkets and health stores. Like many dried pulses, the adzuki bean keeps almost indefinitely if stored in a cool, dark, airy place.

Health benefits The adzuki bean is more than 50 percent starch and contains some protein, fiber, and vitamin B. The bean is considered very healthy and is used in Chinese herbal medicine as an antidote to stomach upsets and laxative.

An

[SWEET ADZUKI PASTE]

An can be eaten on its own or diluted with hot water to make a sweet soup called *zenzai* (a favorite of many women) or used as a filling for different kinds of Japanese confectionery. Although ready-made *an* is available either in tins or in powder form, it is not as good as homemade, nor as economical.

8 oz. (1¼ cups) adzuki beans
8 oz. (1 cup) granulated sugar
A pinch of salt

Put the beans in a saucepan and add enough water to cover. Bring to a boil and drain. Return the beans to the saucepan and add 1¼ pints water and let the beans soak overnight, discarding any that float.

Put the saucepan of beans over a high heat and bring to a boil. Reduce the heat after 5 minutes of rapid boiling and simmer for 1 hour or until the beans are soft. Add 3½ tablespoons water when the liquid is reduced by half and stir. Do this twice more. Add the sugar and salt and stir well to ensure that it all dissolves. The paste will keep for a week refrigerated in an airtight container.

◀ *A confectioner makes cakes filled with sweet adzuki paste.*

Sekihan

[STEAMED GLUTINOUS RICE WITH ADZUKI BEANS]

In the West, people bake cakes to celebrate happy occasions; in Japan, we cook rice with adzuki beans.

Serves 4–6
14 oz. (2 cups) mochi gome (glutinous rice)
4 oz. (⅔ cup) adzuki beans
A pinch of salt
2 tablespoons toasted black sesame seeds

Start by washing the rice. Rinse the rice until the water runs clear and set aside. Wash and rinse the beans and put them in a saucepan with plenty of water. Bring to a boil, cook for 5 minutes and strain off the cooking water. Add 1½ pints of fresh water and bring to a boil over low to medium heat. Turn off the heat, put the lid on and leave for 10 minutes.

Transfer the beans to a larger saucepan that is heavy bottomed and has a tight-fitting lid. Reserve the cooking liquid in a bowl and pour a ladleful of the liquid from a height of 12 inches back into the bowl. Repeat, adding a total of 6 ladlefuls of the liquid—it will intensify the redness of the liquid.

Add the rice to the saucepan and pour in 1¼ pints of the liquid—if there is not enough, add water instead. Put the lid on and add a pinch of salt before placing over a medium heat. Bring to a boil and cook for 5 minutes, then turn off the heat and don't lift the lid until it has steamed for 15 minutes more.

Stir the cooked rice to ensure that the beans are distributed evenly, sprinkle on the sesame seeds and serve.

During the Seventies, when I was at an English boarding school, there were three major air routes between Europe and Japan: the southern route, the route via Moscow, and, the most popular, the route via the North Pole. The long, 16-hour flight was broken midway by a stop-off at Anchorage in Alaska, and I suspect that the true reason for this route's popularity lay in a little noodle stand at the airport transit lounge. I remember watching most of my fellow passengers queue up to get a bowl of 'Alaska Soba' or 'Alaska Udon,' according to which part of Japan they came from. The non-Japanese passengers would be horrified by the sight of the Japanese slurping up their noodles with gusto!

Noodles are among the most popular food in Japan and are eaten everywhere. They are quick to prepare and instantly satisfying, whether eaten at a noodle stand at a busy railway station or at a serene temple ground in Kyoto. Although they originally came from China, noodles have become native to Japan and have developed a national identity of their own. I am happy to see that more kinds of noodle have become available in the West and I hope this section will make Japanese noodles even more accessible.

2 Noodles

蕎麦 Soba [BUCKWHEAT NOODLES]

History Soba noodles are made of flour from the hardy annual soba plant, native to central Asia and found everywhere from Siberia to India. The plant was probably introduced to Japan via the Korean peninsula 10,000 years ago. In Japan the first written record of soba dates from AD 722, when it was planted as an emergency supplementary grain after the rice crop failed. Soba is an ideal second crop since it can be grown practically anywhere; in fact it prefers poorer soil and a cooler climate. It takes just 75 days from sowing to harvesting.

It is widely believed that the technique for noodle-making was brought over from China when Buddhism was first introduced in the middle of the sixth century. Earlier noodles were called *mugi-nawa*, which literally means 'wheat rope.' The soba noodle is likely to have arrived after its counterpart, the udon noodle, which is made from wheat flour, a much easier flour to make into noodles. Traditionally flour from the soba plant was eaten in the form of dumplings or congee, but that changed around the end of the sixteenth century when it was discovered that the addition of a small amount of wheat flour made the otherwise gluten-free soba flour more elastic and workable. In nineteenth-century Tokyo, there were over 3,000 soba-noodle street stands and these noodles were the second most popular snack of the period after sushi.

Soba noodles are an important part of Japanese food culture. Considered auspicious, they are believed to cleanse the five vital organs, so a bowl of hot soba noodles is eaten every New Year's Eve when the temple bells sound at midnight. Traditionally, soba noodles were given when a person moved house—it was a symbolic gesture to wish them long trouble-free relations with their neighbors. Today, soba noodles are eaten all over Japan as a quick snack or a satisfying one-dish lunch. The making of fresh soba noodles is also gaining popularity because of their health benefits.

How they are made Until the late nineteenth century when the soba-noodle machine was invented, every soba noodle was made by hand. Soba seeds are pyramidal in shape, with triangular edges. The seeds are milled and their husks removed. Soba flour is gluten free, so lacks elasticity and is difficult to handle, which is why rice, wheat, or potato flour in a ratio of 1:4 is often added as a binding agent. The soba flour is then mixed with water and made into a dough that is rolled out thinly and cut into thin strands. I had the pleasure of watching a soba masterchef at work, and he transformed every step of noodle-making into an art form. The cutting part was particularly spectacular: each strand was exactly the same thickness with sharp, clean edges. I asked how long it takes to learn to cut and was surprised by his reply—only three days—but blending the soba flour takes over three years of training. He told me that he chose his soba seeds—which particular region, etc—according to each day's temperature and atmospheric conditions.

Appearance and taste Soba noodles vary in color from a light mushroom brown to dark brown, and they may be speckled. Some soba noodles contain green-tea powder and are green, with a mild flavor of tea. Ordinary soba noodles have a distinctive nutty flavor.

Buying and storing Soba noodles are usually sold dried in slim neat bundles tied with thin paper ribbon. One bundle conveniently yields one portion. Dried noodles can be stored for a very long time if kept in a cool, dark, and airy kitchen cupboard.

◂ *Soba fields.*

Health benefits Largely carbohydrate, soba is 13 percent vegetable protein—a very high percentage (though not as high as soybeans). Soba is also particularly high in vitamins B1 and B2, which the typical Japanese rice-based diet lacks, hence the occurrence of rickets. Soba has two and a half times the fiber of polished rice.

Culinary uses In Japan, soba noodle dishes are eaten as snacks or as a one-dish, quick lunch. They are extremely versatile, as good to eat in hot-broth soup as served cold with dashi-based dipping sauce.

Misoka soba

[NEW YEAR'S EVE SOBA]

This is the Japanese equivalent of haggis on Burns' Night in Scotland. The Japanese eat *misoka soba* on New Year's Eve, hoping for a healthy, trouble-free year. Every family has their own recipe—this was my grandmother's.

Serves 4
2 sheets deep-fried tofu
3 oz. chicken breast
14 oz. (about 5–6 cups) soba noodles
For the broth
2 pints (5 cups) dashi broth (see p.169)
5 fl oz. (⅔ cup) mirin
5 fl oz. (⅔ cup) light soy sauce
1 tablespoon granulated sugar
To finish
8 slices kamaboko (fish paste, see p.170)
2 scallions, finely chopped

Place the deep-fried tofu in a strainer, pour over hot water to wash off the excess oil and slice thinly. Cut the chicken breast into thin slices.

Put all the ingredients for the broth in a saucepan, add the tofu and heat over a medium heat. When it is about to boil, add the chicken and cook for 5 minutes more or until the chicken is cooked. Meanwhile, bring a saucepan of water to a boil and add the noodles. When the water is about to come back to a boil, add a cup of cold water and bring it back to a boil again. Drain and rinse the noodles and divide them between 4 large bowls.

Ladle over the hot broth and top with the kamaboko slices. Add the chopped scallion to garnish.

Tororo soba

[CHILLED SOBA NOODLES WITH SHREDDED YAM]

This is a very simple noodle dish and the shredded yam (*yamaimo*) makes a sensuously silky dipping sauce. I hope you will enjoy the texture of this dish.

Serves 4
14 oz. (5–6 cups) dried soba noodles
For the dipping sauce
14 oz. (2½ cups) yam, peeled and shredded
5 fl oz. (⅔ cup) konbu no tsuke dashi (see p.121)
4 tablespoons soy sauce
4 tablespoons mirin
Condiments
4 scallions, finely chopped
4 teaspoons wasabi powder, mixed to a paste with water
4 sheets nori (dried seaweed), finely shredded

Mix together all the ingredients for the dipping sauce and set aside. Next bring a saucepan of water to a boil and add the noodles. As soon as the water begins to boil again, add a cup of cold water and bring back to a boil. Drain, rinse the noodles under cold running water and drain again. Divide the dipping sauce and the noodles into 4 equal portions and serve with the condiments on separate dishes.

Zaru soba

[CHILLED SOBA NOODLES WITH DIPPING SAUCE]

A *zaru* is the bamboo basket or slatted bamboo box in which soba noodles were steamed and served. The most orthodox soba noodles were made of pure buckwheat flour and were susceptible to breaking, so they had to be steamed. A small amount of wheat flour makes the noodles strong enough to withstand boiling, but the traditional *zaru* is still used to serve them. This is the most refreshing and appetizing dish in hot summer.

This recipe suggests you serve the noodles with scallions and wasabi but you can also serve them with shredded nori (dried seaweed), lime (or, better still, yuzu) rind, and shredded daikon (Japanese radish).

Serves 4

14 oz. (5–6 cups) dried soba noodles
4 scallions, finely chopped
4 teaspoons wasabi powder mixed with approximately half the amount of water

For the dipping sauce

2 fl oz. (3½ tablespoons) soy sauce
2 fl oz. (3½ tablespoons) mirin
1 pint (2½ cups) dashi broth (see p.169)

Mix the soy sauce and mirin into the dashi broth and put in the refrigerator.

Meanwhile bring a large saucepan of water to a boil and add the noodles as swiftly as possible. Stir to prevent the noodles from sticking together. Stand by with a cup of cold water and when the water returns to the boil add the water. (This is a classic method of cooking noodles in Japan: the cold water or 'shock water' reduces the temperature so that the inner part of the noodles is cooked at the same speed as the outer part. You may need to do this more than once, depending on the dryness of the noodles.)

Test the readiness of the noodles by cutting a strand with your fingernail—it should be just tender. Drain the noodles in a large strainer and rinse well under cold running water to get rid of the starch. Drain again.

Divide the noodles into four serving dishes or baskets. Arrange the chopped scallions on top and put a mound of wasabi on the side. Serve with a bowl of dipping sauce for each person.

うどん Udon [UDON NOODLES]

As I said earlier, udon and soba noodles are the best-known Japanese noodles. If soba noodles are the working man's fast food in Tokyo, udon noodles are the equally cheap and cheerful equivalent in the southwest of Japan. Together they represent Japan's noodle culture.

History Udon noodles had a noble birth. They were introduced to Japan from China in the eighth century as dumplings to be eaten between meals—an earlier version of dim sum. With the development of noodle-making technique, udon changed their shape from a round dumpling to a noodle. Udon were eaten in the imperial and aristocratic palaces and in Buddhist temples. These noodles became more widely available to ordinary people during the Middle Ages and were one of the most popular street foods by the eighteenth century.

One of my grandmothers lived in Kagawa prefecture on the island of Shikoku, in southwest Japan, which is famous for its delicious udon noodles. Indeed, the province is the spiritual home of udon and Udon Day is celebrated there every year on July 2nd. My grandmother was a pragmatic, no-nonsense widow who ran a successful rice mill by day and a small restaurant in the evening, in order to keep the family estate intact. One of the strongest images of my childhood is of watching my grandmother kneading a generous portion of udon—I always knew a good lunch was on its way when I smelt the slightly sweet aroma of udon dashi broth in the air. How I loved burying my face in a big bowl, blowing on the hot broth to cool it down and slurping up the silky, fat noodles—happiness in a bowl.

How they are made The technique was imported in the sixth century from China. To this day in China there are three basic methods for making noodles: hand-pulling, rolling and cutting, and paring/peeling. Only the first two methods were introduced to Japan, where they can still be seen. Watching hand-pulled noodles being made is like watching a magic trick: a noodle master turns a ball of dough into long strands of noodles after just a few minutes of stretching. It takes years of practice and nowadays, sadly, it is a dying art. One can still see an adaptation of this method, however, in some regions of Japan, where a long noodle rope is suspended between two wooden sticks, which are gradually pulled apart to lengthen and thin the noodles.

The rolled method is less spectacular but perhaps easier to master at home—it is how my grandmother made udon noodles. Udon flour is a combination of equal amounts of strong and all-purpose flour, which is mixed with approximately half its volume of water and a pinch of salt to form a dough. The addition of salt not only gives the noodles more flavor but also breaks down the protein content of the flour making the dough more elastic and workable. The dough is kneaded until the surface becomes slightly glossy, then covered and rested for a few hours before being rolled out with a long rolling pin into a large sheet. The dough sheet is folded and cut into manageable length noodles. Fresh noodles can either be cooked straight away or hung to dry for later use.

Appearance and taste Udon noodles are made from wheat flour. They are white and glossy in appearance, with an ample girth; they feel silky and slippery on the lips, but have a satisfying bite to them. Good noodles are described as 'having a good hip'—an expression perhaps connected to their wholesome nature.

Fresh and frozen udon are thick white strands while the dried version can be flat, square or round. Instant, precooked udon are sold vacuum-packed. Udon noodles have little taste of their own: it is the broth or dipping sauce that gives each dish its character.

Buying and storing Dried varieties are easier to find, and will keep for a long time in a dark, dry cupboard. Some dry udon are sold in neat bundles tied with a strip of paper ribbon.

Culinary use There are three basic methods for cooking udon noodles in Japan, all of which involve boiling them first. They can then be served in hot soup, served hot or cold with a dipping sauce, or stir-fried with other ingredients.

Health benefits Unlike their main rival soba, udon noodles suffer from an unfounded reputation for being fattening. Udon are made of wheat flour, water, and a pinch of salt. In Japan, there are 4 different grades of wheat flour: strong, semi-strong, medium, and plain, depending on the protein content. Strong flour has the highest protein content at around 13 percent and the proportion decreases by 2 percent for each grade, ending with an average of just 7 percent for all-purpose flour. The flour used to make udon is the equivalent of medium flour, with an average protein content of 9 percent—lower than the buckwheat used to make soba noodles. Udon noodles are mainly carbohydrate and in terms of calorific count, udon compare well against soba noodles at 368kcal/100g.

▾ *Men stand around eating noodles at an old-style vending stall.*

Kitsune udon

[UDON NOODLE BROTH WITH DEEP-FRIED TOFU]

In Japanese, *kitsune udon* means 'fox noodles.' Foxes in Japan are revered messengers of the Shinto gods. A pair of stone foxes always stands guard at the entrance to Shinto shrines—a practice I never questioned or thought strange until I came to England. Cultural differences aside, this is a wholesome and delicious one-bowl meal.

Serves 4
2 deep-fried tofu
8 oz. (3 cups) dried udon noodles
For the tofu broth
8 fl oz. (1 cup) dashi broth (see p.169)
1 tablespoon granulated sugar
1 tablespoon mirin
2 teaspoons light soy sauce
For the noodle broth
2½ pints (6 cups) dashi broth (see p.169)
2 tablespoons light soy sauce
1 tablespoon mirin
½ teaspoon salt
1 teaspoon granulated sugar
To garnish
4 slices of kamaboko (fish paste, see p.170)
2 scallions, finely chopped
Shichimi togarashi (Japanese chili pepper, see p.210)

Blanch the tofu in boiling water to remove its excess oil. If the tofu is a rectangle, cut it into two squares or triangles. Meanwhile, combine the tofu broth ingredients and bring to a boil. Simmer the tofu triangles in the broth until the liquid is reduced by half, then set aside.

Bring a saucepan of water to a boil and add the noodles for 2–3 minutes, stirring them with a pair of chopsticks to separate them. Add a cup of cold water when the water returns to the boil—a step you may have to repeat, depending how dry the noodles are. Drain the noodles and divide them between 4 bowls.

Meanwhile, heat all the ingredients for the noodle broth in a separate saucepan—but don't let it boil. When it is hot, ladle it over the noodles. Place the cooked tofu in the bowls and top with the kamaboko slices. Garnish with the scallion and hand around the shichimi togarashi.

Nabeyaki udon

[POT-COOKED UDON NOODLES]

This dish is often translated as 'pot-cooked noodles' because of the heavy earthenware pot used to cook the noodles. My mother used to make it for me when I was studying late at night for my many examinations. It is a deeply warming dish yet very digestible, and it got me through my exams! Unusually, this recipe serves just one.

Serves 1

1 dried shiitake mushroom, soaked in hot water for
   15 minutes
1 boneless, skinless chicken thigh
1 tablespoon soy sauce
1 tablespoon mirin
1 tablespoon saké
1 bunch dried udon noodles, weighing 3–4 oz.

For the noodle broth

10 fl oz. (1¼ cups) dashi broth (see p.169)
6 tablespoons soy sauce
3 tablespoons mirin

To finish

1 egg
1 scallion, finely chopped
3 slices kamaboko (fish paste, see p.170)

Drain the mushroom, reserving the liquid. Cut off the stalk and slice the cup in half. Cut the chicken into bite-size pieces and let it marinate with the soy sauce, mirin, and saké while you cook the noodles. Bring a pot of water to a boil and add the noodles. When the water has returned to a boil, add 1 cup of cold water. Drain the noodles and rinse them in cold running water to wash off the starch. Drain well again and set aside.

Put all the ingredients for the noodle broth in a small sturdy casserole, together with the mushroom-soaking liquid and the chicken. Bring to a boil, skim off any scum that rises to the surface and add the mushroom.

If the noodles have stuck together, rinse in boiling water to separate. Add the noodles to the casserole and cook for 3 minutes before turning off the heat. Break the egg into the soup, add the scallion and kamaboko slices and cover for about a minute. The egg will cook in the residual heat to a poached state.

Shoyu kake udon

[WARM UDON NOODLE SALAD]

This is an easy-to-prepare noodle salad—it is worth making it with fresh udon, which have a better texture.

Serves 4

7 oz. (2½–3 cups) fresh udon noodles
2 tablespoons sesame oil
2 tablespoons soy sauce

For the topping

14 oz. fresh daikon (Japanese radish), peeled
   and shredded
8 green shiso (perilla) leaves, finely chopped
8 scallions, finely chopped
½ oz. dried wakame (seaweed), reconstituted in water
   and drained
¾ oz. fresh ginger root, peeled and finely shredded

Bring a saucepan of water to a boil and add the noodles. Cook them for 2–3 minutes. Drain but do not rinse, and keep warm. Heat a large skillet over a medium heat and add the sesame oil. Add the drained noodles and toss lightly to coat with the oil. Divide the noodles into 4 equal portions. Arrange some of each topping on the noodles and drizzle with the soy sauce.

▲ *Pot-cooked udon noodles.*

そうめん Somen [SOMEN NOODLES]

Fine, elegant somen noodles have the same origin as robust udon noodles. But while udon noodles left their aristocratic birthplace to become the working man's food, somen noodles remained true to their upper class roots, staying within the walls of the imperial palaces and Buddhist temples as the nobility's favorite noodle. Somen is undoubtedly the queen of all noodles.

History Traditionally, somen noodles were regarded as noble and auspicious on account of their length and it was considered bad luck to cut or bite them short. There are some comical woodblock prints from the nineteenth century depicting men struggling to eat somen noodles that were more than 6 feet long. Luckily, these days they come in the more manageable length of 10 inches.

In the past somen noodles were made by women in farming villages to supplement their meager income during the cold winter months. The dry atmosphere and low temperature of a typical Japanese winter suits somen making. All the most famous somen producing areas, such as Miwa in Nara prefecture and Shodo Island, are found in southeast Japan.

Somen noodles are the main dish of Japan's Star Festival. The festival of Tanabata is based on an old, romantic, Chinese legend. Once a year, on the evening of July 7th, a young cattleman, the star of Altair, is allowed to cross the Milky Way to meet his beloved, the beautiful weaver Vega. All over Japan, children used to decorate bamboo branches with their origami creations and tie on colored paper tags which bore their wishes. On the following morning, the decorated bamboos were thrown into nearby rivers, down which their wishes would float. Unfortunately, but perhaps understandably, the practice was banned long ago for environmental reasons.

How they are made Somen noodles are made from wheat flour, salt, and water, in a similar method to hand-pulled udon noodles. The major difference is that slim somen noodles take much longer, and require a long pulling and resting process. Also, the noodles are moistened with sesame or cottonseed oil to prevent them from breaking while they are being pulled and lengthened. Today, many forms of somen noodles are machine-made, but the handmade version, made the previous year, is the most highly prized. This is because noodles dry out during storage and that improves the texture.

Appearance and taste Somen noodles are elegantly thin and mostly white in color. The dried kind is far more common and is more practical than fresh somen. The noodles are sold in packs, very often in bundles tied with neat paper ribbons, and there are three pretty versions: *cha somen* (light green from the addition of green tea powder); *tamago somen* (yellow from the addition of egg yolk); and *ume somen* (pale pink from the addition of plum). Like udon, somen have very little taste of their own but they are enjoyed for their fineness, which brings a light, shower-like sensation to the tongue.

Buying and storing Even in Japan, somen noodles normally come in dried form and are likely to be machine-made. If you are lucky enough to find a hand-made version, resist the temptation to eat them straight away and keep them for another year or two. My grandmother 'overwintered' her somen but always used them within three years, as the tiny amount of oil on them changes their taste. Machine-made somen do not improve with time, so use them by the date shown.

Culinary uses Somen noodles are usually served chilled and eaten with a cold dipping sauce with many different condiments and garnishes. Somen in hot broth, served in winter, are called 'new men.'

▸ *Somen with eggplant and myoga.*
▸ *Stretching somen noodles by hand.*

Somen to yaki nasu

[SOMEN WITH EGGPLANT AND MYOGA]

I invented this dish to combine the Italian way of cooking with Japanese ingredients. If you are unable to find somen noodles, you can substitute spaghetti or linguini.

Serves 4
4 tablespoons olive oil
2 garlic cloves, lightly crushed
1 eggplant, peeled and cut into ½ inch cubes
14 oz. (5–6 cups) dried somen noodles
2–3 myoga, blanched in cold water and finely chopped
2 umeboshi (pickled plums), pit removed, squashed to a paste
Salt and pepper to taste
To finish
8 green shiso (perilla) leaves, finely torn

Heat the oil in a skillet over a low heat and add the garlic. Stir until the oil is infused, then remove the garlic and add the diced eggplant. Meanwhile, bring a saucepan of water to a boil and cook the noodles, adding a ladleful of the cooking water to the pan.

When the noodles are cooked, drain and add to the eggplant. Turn up the heat and quickly sauté the sauce and the noodles together. Cook until the liquid has reduced, then add the myoga and the umeboshi paste. Stir to ensure that the noodles are well coated with the sauce, then turn off the heat, taste, and season with the salt and pepper. Divide the noodle mixture between 4 serving bowls and garnish with the shiso.

Hiyashi somen

[CHILLED SOMEN NOODLES]

This brings back happy memories of warm summer evenings spent with my family. We used to change into a crisp *yukata* (cotton or linen kimono) after bathing and sit out on wooden benches in the garden. There would be mosquito repelling incense burning under the benches and we would cool ourselves with our *uchiwa* (bamboo and paper fans). My grandmother would bring out a big lacquered tub of somen noodles floating in ice cold well water. We always rounded up the evening with fireworks.

Serves 4
14 oz. (5–6 cups) dried somen noodles
For the dipping sauce
8 dried shiitake mushrooms, soaked in 4 fl oz. hot water for 15 minutes
8 fl oz. (1 cup) dashi broth (see p.169)
2 fl oz. (3½ tablespoons) mirin
2 fl oz. (3½ tablespoons) soy sauce
Condiments
1 oz. (2-inch piece) fresh ginger root, peeled and shredded
Finely shredded yuzu peel (lime or lemon will do)
1 sheet nori (dried seaweed), finely shredded
4 scallions, finely chopped

Put the mushrooms, their soaking liquid and all the other dipping sauce ingredients in a saucepan and heat over a medium heat. Simmer gently until the mushrooms are soft, then let cool.

Remove the mushrooms and chop them finely. Bring a saucepan of water to a boil and add the noodles, stirring with a pair of chopsticks to separate them. When the water is about to boil, add 1 cup of cold water and let it return to a boil. Drain, rinse under cold running water and drain again. Serve the noodles floating in a big bowl of ice water or pile them on a bed of ice. Serve with a cup of dipping sauce, the mushrooms and all the condiments on the side.

冷や麦 Hiyamugi [HIYAMUGI NOODLES]

The origin of hiyamugi is the same as that of the famous udon noodles, hiyamugi's robust big brother. *Hiyamugi* literally translates as 'cold wheat' and traditionally meant chilled udon noodles as opposed to *atsu mugi* (hot wheat), meaning hot udon noodles. However, sometime during the fifteenth century the term 'atsu mugi' disappeared, to be replaced by 'udon,' but the term 'hiyamugi' survived.

Appearance and taste Hiyamugi noodles are a cross between thick udon and fine somen noodles. According to the Japan Agricultural Standard (JAS), hiyamugi noodles measure about ⅟₁₆ inch in width and about ⅟₂ inch in thickness if the noodles are rectangular in cross section. For the round noodles to classify as hiyamugi, they have to measure about ⅟₁₆ inch in diameter. Hiyamugi is made of wheat flour, salt, and water and, as with udon and somen, it has very little taste of its own, rather it is the dipping sauce that determines the character of the dish. It is for the sensation and the texture of the noodles that hiyamugi are enjoyed during the hot summer season in northeast Japan.

Buying and storing Personally I have yet to come across a fresh version of hiyamugi but that is probably because I come from the Kansai region (in the southeast of Japan) where udon and somen noodles dominate the noodle culture. The dried version is widely sold in Japanese food stores. They keep very well for up to a year if stored in dry kitchen cupboards.

Culinary use Hiyamugi noodles are, as the name implies, eaten cold with dipping sauce. They are boiled briefly, rinsed to wash off the sticky gluten, and then drained. The accompanying dipping sauce is similar to that served with soba noodles but less seasoned.

Natto oroshi hiyamugi
[HIYAMUGI NOODLES WITH FERMENTED SOYBEANS]

This is an easy to prepare noodle dish using natto (fermented soybeans, see p.36).

Serves 4
14 oz. (5–6 cups) dried hiyamugi noodles
2 packets natto
7 oz. daikon (1 cup), shredded
For the sauce
16 fl oz. (1¾ cups) konbu no tsuke dashi (see p.121)
4 fl oz. (½ cup) mirin
2 tablespoons saké
4 fl oz. (½ cup) soy sauce
To finish
4 scallions, finely chopped
½ teaspoon shichimi togarashi (Japanese chili pepper)

Bring a large saucepan of water to a boil and add the noodles. When the water is about to boil over, pour in 1 cup of cold water and return to a boil. Drain, rinse under cold running water, drain again, and set aside.

Empty the natto into a mixing bowl and stir well with a fork until it becomes sticky. Stir in the shredded daikon. Combine all the sauce ingredients. Divide the cooked noodles between 4 serving bowls and add the natto mixture. Pour in the sauce. Garnish with chopped scallion and a sprinkling of shichimi togarashi and serve.

◀ *A big noodle delivery.*

Chilled hiyamugi noodles with tomato sauce

This is not a traditional recipe for it treats hiyamugi noodles like pasta—noodles and pasta are, after all, long lost cousins. If you wish to serve the noodles in a traditional manner, cook them in the same way as soba and serve with the *zaru soba* dipping sauce (see p.44).

Serves 4

14 oz. (5–6 cups) dried hiyamugi noodles

For the tomato sauce

7 oz. (2 medium) ripe vine tomatoes, seeded

1 shallot, peeled and roughly chopped

½ red bell pepper, seeded

½ yellow bell pepper, seeded

½ celery stick, roughly chopped

½ baby cucumber, peeled and chopped

2 tablespoons extra virgin olive oil

Salt and pepper to taste

Prepare all the vegetables for the sauce and roughly chop them. Put them in a food processor and whizz for one or two seconds—the vegetables should be in small bits, not puréed. Add the olive oil and season with salt and pepper, if needed. Refrigerate the sauce while you cook the noodles.

Bring a saucepan of water to a boil and add the noodles. Stir with chopsticks to separate them and when the water returns to a boil, add 1 cup of cold water and bring back to a boil. You may have to repeat this once or twice more, depending how dry the noodles are. Drain, rinse under cold running water, and drain well again. In a big bowl, combine the sauce and the noodles and serve.

▲ *Chilled hiyamugi noodles with tomato sauce.*

ラーメン Ramen [RAMEN NOODLES]

Ramen are not truly Japanese, but an adaptation of Chinese wheat noodles (the word ramen is most likely derived from a Cantonese word, *raomin*). The word literally means 'stretched noodles' and they are also called *Chuka soba* or *Shina soba*, meaning 'Chinese noodles.' Noodle-making techniques, as has been said, were introduced from China over 1,400 years ago to the devoutly Buddhist imperial court of Nara. While noodles such as udon and somen were popular first with Buddhist monks and religious aristocrats and later with the rest of the population, direct copies of Chinese noodles that were often served with meat never caught on.

History Chinese cooking did not become popular until the Meiji Restoration in the late nineteenth century when the ban on meat consumption was lifted. By 1870 there were 515 foreigners living in the designated foreign settlement area of Nagasaki, of whom 338 were Chinese. The majority of those Chinese inhabitants were employed as domestic servants by European and American trading merchants and mostly came from the Canton or Hokkien regions of China. In the following year the Japan–China treaty was signed, granting the Chinese in Japan the freedom to work and move around as they liked. Soon they began opening Chinese restaurants serving southern Chinese home cooking. The popularity of Chinese cuisine grew gradually over the next 50 years.

Ramen are sold by late-night street vendors and by specialist *Ramen ya*, and are dismissed by purists as the worst kind of junk food. However, a highly entertaining film by the late Juzo Itami called *Tampopo* (*Dandelion*) casts a Zen philosophical angle on ramen.

Ramen, or, more accurately, instant ramen, took the whole country by storm when one of the largest flour millers launched chicken ramen in 1958. This revolutionary form of fast food involved no cooking: you just poured boiling water over the dried noodles in a bowl and waited a few minutes. Other manufacturers quickly followed and introduced many varieties, including some with regional flavors. Today, sadly, Japanese instant ramen (often known as pot noodles) are found not only all over Japan but also on supermarket shelves around the world.

Appearance and taste The appearance of ramen differs according to variety: fresh, semi-cooked, and the dreaded instant version. The instant comes in either a cup or a plastic pack, usually with a sachet of powdered broth. Prepare them according to the directions on the package—you will not find a real noodle lover anywhere near them.

Although the fresh variety is more difficult to find, undoubtedly it is the best. Fresh ramen are about the thickness of a soba noodle, pale yellow in color and come in one serving portion. They are not dissimilar to their long-lost Chinese cousins, Shanghai or Hokkien noodles. They can happily be cooked in many different ways: in hot broth, stir-fried, or deep-fried. Their robust meaty texture goes well with a variety of sauces and ingredients.

The semi-cooked variety is normally sold vacuum-packed. It is paler than the fresh variety and looks glossy, as though it were coated with oil. You may come across semi-cooked ramen labeled *yakisoba*: they are not soba but ramen for stir-fries.

Sapporo miso ramen

[SAPPORO MISO SOUP WITH RAMEN]

This is a gutsy, heart-warming miso soup with attitude. Sapporo is the regional capital of Hokkaido, Japan's northernmost island. In the mid nineteenth century, when the newly formed Meiji government, eager to modernize the country, encouraged large numbers of pioneering farmers and miners to go north in search of a new life, Hokkaido was the Japanese equivalent of the Wild West. In the harsh winters, garlic and chili oil warmed the bodies and souls of the new settlers.

Serves 4
2 tablespoons vegetable oil, e.g. groundnut oil
1 tablespoon sesame oil
7 oz. boneless, skinless chicken thighs, thinly sliced
1 onion, peeled and thinly sliced
1 leek, washed and finely sliced
1 carrot, peeled and cut into matchstick strips
5 oz. canned, sliced bamboo shoots, drained
16 snow peas, coarsely chopped
9 oz. (4½ cups) bean sprouts, rinsed and trimmed
4 garlic cloves, peeled, crushed, and finely chopped
Salt and pepper

7 oz. (2½ cups) dried ramen noodles

For the miso soup

1¾ pints (4 cups) chicken broth (preferably home-made)

4 tablespoons soy sauce

4–6 tablespoons medium colored miso paste

To finish

2 scallions, finely chopped

4 teaspoons chili oil (optional)

4 teaspoons sesame seeds, dry roasted

Heat both oils in a wok and swirl to coat. Add the chicken and all the vegetables and stir-fry for 5 minutes over high heat. Adjust the seasoning with salt and pepper and turn down the heat to low. Bring a large saucepan of water to a boil, add the noodles and cook for 3 minutes or until the noodles are soft but firm. Drain and divide them between 4 individual bowls. Add the chicken broth to the wok, turn up the heat and bring to a boil. Add the soy sauce and miso paste, stirring well to ensure that the miso is thoroughly dissolved. Return to a boil and turn off the heat. Ladle the soup over the noodles. Garnish with the chopped scallions, drizzle over the chili oil (if using), sprinkle with sesame seeds, and serve immediately.

Yakisoba

[STIR-FRIED NOODLES WITH SEAFOOD]

This Japanese adaptation of Chinese stir-fried noodles is a popular snack or lunch dish sold by all street vendors. Yakisoba sauce is sold in Japanese grocery stores (use 8 tablespoons), if you don't feel like making your own.

Serves 4

14 oz. (5–6 cups) vacuum-packed yakisoba noodles or fresh ramen noodles

2 tablespoons vegetable oil

1 tablespoon sesame oil

4 oz. (1 cup) large shrimp, shelled and de-veined

4 oz. (1 cup) squid, cut in stamp-size pieces with criss-cross scoring

1 onion, peeled and sliced

1 carrot, peeled and sliced

4 oz. (1–1¼ cups) cabbage leaves, roughly chopped into stamp-size pieces

7 oz. (3½ cups) bean sprouts, trimmed

For the yakisoba sauce

5 tablespoons brown sauce (British HP sauce)

4 tablespoons soy sauce

2 tablespoons tomato ketchup

2 tablespoons oyster sauce

4 tablespoons superfine sugar

To finish

4 teaspoons ground nori (dried seaweed)

4 teaspoons sesame seeds, toasted

4 tablespoons red pickled ginger (optional)

Mix together all the sauce ingredients, if making your own. If using vacuum-packed yakisoba noodles, rinse in hot water, separate the noodles with a pair of chopsticks, drain and set aside. (If using fresh ramen noodles, cook in the usual way.) Heat both oils in a wok and swirl to coat. Add the prawns and squid and stir-fry for 2 minutes before putting to one side. Add all the vegetables and stir-fry for 5 minutes, then mix in the seafood and add the noodles. Toss the noodle mixture well and season with the yakisoba sauce. Divide between 4 individual serving bowls and garnish with the ground nori and sesame seeds, with the pickled ginger in the middle.

◂ *Stir-fried noodles with seafood.*

春雨 Harusame [HARUSAME NOODLES]

History Harusame literally means 'spring rain,' which is a fitting description for this elegant noodle made from potato, sweet potato and cornstarch or mung-bean starch. Harusame noodles are relatively new to Japan, for potatoes and sweet potatoes were late arrivals, introduced by the Portuguese in the sixteenth century.

Manufacture The various starches are mixed with water and then extruded through small holes into boiling water. They are boiled to harden them, then cooled quickly and freeze-dried into crisp, thin filaments.

Appearance and taste Delicate and fine with a translucent, white appearance, harusame are Japan's answer to Thailand's famous cellophane noodles. They vary in length from 5 to 6 inches and can be thread-like or flat and thin.

Buying and storing Harusame are sold dried in manageable-size packets of about 4 oz.

Culinary uses Harusame are often used as a substitute for shirataki noodles in the famous *sukiyaki* (Japanese beef stew, see p.56). Despite their delicate appearance, the noodles have a chewy texture once reconstituted in hot water and can withstand vigorous treatment such as stir-frying. Other culinary uses include soup and salad. Though decidedly Japanese in nature, harusame are also popular in Korea, perhaps because they are not dissimilar to Korean *dang myun* noodles. In Korea they are mixed mainly with shellfish, such as crabs, shrimp, and clams, but my favorite method is to deep-fry them, treating them like unusual tempura batter. They puff up to a fluffy, white bird's nest, giving a highly theatrical appearance and a wizardly satisfaction to anyone cooking them.

Harusame no sunomono

[HARUSAME NOODLE SALAD WITH SHRIMP AND CUCUMBER]

Sunomono means 'vinegary thing'—in other words, the Japanese idea of salad. The slightly resilient texture of harusame noodles adds to this refreshing dish.

Serves 4
7 oz. (1¾ packets) dried harusame noodles
½ oz. dried wakame (seaweed), reconstituted in water and drained
12 large cooked shrimp, heads removed but tails intact
2 baby cucumbers, peeled and finely sliced
1 oz. fresh ginger root (2-inch piece), peeled and finely shredded
For the vinegar dressing
4 tablespoons rice vinegar
1 tablespoon soy sauce
1 tablespoon granulated sugar

Place the noodles in a large bowl and cover with boiling water for 10 minutes or until the noodles are soft. Drain, rinse under cold running water and drain well again. Put the noodles back in a large bowl and chop them roughly into manageable lengths—about 2 inches —with a pair of kitchen scissors. Add the rest of the salad ingredients. Mix all the dressing ingredients together and pour over the salad. Toss lightly, divide between 4 bowls and serve.

Deep-fried prawns with harusame batter

This is a tempura batter with a difference: the pieces of harusame puff up to give a highly dramatic effect. Whether you serve this as a beautiful canapé or an appetizer, this dish is guaranteed to impress your guests.

Makes 16 canapés
16 large shrimp
For the tempura batter
1 egg white
2 fl oz. (3½ tablespoons) cold water
2 oz. (½ cup) plain flour
2 oz. (½ packet) dried harusame noodles, chopped or cut into very small pieces
Vegetable oil, for deep-frying e.g. corn oil
To season
Salt mixed with sansho pepper

Prepare the shrimp and pat dry on paper towels. Mix the egg white with the cold water in a bowl and add the flour. (Don't worry too much about small lumps.) Put the chopped noodle pieces on a plate.

Heat a panful of cooking oil. To test the temperature of the oil, drop in a teaspoonful of batter—if the batter sinks to the bottom and then rises, it is about the right temperature: 310°F. (This is slightly lower than the normal temperature for tempura, because if the oil is too hot it will discolor the batter.)

Holding the shrimp by the tail, dip them in the batter mixture and roll them in the noodles. Deep-fry the shrimp—the noodle pieces will puff up almost straight away but leave them to fry for 1 minute more—then remove and drain well on kitchen paper. Sprinkle with salt mixed with sansho pepper and serve.

白滝 Shirataki [SHIRATAKI NOODLES]

History Shirataki are not truly noodles: they are made from the root of *Amorphophallus konjac*, a Japanese yam known more commonly as konnyaku (devil's tongue). A perennial from Indo China, this yam was first introduced to Japan in the sixth century as an ingredient in Chinese herbal medicine; records show that it was being eaten by the tenth century.

Manufacture These fine strands of konnyaku (see p.182) are sometimes called *ito konnyaku*, meaning 'thread konnyaku.' The bulbous root of the plant is first boiled, then stripped of its black skin and ground to a sticky paste. The paste is extruded through small holes into heated lime water, which works as a coagulant.

Appearance and taste The name *shirataki*, meaning 'white waterfall,' is a fitting description of their shimmering appearance. They come suspended in water in giant, transparent, sausage-shaped plastic tubes or ordinary plastic packs. Like other 'noodles,' shirataki have virtually no taste of their own but are appreciated for their texture. They are best described as fine and jelly-like, slippery but with a certain chewiness.

Culinary uses Their most common use is in *sukiyaki*, a famous Japanese dish of beef and vegetables cooked at the table. While purists believe that *sukiyaki* is incomplete without shirataki, harusame noodles or bean vermicelli noodles make good substitutes.

Health benefits Shirataki are mostly water, 97 percent to be precise, have almost no calories and are fat-free, so are an ideal slimming food. They contain a great deal of indigestible fiber, which cleans the intestines.

Sukiyaki

[JAPANESE BEEF STEW]

Sukiyaki came about when the Japanese, having not eaten beef for over 1,000 years, adopted what is essentially a beef stew with vegetables and transformed it into something more Japanese. This is an easy dish to prepare: you arrange all the sliced ingredients on a large platter, then you and your guests cook everything together at the table. The traditional dipping sauce is raw beaten egg— I have never much cared for it, but I leave you to decide.

Serves 4
2 white onions, peeled and thinly sliced
8 negi or baby leeks, chopped into 1-inch lengths
1 packet shirataki noodles, about 7 oz., drained
8 fresh enoki mushrooms, stalks removed, caps cut in half
7 oz. (2–2½ cups) Chinese cabbage, blanched and roughly chopped
7 oz. (2–2½ cups) Japanese greens, such as shungiku (see p.76), mizuna (see p.78) or mibuna (see p.75)
1 lb. top-quality sirloin beef, cut into thin slices
1 tablespoon saké
6 tablespoons vegetable oil
For the Kansai-style warishita cooking sauce
8 fl oz. (1 cup) soy sauce
9 oz. (1¼ cups) sugar
8 fl oz. (1 cup) mirin

Arrange all the dry ingredients on a large plate, sprinkle the saké over the beef and set aside. Mix all the ingredients for the cooking sauce in a jug, stir until all the sugar has dissolved and set aside. (This is quite a sweet cooking sauce—if preferred, reduce the amount of sugar or use saké instead of mirin.)

Set the table-top hob in the middle of the table. Place a heavy, shallow, cast-iron skillet on it to heat up and add enough oil to coat the surface. Add about half of the beef and let it brown before pouring on about half the cooking sauce. Add the onion and leeks and cook them for 2–3 minutes, then add the noodles. Cook for 2 minutes more before adding the rest of the vegetables and the remaining cooking sauce. Your guests should help themselves as soon as the beef and vegetables are cooked.

Shirataki to kinoko no ni-mono

[SHIRATAKI NOODLES WITH MUSHROOMS]

This is a quick one-pot dish using shirataki noodles, which absorb all the flavor of the mushrooms and seaweed. This dish can be prepared in advance and reheated.

Serves 4

7 oz. (1 packet) shirataki noodles, blanched in boiling water
2 tablespoons vegetable oil
1 teaspoon sesame oil
8 fresh shiitake mushrooms, stalks removed, sliced
4 oz. shimeji mushrooms, trimmed and separated
1 piece konbu (dried kelp), 1x3 inches, thinly torn

◄ A noodle stand at a railway station.

▲ Sukiyaki. The raw beaten egg dipping sauce is optional!

For the cooking broth

3 fl oz. (⅓ cup) water
4 fl oz. (½ cup) saké
2 tablespoons mirin
2–3 tablespoons soy sauce

Roughly chop the blanched shirataki noodles into easy-to-eat lengths of 1 inch. Heat both oils in a saucepan over medium heat. Add the noodles and mushrooms and sauté briskly for 2 minutes.

Pour in all the ingredients for the cooking broth and add the konbu. Turn down the heat and simmer, removing any scum that forms on the surface, until the liquid has reduced by half. Serve hot or at room temperature.

The most basic and quintessential Japanese food is *ichijuissai*: one soup and one vegetable dish to accompany a bowl of plain boiled rice. Vegetables have always been central to Japanese cuisine, as appetizers, as side dishes, and as main courses. Buddhist teaching prohibited Japanese people from eating meat for some 1,200 years, and they had to rely on vegetable protein. Surprisingly enough, only a handful of vegetables are true natives and many vegetables that are integral to Japanese cuisine are of foreign origin. Included in this section are typical 'Japanese' vegetables, which are becoming increasingly familiar and easy to obtain in the West.

3 Vegetables

牛蒡 Gobo [BURDOCK]

Burdock is native to the Mediterranean, western Asia, Siberia and northern China, but only in Japan has burdock been bred and cultivated as a vegetable. This thin, brown root vegetable has been used in Chinese herbal medicine since ancient times. In Japan, too, it was originally used as a medicine: archaeologists found a large quantity of seeds in a 3,000-year-old village. Burdock was not cultivated in Japan until the eleventh century but, despite its slow start, burdock has been naturalized and now features in many Japanese dishes.

How it grows Burdock is a hardy biannual belonging to the chrysanthemum family, but the edible annual varieties are preferred in Japan. The spring-sown ones are ready for lifting from midsummer until autumn, and the autumn-sown varieties are harvested the following spring or summer.

Appearance and taste Burdock roots can measure as long as 4 feet, but those sold in shops are normally about 12–18 inches. The outer skin is usually brown, but paler-skinned varieties are being developed. The root is covered with characteristic hairy, short rootlets. The flesh is white when it is first cut but quickly turns grey unless put in water. Burdock root has a distinctive smell. When cooked, the slightly bitter taste changes, ranging from mild to sweet to strong, depending on the age and quality of the plant.

Buying and storing In the West, burdock is most likely to be sold cut into lengths in a packet. Don't buy very thick ones with darker centers as they can be rather woody and taste of mud. The traditional way to keep burdock roots is to bury them in the ground, but they keep for a few weeks if wrapped in paper and refrigerated.

Health benefits Burdock is rich in fiber—effective for curing constipation, restoring healthy digestion, and lowering cholesterol. Regular consumption of burdock is known to prevent diabetes.

Culinary uses Burdock has never been eaten for its nutritional value but for its unique flavor and texture. The most popular way to cook burdock, called *kimpira*, is to shred and stir-fry it with a small portion of shredded carrot seasoned with soy sauce and chili powder.

Gobo no kimpira

[BURDOCK STIR-FRY]

Kimpira is a general cooking term, meaning to cook and season with sweet soy sauce, and burdock is the most popular ingredient for *kimpira*.

Serves 4
7 oz. (1 cup) burdock
2 tablespoons vegetable oil
1 tablespoon sesame oil
2 tablespoons soy sauce
1 tablespoon granulated sugar
1 tablespoon mirin
½ teaspoon dry chili flakes

If you have bought fresh burdock with a dark brown skin, scrub with a nailbrush or kitchen scourer until it becomes pale cream, then cut the burdock into thick matchsticks, soak in cold water very briefly and drain. (This is unnecessary if you have bought ready-washed and chopped roots.)

Heat a wok or skillet, add both oils and swirl. Add the drained burdock and stir. Add the soy sauce, sugar, and mirin and cook over a medium heat until most of the liquid has evaporated. Sprinkle on the chili flakes and serve.

▸ *Mackerel and burdock deep-fried dumplings.*

Kenchin jiru

[KENCHIN SOUP]

This is a hearty, country-style vegetable soup. One of my grandmothers, who was a great udon-noodle maker, used to cook large quantities of this soup, so that any leftover could be served with udon noodles the following day.

Serves 4

1 sheet deep-fried tofu
1 firm 'cotton' tofu, wrapped in paper towels to drain
1 burdock root, scrubbed clean and roughly chopped
4 oz. (1¼ cups) daikon (Japanese radish), peeled and roughly chopped into bite-size pieces
1 carrot, peeled and chopped into bite-size pieces
2 tablespoons sesame oil
1½ pints (4 cups) konbu no tsuke dashi (see p.121)
2–3 tablespoons soy sauce
2 tablespoons mirin
Salt
4 scallions, roughly chopped

Pour boiling water over the deep-fried tofu to remove the excess oil and cut it and the 'cotton' tofu into bite-size pieces. Soak the chopped burdock, daikon, and carrot in a bowl of cold water for 10–15 minutes to remove their strong tannin. Drain and set aside. Heat the oil in a large saucepan and fry the burdock, daikon, and carrot until they become soft. Add both kinds of tofu and pour in the dashi, soy sauce, and mirin. Turn down the heat and bring to the boil. Taste and add salt if necessary, then add the chopped scallions and serve.

Saba to gobo no dango

[MACKEREL AND BURDOCK DEEP-FRIED DUMPLINGS]

My family is reluctant to eat either burdock or mackerel on its own but it is a completely different story if I put them together and turn them into easy-to-eat dumplings.

Serves 4

1 fresh mackerel, filleted
1 burdock, peeled and finely shredded
4 oz. ground chicken
1 onion, peeled and finely ground
½ carrot, peeled and finely chopped
1 oz. (2-inch piece) fresh ginger root, peeled and ground
1 egg yolk
1 tablespoon miso paste
Salt and pepper

Place the mackerel skin side down on a chopping board with its tail towards you. With a spoon, flake the fillet—you may be pleasantly surprised just how easily a mackerel flakes. Discard the skin and any bones. Blanch the shredded burdock briefly in cold water to remove the tannin and drain. Put all the ingredients in a large bowl and mix well. Heat a saucepan of vegetable oil to 350°F, gently drop in a dessertspoonful of the mixture and deep-fry for 3 minutes. Drain on paper towel and serve with a vinegar and soy dipping sauce.

蓮根 Renkon [LOTUS ROOT]

Anyone who has seen a lotus flower would agree that it is gloriously beautiful. No wonder it has become the symbol of Buddhist purity. The lotus, a perennial aquatic plant and a member of the water lily family, is a native of Asia. It has long been associated with Buddhism and statues of Buddha are always seated on a cushion that depicts a lotus flower. Man's struggle to redeem himself and to rise above the material world to realise his divine potential of purity is reflected in how the lotus grows in a muddy pond and yet produces the most beautiful flowers. In Japan, the spread of Buddhism made lotus an important ingredient and it is regarded as an auspicious root vegetable gracing many ceremonial and festival tables.

History For a long time it was believed that the lotus was first introduced to Japanese soil from China, together with Buddhism in the mid sixth century. The discovery of 2,000-year-old lotus seeds in 1951 casts a completely new light on its history. It is now understood that there were native varieties of lotus in Japan before the Chinese varieties were brought in as ornamental plants. Today both native and Chinese varieties thrive all over Japan. Although it is not entirely clear when lotus roots began to be eaten, the menu of a Buddhist temple in 1118 AD includes lotus roots and, from the mid fifteenth century onwards, lotus was grown in castle moats as a valuable emergency food.

How it grows Although the leaves, flowers, flower buds and seeds are all edible, it is mainly for the roots that the lotus is grown. Rhizomes with several segments are planted in mud in March and April. Although lotus roots can be harvested any time of the year, the best time is after the flowers have died down in the fall and before the water freezes in winter.

Appearance and taste In complete contrast to its graceful flower, lotus roots are bizarre looking; they resemble a string of giant muddy sausages. Those buff-colored, rather wooden-looking rhizomes measuring around 2⅛ inch diameter and nearly 3ft long are divided into cylinder-like segments, each up to 6 inches long. Air passages run though the length of the rhizomes, giving them a beautiful paper-chain-like cross section. The young lotus roots have a crunchy texture with a mild sweet flavor.

Health benefits The lotus root contains carbohydrate, protein, vitamin C, calcium, iron, and phosphorous. Despite its muddy habitat, it is regarded as the symbol of purity and thought to cleanse the body. A mixture of raw, shredded root and hot water is an old-fashioned remedy for cough and catarrh. Because it is fibrous, the lotus root is an effective natural remedy for constipation. Both the seeds and roots refresh the body and improve blood circulation and, for this part, I am unable to resolve the contradiction, but they are supposed to increase sexual virility!

Culinary uses All parts of the lotus are edible, both raw and cooked. The young leaves and stems cooked with rice is a well-known vegetarian dish. The seeds are eaten fresh in the summer as a sweet snack and flour made from seeds is used to make fillings for Japanese candies and cakes. The root is by far the most widely used part of the lotus in the Japanese kitchen. It is pickled, stewed, stir-fried, deep-fried, dressed with sesame seeds, cooked with rice, and mixed with sushi rice.

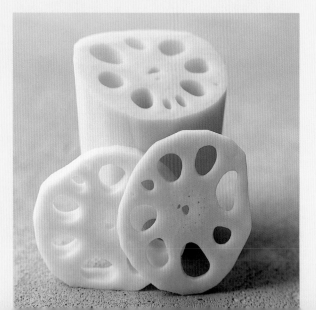

Renkon no kimpira

[SIMMERED LOTUS ROOT]

Serves 4–6

14 oz. (2–2½ cups) lotus root, peeled and thinly sliced
1 tablespoon each sesame oil and vegetable oil
2 tablespoons each mirin and soy sauce
1 teaspoon toasted sesame seeds
Pinch of shichimi togarashi (Japanese chili pepper) to
    taste, finely chopped

Soak the lotus slices in cold water for 10 minutes and
drain. Heat both oils in a saucepan and sauté the slices
over a high heat until they become soft. Add the mirin
and soy sauce and reduce the heat to low. Cook until
the juice has almost disappeared, then add the sesame
seeds and stir well. Transfer to a serving dish, sprinkle
with shichimi togarashi, and serve.

▸ *The beautiful flower of the lotus plant.*

▴ *Simmered lotus root.*

Subasu

[LOTUS ROOT IN SWEET VINEGAR]

Serves 4–6

14 oz. (2–2½ cups) lotus root, peeled and cut into
    ¼-inch slices
1 tablespoon rice vinegar
For the sweet vinegar
8 fl oz. (1 cup) water
8 fl oz. (1 cup) rice vinegar
2 oz. (¼ cup) granulated sugar
1 teaspoon salt

Put the sliced lotus root in a saucepan and cover with
cold water. Add the rice vinegar (to stop discoloration)
and bring to a boil. Meanwhile, combine all the sauce
ingredients in a bowl. When the lotus slices have
become translucent, drain well and transfer them to
the bowl of sweet vinegar mixture. Leave to soak for
30 minutes, then drain and serve.

里芋 Sato imo [TARO]

Taro is one of Japan's oldest vegetables, though it is not a native plant. It originates in India and southern China, where wild varieties of taro have been growing since long before rice cultivation started in the thirteenth century BC. Partly because of the tuber's history and also because of how it multiplies, the taro has long been considered auspicious: it is seen as a symbol of family prosperity and features in many Japanese religious and seasonal festivals.

How it grows Although of tropical origin, taro is robust and is cultivated in almost every part of Japan. It prefers warm, moist conditions and requires a lot of water during its seven-month growing period. In Japan, starter tubers are planted in early spring and lifted before the first frost. Like other root vegetables such as potatoes and burdock, taro is available almost all year round.

Appearance and taste The taro leaves are similar to those of banana plants, and both young leaves and stalks are eaten. There are many varieties but in Japan the smaller ones are preferred. Tubers vary in shape but are usually spherical, tapering at one end. They have stripy, brown, hairy skin; the flesh is white with a slight purple tinge. Peeled tubers are very slippery, with a taste not dissimilar to that of potatoes but sweeter and creamier in texture.

Health benefits Taro is 14 percent carbohydrate, with a trace of protein, and is easy to digest. Burns and tumors used to be treated with a mixture of shredded taro, flour, and ginger juice. Shredded taro is also known to reduce fever.

Buying and storing Taro is available almost all year round in the West from Asian grocery stores. Choose ones that feel solid and therefore haven't dried out. Taro keeps for a week or two if wrapped in paper that keeps it moist and stored in a cool dark place—do not refrigerate.

Culinary uses There is a famous taro dish in Kyoto called *imobo*, in which taro is cooked slowly with salt-cod and seasoned with soy sauce and sugar. Simmered with dried kelp seaweed, taro makes a subtle and delicious vegetarian dish. It is also used raw in salad, and can also be broiled or baked.

Sato imo no dengaku

[BROILED TARO WITH SWEET MISO PASTE]

Dengaku is sweet, seasoned miso paste, which goes very well with the subtle flavor of broiled taro. Cut the taro into small bite-size pieces to make a delicious canapé with a difference.

Makes 10 canapés
10 sato imo (taro)
2½ pints (6 cups) water
1 teaspoon salt
2 oz. (¼ cup) granulated sugar

▸ *A farmer attending his flooded taro field.*

For the dengaku paste
2 oz. miso paste
2 oz. (¼ cup) granulated sugar
3 tablespoons soy sauce
3 tablespoons mirin
1 tablespoon sesame oil
1 egg yolk

Peel the taro and cut each tuber in half. Cook the taro in
a saucepan of water with the salt and sugar until al
dente. Drain and set aside. Preheat the broiler. Combine
all the ingredients for the dengaku paste in a mixing
bowl, adding the egg yolk at the end to thicken the
mixture. Spoon some of the mixture onto each piece of
taro, broil for 5 minutes or until lightly toasted and serve.

◂ *Oven-baked taro with sage.*

Oven-baked taro with sage

This is an Italian-influenced dish—sage and garlic add
an appetizing flavor to the otherwise bland taro.

Serves 4
16 sato imo (taro)
16 fl oz. (2 cups) olive oil
4 garlic cloves, peeled but left whole
8 sage leaves
Salt

Preheat the oven to 350°F. Peel the taro. Pour the oil into
a small baking pan and put it in the oven to heat. Add
the taro, garlic cloves, and sage leaves and bake for
20 minutes or until the taro is cooked. Sprinkle with
salt and serve.

山芋 Yama imo [YAM]

The yam originates in southwest China. There are more than 600 varieties growing all over Asia, of which 500 are edible. One of its Japanese names, *yama imo*, literally means 'mountain potato,' for it has been growing in the wild since prehistoric times. Another Japanese name, *naga imo*, means 'long potato,' a name derived from its shape. To confuse matters further, the yam is sometimes called *san yaku*, meaning 'mountain medicine,' because of its high nutritional value and widespread medicinal use. The elongated wild variety was most probably native to Japan, while the varieties now cultivated were introduced from China. Its different names aside, the yam is one of the most highly prized vegetables in Japan and, unlike in China, where the vegetable is more a medicine than a cooking ingredient, both wild and cultivated varieties are widely used in Japanese cuisine.

How it grows In the wild, this attractive perennial scrambles up trees, sometimes as high as 20 feet, and bears two or three elongated tubers. Cultivated varieties are propagated by using sprouting tubers.

Appearance and taste The different varieties are a long truncheon shape, a large gingko-leaf shape, and giant potato shape. The most common variety of yam is truncheon shaped with a rough brown skin. Its flesh is nearly pure white and has a sticky, almost slimy feel. The yam has almost no smell, and is rather bland. It is valued not for its flavor but because it goes with anything, taking on the flavor of its cooking partners.

Health benefits As one of its names suggests, the yam has many medicinal uses. Its enzymes make it an effective digestive; like many naturally sticky vegetables, the yam helps to maintain supple skin; and regular consumption is believed to slow down the ageing process and prevent symptoms of old age. The yam is rich in fiber, so relieves constipation, reduces cholesterol, and helps to lower blood pressure.

Buying and storing Although the yam is available all year round from Asian grocery stores, the best seasons are autumn and winter. Choose ones that feel solid and weighty and are free of bruises. Wrap them in newspaper to stop them drying out and keep them in a cool dark place. Shredded yam can be frozen.

Culinary uses The simplest and most popular way to use yam is shredded, to make a sticky sauce that is seasoned with a soy sauce-based broth and served with boiled rice or soba noodles. Shredded yam mixed with vinegar makes a refreshing salad. Dried, powdered yam is used as a binding agent in soba noodles and deep-fried fish cakes. The powder is also used to make sweet cakes.

Yamaimo no salada

[FRESH YAM SALAD]

Yam's stickiness makes it rather tricky to cut—sprinkle some salt on the chopping board as grit.

Serves 4
10 oz. (1½–1¾ cups) yam, peeled
3 tablespoons soy sauce
2 tablespoons rice vinegar
1 tablespoon granulated sugar

Cut the yam into thick matchsticks and rinse under cold running water.
Drain and set aside. Put the soy sauce, rice vinegar, and sugar in a bowl and mix well.
Add the drained yam to the soy mixture and mix until the yam becomes elastic. Transfer to a large serving bowl or divide into four equal portions and serve.

Maguro no tororo ae

[DICED TUNA WITH YAM SAUCE]

The yam's sticky consistency makes it a perfect ingredient in a sauce. The sauce can be served on plain boiled rice or with chilled soba noodles.

Serves 4

10 oz. (1½–1¾ cups) yam, peeled
16 fl oz. (1¾ cups) dashi broth (see p.169)
5 tablespoons soy sauce
1 tablespoon granulated sugar
½ tablespoon mirin
14 oz. fresh tuna, cut into bite-size cubes
½ teaspoon salt

To garnish

2 teaspoons wasabi powder mixed with the same amount of water
2 scallions, finely sliced into rings
1 sheet nori (dried seaweed), finely torn

Shred the peeled yam into a large mixing bowl. Add the dashi broth, soy sauce, sugar, and mirin and mix well. Put the tuna in a separate bowl, sprinkle with the salt and pour in the yam mixture. Stir to combine. Divide the tuna and yam mixture between four serving dishes and garnish with small mounds of wasabi, chopped scallion, and torn nori.

▼ *Diced tuna with yam sauce.*

薩摩芋 Satsuma imo [SWEET POTATO]

History It is well known that the sweet potato is a South American native that was first introduced to Europe by Christopher Columbus in the late fifteenth century. Its other, less famous, journey was across the Pacific Ocean to China. In the seventeenth century it came to the southern region of Satsuma via the island of Okinawa, hence its Japanese name. It quickly spread across the island of Kyushu, where the warm climate suited its cultivation and saved the islanders from famine when the rice crop failed. Ever since then it has been cultivated as a supplementary crop to rice in the warmer parts of Japan.

How it grows Numerous varieties of sweet potato are grown in the southwestern regions of Japan, where the climate is warm and free from frost until late autumn. The starter tuber is planted in nursery beds in March and young shoots are transplanted one month after germination. In warm areas it is harvested from May right through to November.

Appearance and taste Skin and flesh color of the sweet potato varies from cream to pale yellow, orange, bright red, and maroon. It has a rich, sweet aroma and tastes, as the name suggests, sweet.

Health benefits Sweet potato is regarded as a health-giving and high-energy food. It is over 30 percent carbohydrate, which is nearly twice as high as ordinary potatoes. It is also rich in fiber, promoting healthy bowels.

Buying and storing Similar to ordinary potatoes, sweet potato keeps well for up to a week or so if stored in a cool, airy place away from direct sunlight. Do not put it in the refrigerator.

Culinary uses The sweet potato was traditionally used to bulk out rice or rice porridge. This saved the nation from starvation during the acute food shortages of the immediate post-war period and, for this reason, sweet potato has always been associated with times of scarcity and rather looked down upon as a food for the poor. My childhood memories of sweet potato are happy but mixed with a sense of naughtiness—perhaps because of its poor image.

The sweet potato vendor was a popular winter sight in Japan and women and children would stop him outside their houses to buy piping hot, stone-baked sweet potatoes wrapped in old newspaper. Today, because of its sweet flavor, it is often used in desserts. It is also used for distilling *shochu*, a potent spirit. A flour made from powdered sweet potato is often used as a thickening agent.

Satsuma imo no shojin age
[DEEP-FRIED SWEET POTATO IN BATTER]

The difference between *tempura* and *shojin age* is that the latter is for deep-frying vegetables. In order to enhance the delicate flavour of vegetables, the batter for *shojin age* is thicker but more thinly applied and the temperature of the oil is lower.

Serves 4
1 sweet potato, scrubbed clean
Vegetable oil, for deep-frying
Salt
For the batter
7 fl oz. water
1 egg white
4 oz. (1 cup) all-purpose flour

▸ *Vanilla-flavored*
sweet potato
with oranges.

Cut the sweet potato into slices ½ inch thick. Now make the batter. Combine the water and egg white in a mixing bowl. Add the flour and stir to mix—but do not over-stir as it will make the batter sticky. Heat the oil in a wok or deep-fat fryer to 300°F. Coat the slices of sweet potato with the batter, taking care not to over-coat them. Gently submerge the slices in the oil and deep-fry them until the batter turns pale cream in color. Turn them over to cook the other side. Drain on paper towels and serve with a small dish of salt.

Vanilla flavored sweet potato with oranges

Traditionally, sweet potatoes are stone-baked and eaten hot on their own as a snack. This makes an elegant change with its refreshing orange and vanilla flavor.

Serves 4
8 oz. (1 medium) sweet potato, peeled
1 orange, sliced
1 vanilla bean, slit lengthways
2 oz. (¼ cup) granulated sugar

Chop the sweet potato into chunks 1 inch thick and soak in cold water. Drain, then put the chunks in a saucepan with enough water to cover. Bring to a boil, then reduce the heat and simmer for about 10 minutes. Drain off the cooking water. Add the orange slices, vanilla bean, sugar, and 1¾–2 cups of fresh water and cook until the potato is soft. Remove the chunks of potato and transfer them to a serving dish. Reduce the liquid by half and drizzle it over the potato.

◂ ◂ *Farmers on Kyushu Island harvesting sweet potatoes.*

大根 Daikon [JAPANESE RADISH/MOOLI]

Daikon means 'big root,' an apt name for this popular vegetable. Although not native to Japan, it is the country's most widely cultivated vegetable. It was grown in ancient times around the Mediterranean and in central Asia—ancient Egyptian texts record that the slaves conscripted to build the pyramids were given a variety of radish (probably something similar to the modern breakfast radish)—and the larger varieties are believed to have been developed in China around the fourth century BC. There is no record of its first arrival in Japan but by the sixth century AD it was already considered to be a noble vegetable and since then it has become deeply incorporated in Japanese cuisine.

How it grows Many varieties are grown in Japan, some long, some thick, some round. Although it used to be grown as a winter vegetable, it is now grown all year round with three main sowing seasons: spring, summer (the main one), and autumn.

Appearance and taste The Japanese radish is very different from the little, round, red radishes of the West. Imagine a giant white carrot: it is large, anything between 8 inches and 2 feet long. The roots are tapered or cylindrical and can be pointed or rounded at the end, sometimes with a few white whiskers. The skin is a translucent white but many varieties are green-shouldered at the top. Inside they are normally white but some green-shouldered varieties have a green tinge. Pure white varieties are generally more pungent and peppery than the green-shouldered ones, which can even be faintly sweet in flavor.

Buying and storing Japanese radishes are available all year round from Asian grocery stores, but are particularly plentiful between autumn and early spring. Choose ones that feel heavy and solid, and are rigid, with unblemished skin and a pungent radish smell. If possible, buy one with plenty of green leaves on top, as the leaves are also edible. It will keep for four to five days refrigerated.

Health benefits In Japan, daikon has long been considered a detoxicant and digestive aid. In fact, it is a bit of an all-round home remedy: shredded daikon with hot water is taken for colds and applied locally for burns or bruises, while sugared daikon is used as a cough medicine. Daikon is 95 percent water and has a very low calorie count.

Culinary uses Daikon appears in a variety of forms in the Japanese kitchen. Young seedlings called *kaiware daikon*, meaning 'opening-shell radish,' are as commonplace in Japanese supermarkets as cress in the West; they are used mostly in salads or as a garnish but can also be used in soups and sauces. The

green leaves are used raw in salad, pickled, simmered in soup, and stir-fried—there are a few varieties grown especially for their leaves. It is for the big root, however, that the vegetable is usually grown. The root is sliced very finely as a garnish for sashimi (slices of raw fish); shredded it is used as a dipping sauce for the famous tempura dishes and is often served with soba noodles or as an essential accompaniment for broiled fish dishes. Daikon is used in simmering dishes either on its own or with meat or poultry as it can withstand long slow cooking and absorbs the flavor and juice of other ingredients without disintegrating. Dried sliced daikon, *kiriboshi daikon*, was once important as a preserved vegetable and was used as an army field ration. Today dried daikon is appreciated more for its distinctive flavor. Most of all, daikon is used to make the famous *takuan* (yellow pickled radishes), one of the most popular pickles in Japan.

Oroshi daikon no salada

[SHREDDED DAIKON SALAD DRESSING]

Daikon has a refreshing flavor and aroma that makes it perfect for salad dressing, especially for dishes that contain oily fish or meat.

7 oz. (1 cup) daikon, peeled and shredded
Juice of ½ lemon
2 tablespoons granulated sugar
2 fl oz. (3½ tablespoons) soy sauce
2 tablespoons rice vinegar
1 teaspoon sesame seeds, toasted
4 tablespoons virgin olive oil
1 teaspoon sesame oil

Mix all the ingredients together in a jam jar, put the lid on and shake vigorously to blend. The dressing will keep for several days refrigerated. Use it to dress any salad containing cooked meats or oily fish such as salmon and sardines.

◣ *Simmered daikon with grainy mustard and miso.*
◂ *Farmer's wives hanging daikon out to dry on huge wooden frames. Once dry, the daikon will be pickled.*

Horofuki daikon

[SIMMERED DAIKON WITH GRAINY MUSTARD AND MISO]

This modern adaptation of an old traditional recipe combines Western grainy mustard with traditional Japanese miso.

Serves 4
10 inches daikon, peeled and cut into eight slices approx 1 inch thick
1 sheet konbu (dried kelp), postcard size
3 tablespoons grainy mustard
1 tablespoon mirin
1 teaspoon soy sauce
1 tablespoon white miso paste
1 tablespoon virgin olive oil

Put the daikon chunks in a saucepan, cover with water, add the konbu and bring to a boil over a medium heat. Turn down the heat when it reaches boiling point and let it simmer for 10 minutes or until the daikon becomes almost translucent. Leave to cool overnight.

Just before serving, put 2 tablespoons of the cooking liquid in a separate saucepan and heat. Add the mustard, mirin, and soy sauce before stirring in the miso paste. When the miso paste has dissolved, simmer the mixture for 5 minutes to reduce it, then turn off the heat. Meanwhile, re-heat the daikon. When it is warm, divide the chunks between four individual dishes. Put a tablespoon of sauce over each chunk of daikon, drizzle with olive oil, and serve.

蕪 Kabu [TURNIP]

Kabu originally came from the Mediterranean and Afghanistan. It arrived in China 2,000 years ago but there is no clear record of its entry into Japan. By the seventh century, however, it had become an important vegetable and many different varieties are grown all over Japan.

How it grows Traditionally it was grown in northeast regions of Japan by the primitive slash-and-burn method: a field was cleared and burnt in mid July, with mature turnips being harvested in the late fall. Today it is grown more or less all year round except in midsummer.

Appearance and taste Nearly forty varieties, of varying shapes, sizes and colors, are grown in Japan. The biggest variety, *shogoin*, is grown in the Kyoto region. It has an almost pure white global root, typically weighing 2¼–4½ pounds and is used for making pickles. The most commonly seen type has jagged green leaves and a round white root which tapers off at the end. The size can vary from ping-pong ball to tennis ball and some kinds have flatter roots than others. One other

famous variety, *hinona kabu*, deserves a mention: it is the same shape and size as a baby carrot and has a pink top. This variety has been grown for more than 500 years for making pretty *sakura zuke*, reputedly named for its cherry-blossom color by an emperor. Although Japanese turnips come in different varieties, they all taste like mild radishes.

Buying and storing If possible, choose ones which still have their green leaves as the leaves can also be used in cooking. The round root part should be unblemished and feel solid. Kabu will keep fresh for a few days in the refrigerator.

Health benefits Nutritionally, kabu is similar to the Japanese radish and, like daikon, is considered an effective digestive aid. The root is rich in vitamin C, iron and fiber. The green leaves are also nutritious, being rich in vitamin A, and are believed to reduce high blood pressure and help prevent hardening of the arteries. The leaves have a high calcium content, so are good for bones and teeth.

Culinary uses Both leaves and root are pickled—there are many regional specialities—and can also be used in soups, simmered dishes, and salads.

Kabu no miso shiru
[MISO SOUP WITH TURNIPS]

This is a heartwarming winter soup, which uses both the leaves and roots of newly harvested turnips. Stir-frying the turnips in sesame oil brings out their subtle sweetness and flavor.

Serves 4
1¾ pints (4 cups) dashi broth (see p.169)
4–6 tablespoons light brown miso paste
3–4 tablespoons sesame oil
7 oz. (1–1½ cups) turnips, chopped, the root roughly and the leaves finely
2 tablespoons soy sauce
Salt

▸ *Japanese Kabu being dried ready for pickling.*

Heat the dashi broth in a saucepan over a medium heat and add the miso paste just before the broth reaches boiling point. (Adding the miso through a small tea strainer will ensure that it dissolves evenly.) Turn off the heat and set aside. Heat the oil in a skillet and quickly sauté the chopped turnips until they are cooked. Turn off the heat and stir in the soy sauce. Transfer the turnips to the saucepan of miso soup and return to a boil. Take off the heat as soon as the soup begins to boil and add salt if required.

Turnips marinated in sweet vinegar with smoked salmon

This is an adaptation of a pickled turnip dish called *senmai zuke,* which means 'thousand layers pickle.' If cooking for vegetarians, omit the smoked salmon.

Serves 4
1 lb. (2½–3 cups) turnips, preferably large ones, peeled
1 piece konbu (dried kelp), postcard size
1¾ pints (4 cups) slightly salted water

For the pickling mixture
2 dried bird's-eye chiles
2 tablespoons salt
1 piece konbu, postcard size, roughly chopped
2 oz. mirin
2 oz. rice vinegar
4 oz. smoked salmon

Cut the turnips into slices ⅛ inch thick. Put the slices in a large bowl, add the piece of konbu and pour over enough saltwater to cover. Leave to soften for about 1 hour. Drain, then make a single layer of the softened turnip in a flat-based non-metallic container.

Sprinkle with salt, add the konbu pieces and pour over some mirin and vinegar. Repeat this process until you have used all the ingredients.

Place the chiles on top and cover with a plastic or non-metallic plate small enough to fit in the container and put a weight (a large can of tomatoes is ideal) on top of that. Leave overnight or for up to 3 days in a cool dark place. Take out the pieces of turnip (they should feel slippery) and layer with smoked salmon slices.

▼ *Turnips marinated in sweet vinegar with smoked salmon.*

うど Udo [UDO]

This huge, pale-colored stalk is one of a handful of vegetables native to Japan, and it has no name in English: its Latin name is *Aralia cordata*. It grows wild all over Japan or is cultivated, often near large cities. Although it has rather unfortunate connotations—it is used as a euphemism for a useless giant—it is a highly prized vegetable of ancient origin and features in many traditional dishes.

How it grows Wild udo grows in the mountains all over Japan, as well as in Korea and China. It is a large-leaved perennial plant. Cultivated varieties are grown in the dark and can be up to 5 feet long.

Appearance and taste Even Japanese people fail to recognise udo, as it is a rare sight in ordinary Japanese fruit and vegetable stores. It is sometimes called Japanese asparagus, but that is stretching the imagination a little too far. The wild variety is blanched by partially covering it with earth, while cultivated varieties are grown in the dark to keep them soft and pale colored. Udo's pale flesh has a mild and subtle flavor and a refreshingly crunchy texture.

Health benefits Udo is not eaten for its nutritional value but for its taste and texture. It does however help to rid the body of excess fluid—it is an effective natural diuretic. It can be used as a painkiller, too, and will bring down a fever.

Culinary uses Udo appears widely in many of the more traditional dishes: it is used in soups, salads, simmered dishes, and is pickled or finely shredded as a garnish for fish dishes. Spring varieties are preferred because of their more delicate flavor.

Carpaccio of udo with tomato and basil

Serves 4
1 large, ripe beef tomato
1 teaspoon salt
3 tablespoons extra virgin olive oil
7 oz. udo
Juice of ½ lemon
Freshly ground pepper
A few fresh basil leaves

Skin the tomato by submerging it in boiling water. Peel off the skin, seed, chop coarsely and put in a bowl. Add ½ teaspoon salt and 1 tablespoon of extra virgin olive oil and mix well. Refrigerate for at least 30 minutes to let the flavor develop and infuse. Put the serving plate in the refrigerator to chill, too. Peel the udo and slice it lengthways into 2-inch long, 1⁄16-inch thick rectangular pieces. Put all the udo in a bowl and add the remaining ½ teaspoon salt, olive oil and the lemon juice, and mix well. On the chilled serving plate, arrange the slices of udo, spoon over the tomato, sprinkle with freshly ground pepper and basil leaves, and serve.

◀ *Harvesting soft, pale udo that has been cultivated in the dark.*

壬生菜 Mibuna [MIBUNA]

Mibuna is a relatively new vegetable. Like its elder brother mizuna (see p.78), from which mibuna was developed in the nineteenth century, it belongs to the *tsuke na* family. Both mizuna and mibuna are regarded as Japanese vegetables, even though they originated in China.

How it grows Like mizuna, it is a vigorous, hardy annual that grows almost all the year round. However, its best season is traditionally late autumn to early spring.

Appearance and taste Mibuna is an attractive vegetable that grows in a very elegant and striking spray-like clump. Each one of its long, narrow leaves measures ½–1½ inches wide and 12–18 inches long, depending on variety, and has a rounded tip. Mibuna has a slightly stronger flavor than mizuna.

Health benefits Nutritionally and medically, mibuna is very similar to mizuna.

Culinary uses In Japan, mibuna is eaten fresh and pickled. In the West, both mibuna and mizuna make excellent salad greens, especially in winter and early spring when the range of salad vegetables is limited.

Mibuna to abura age no nimono
[SIMMERED MIBUNA WITH DEEP-FRIED TOFU]

This is another homely dish that used to appear regularly at my grandmother's.

Serves 4
2 sheets deep-fried tofu
1 tablespoon vegetable oil
7 oz. (2–2½ cups) mibuna, cleaned and roughly chopped
3 tablespoons soy sauce
1 tablespoon granulated sugar
3 tablespoons mirin
Salt

Put the deep-fried tofu in a colander and pour boiling water over it to remove the excess oil. Drain and slice it into ½-inch wide strips.

Heat the oil in a wok or large, shallow pan and stir-fry the tofu strips and mibuna over a medium heat for 2–3 minutes. Add the soy sauce, sugar, and mirin. Reduce the heat to low and simmer for 10 minutes. Add salt to taste and serve.

春菊 Shungiku [CHRYSANTHEMUM GREENS]

This is an edible chrysanthemum of Mediterranean origin. The plant spread across Europe, Africa, and Asia but only in China, Japan, and some other Southeast Asian countries has it been cultivated as a vegetable. The date of its first arrival in Japan is not clear but it is believed to have come from China some time during the sixteenth century, and was first cultivated as a popular spring vegetable (its Japanese name means 'spring chrysanthemum') in southwest Japan.

How it grows Shungiku is a relatively hardy, undemanding, annual plant. It grows to about 1 foot tall. Its flowers are small, single and daisy-like in appearance and the color of the petals varies from white and yellow to orange. Its preferred climate is cool and temperate: it does not grow in temperatures above 77°F.

Appearance and taste The edible leaf resembles that of the ornamental chrysanthemum in size, shape, color, and smell, but is perhaps slightly softer in texture.

Health benefits Over 90 percent of the plant is water. Its high carotene content allows the body to produce vitamin A, and its chlorophyll, which helps to lower cholesterol, is relatively heat resistant and is not destroyed by cooking. Soups containing edible chrysanthemum help to cure respiratory disorders and have a 'cooling' effect on those suffering from menopausal flushes.

Buying and storing Although it's best in the early spring, the edible chrysanthemum is now available almost all year round from Asian fruit and vegetable stores. As with any leafy green vegetables, choose ones that feel crisp and are a deep green, avoiding limp or yellowish ones. It will keep for a few days in the refrigerator.

Culinary uses Young leaves are excellent raw in salads. They are also used in soups and simmered with other vegetables. More mature ones should be stir-fried, as they can withstand robust cooking and more seasoning.

Shungiku no goma itame

[STIR-FRIED CHRYSANTHEMUM GREENS
WITH SESAME SEEDS]

Sesame seeds are widely used in the Japanese kitchen for their rich nutty flavor and the extra texture they bring. In this recipe, instead of the sesame seeds being added at the end, the shungiku is coated with the seeds before being cooked.

Serves 4
14 oz. (4–5 cups) shungiku (chrysanthemum greens), trimmed
6 tablespoons toasted sesame seeds
2 tablespoons vegetable oil
1 tablespoon soy sauce
Salt and pepper

Bring a saucepan of water to a boil and blanch the shungiku briefly. Transfer to a bowl of ice-cold water and drain well. Chop the shungiku roughly and coat with the sesame seeds. Heat the oil in a wok and stir-fry the shungiku for 2–3 minutes or until it becomes soft. Add the soy sauce, adjust the seasoning with salt and pepper, and serve.

◂ *Produce spills out on to the street at a vegetable shop in Japan.*

Shungiku to kani, shimeji no ohitashi

[DASHI-STEEPED SHUNGIKU]

Ohitashi is a dish containing cooked vegetables immersed in a subtle mixture of dashi broth, soy sauce, and mirin.

Serves 4
2 oz. (⅔ cup) shungiku (chrysanthemum greens)
2 oz. (⅔ cup) shimeji mushrooms (or sliced shiitake)
2 oz. (⅔ cup) cooked white crabmeat, flaked
For the *ohitashi* mixture
8 fl oz. (1 cup) dashi broth (see p.169)
2 tablespoons soy sauce (preferably light soy sauce)
1 tablespoon mirin

▴ *Dashi-steeped shungiku.*

Bring a saucepan of water to a boil and blanch the shungiku briefly. Transfer to a bowl of ice-cold water, drain well and chop into 1-inch lengths. Using the same boiling water, blanch the shimeji mushrooms and separate them.

In a separate bowl, mix the dashi broth, soy sauce, and mirin. Immerse the shungiku, mushrooms, and flaked crabmeat in the dashi mixture and stir to combine. Using your hand, squeeze out any excess liquid, divide between 4 individual bowls and serve.

水菜 Mizuna [MIZUNA]

Mizuna originates in ancient China and Japan, belonging to the *tsuke na* group that includes many varieties of greens. It is also sometimes called 'kyo na', meaning 'green of Kyoto,' because it has been cultivated in the ancient capital Kyoto and its surrounding areas since the seventeenth century. Botanically, it is a close relative of the leafy turnip. Mibuna (see p.75) is a derivative of this vegetable.

How it grows It acquired the name *mizuna* (meaning 'water green') because it was grown in water-filled furrows in fields. It is one of the easiest and most tolerant cultivated green vegetables: it quickly grows back after being cut and does not bolt even in high summer temperatures of over 90°F. Although its best season is between October and March, in Japan it is grown almost all year round.

Appearance and taste Mizuna is a very pretty vegetable. It forms a bushy clump—a giant green rosette with 600–1,000 finely dissected, dark, glossy-green leaves. The lower part of each leaf is a slender white stalk with a juicy and crunchy texture. Slightly peppery, like very mild rocket, mizuna has a refreshing taste.

Health benefits Mizuna is about 95 percent water. It is rich in various vitamins, especially vitamin A, and contains iron and other minerals. Its high chlorophyll content helps reduce cholesterol and cleanse the blood.

Culinary uses Mizuna's main culinary benefit is to reduce the strong smell of meat. One of the specialities of the island of Kyushu is a dish containing mizuna and politically incorrect whale meat. Mizuna is also eaten pickled, simmered, and stir-fried.

Spaghetti with mizuna and deep-fried tofu

Although I grow my own mizuna, it is not always so easy to persuade my family to eat it. However, I have hit upon a winning formula by cooking this traditional Japanese green with familiar spaghetti.

Serves 4
7 oz. (2½–3 cups) spaghetti
4 tablespoons olive oil
2 garlic cloves, peeled and gently crushed
1 sheet deep-fried tofu, roughly chopped
2 oz. (⅔ cup) fresh mizuna, cleaned and roughly chopped
Salt and pepper

Bring a large saucepan of water to a boil and add the spaghetti to cook. While the spaghetti is cooking, heat the olive oil in a skillet over low heat, add the garlic cloves to flavor the oil. When the garlic cloves have turned golden, remove from the pan and discard. Quickly sauté the chopped deep-fried tofu. Ladle in about 3 fl oz. cooking water from the spaghetti, add the chopped mizuna and cook until soft. Drain the spaghetti and toss it with the contents of the skillet. Adjust the seasoning with salt and pepper and serve immediately.

Mizuna to ebi no salada

[WARM SALAD OF MIZUNA AND LARGE SHRIMP]

▲ Warm salad of mizuna and giant shrimp.

I often make this warm salad dish in the middle of winter when my homegrown mizuna is in season.

Serves 4

7 oz. (2–2½ cups) fresh mizuna, cleaned and roughly chopped

1–2 sticks celery, strings removed, finely chopped into matchsticks

1 oz. (2-inch piece) ginger root, peeled and finely chopped into matchsticks

7 oz. (1½–2 cups) cooked large shrimp, peeled, heads and tails removed

For the salad dressing

4 tablespoons rice vinegar

2 tablespoons soy sauce

1 tablespoon granulated sugar

Juice of 1 lime

To serve

4 tablespoons sesame oil

Put the mizuna, celery, and ginger on a large serving dish. Arrange the shrimp on top. Make the salad dressing and drizzle it over the salad. Just before serving, heat the sesame oil in a ladle until it is almost smoking. Drizzle the hot oil over the salad and serve immediately.

小松菜 Komatsuna [MUSTARD SPINACH]

Komatsuna is named after its seventeenth-century birthplace, the Komatsukawa region of Greater Tokyo. It is sometimes called *uguisuna* (Japanese bushwarbler green) and also *fuyuna*, (winter green). Komatsuna is still relatively unknown in the West but deserves more attention, as it is one of the hardiest, most nutritious, and most productive winter vegetables cultivated in Japan.

How it grows If mizuna and mibuna are Kyoto's most famous green vegetables, komatsuna is Tokyo's answer. Able to withstand severe winter temperatures and frost, it is at its best between October and April, though nowadays it is grown all year round. It is a fast-growing plant and can be harvested 20–30 days after sowing.

Appearance and taste Komatsuna looks like a cross between pak choi and spinach. Its leaves are larger than the average spinach leaf, and its leaf stalk is usually light green and much thinner than the swollen leaf stalk of pak choi. The flavor of komatsuna can best be described as a mixture of cabbage and mustard green with a hint of spinach.

Health benefits Komatsuna's nutritional value compares favorably with spinach: it has five times more calcium, and it contains more vitamin C and carotene, which allows the body to produce vitamin A. It is known in Japan as a warming vegetable that wards off cancer,

strengthening the body's immune system and cleansing the blood.

Culinary uses In the Japanese kitchen, komatsuna is particularly highly valued during winter when fresh greens are scarce. It is lightly steamed, simmered, or stir-fried with other vegetables or meat. A variety called *nozawana* is used exclusively for pickling.

Komatsuna to age-dofu ni

[SIMMERED KOMATSUNA WITH DEEP-FRIED TOFU]

Golden strips of deep-fried tofu and leafy green komatsuna are braised together—this is real home cooking. This works well with other greens, such as spinach or savoy cabbage.

Serves 4
2 sheets deep-fried tofu
7 oz. (2–2½ cups) komatsuna (mustard spinach), cleaned and trimmed
Pinch of salt
For the simmering broth
16 fl oz. (1¾ cups) dashi broth (see p.169)
1 tablespoon saké
1 tablespoon mirin
2 tablespoons light soy sauce
Pinch of salt

Place the tofu in a colander and pour boiling water over it to remove the excess oil. Cut lengthways in half and slice thinly.

Discard the roots of the komatsuna and wash. Bring a large saucepan of water to a boil and add a pinch of salt. Blanch the komatsuna and transfer immediately to a bowl of cold water. Squeeze the komatsuna dry and chop it into 1-inch lengths.

Put all the ingredients for the simmering broth in a large saucepan and bring to a boil. Add the tofu strips and simmer over medium heat for 2 minutes before adding the chopped komatsuna. Simmer for another 2–3 minutes and serve.

▸ *A woman sells vegetables at a street market.*
▸ *Mustard spinach with black sesame dressing.*

Komatsuna no kuro goma ae

[MUSTARD SPINACH WITH BLACK SESAME DRESSING]

I often use sesame dressing on steamed vegetables but one day I had run out of white sesame seeds and used black ones instead—the result is a rich nutty dressing that can be used over any vegetables.

Serves 4

7 oz. (2–2½ cups) fresh komatsuna, cleaned and trimmed

For the dressing

4 tablespoons toasted black sesame seeds
1 tablespoons granulated sugar
2 tablespoons balsamic vinegar

To garnish

1 tablespoon pine nuts

Bring a saucepan of water to a boil and add the komatsuna, root first. Let the water return to a boil, then quickly transfer the komatsuna to a bowl of ice-cold water.

With a pestle and mortar, grind the sesame seeds until you have a smooth paste, then add the sugar and balsamic vinegar and mix well. Drain the komatsuna thoroughly, chop roughly and transfer to a serving dish. Drizzle with the dressing, garnish with pine nuts and serve.

白菜 Hakusai [CHINESE CABBAGE]

Chinese cabbage is called hakusai, meaning 'white leaves' in Japanese. Despite its relatively late introduction from China in 1895, it has become one of the most widely cultivated vegetables in present-day Japan and, as in China, many new varieties have been developed.

How it grows Hakusai prefers a cooler climate with limited daylight. Although it is available all year round, the principal planting time is between September and March, giving a main season of late autumn through to spring.

Appearance and taste Although there are many varieties cultivated in Japan, the most popular ones have yellowish central leaves. A hakusai looks quite different from the round, green cabbages grown in the West—more like a larger version of the cos lettuce—with white or pale-green, upright leaves that form a tight head. The leaves are crispy with a very mild, slightly sweet flavor.

Health benefits Hakusai is more than 95 percent water but it has a high vitamin C content and is a source of minerals such as calcium, iron and potassium, which helps rid the body of excess salt. Shredded hakusai is used to treat rashes and burns.

Buying and storing Traditionally hakusai was grown as a winter vegetable, but today it is available almost all year round from Asian grocery stores. Choose one that feels solid and heavy, as it will contain more moisture. It keeps well for up to a week in the salad compartment of the refrigerator.

Culinary uses Hakusai is a versatile vegetable and has a wide range of uses in the Japanese kitchen. It can be simmered, steamed, used in soups, or stir-fried and because of its mild flavor it is often used to bulk out meat, poultry, or fish. Raw hakusai makes a refreshing salad leaf. Traditionally, hakusai is pickled in salt or rice bran to serve as a source of vitamins during winter.

Hakusai no miso shiru
[CHINESE CABBAGE MISO SOUP]

Creeping westernization means that coffee and toast have become a familiar sight at the breakfast table, but millions of Japanese people still start their day with a bowl of miso soup. Hakusai is one of the most common ingredients of the Japanese kitchen: there's always some lurking in the refrigerator.

Serves 4
4 oz. (1–1½ cups) hakusai, finely chopped
32 fl oz. (3¾ cups) dashi broth (see p.169)
4 tablespoons light colored miso paste

Put the chopped hakusai in a saucepan and add enough water to cover. Bring to a boil over a medium heat, skimming off any scum that rises to the surface. Add the dashi broth and bring back to a boil. Reduce the heat to low and gradually add the miso paste through a small strainer—a tea strainer is ideal for this job. Do not drop a lump of miso paste into the soup and expect it to dissolve by itself— it won't. Bring the soup back to a boil, turn the heat off immediately and serve.

Hakusai no bacon maki

[CHINESE CABBAGE AND BACON ROLLS]

I have adapted this recipe, which traditionally calls for very thinly sliced pork. In Japan, meat is sold in thin slices rather than in lumps or rolled for roasting. This is because we do not have ovens in our kitchens and most of our cooking is done over a surface heat.

Serves 4

6 leaves hakusai, blanched to soften and cut in half lengthways

12 slices rindless, green bacon

32 fl oz. (3¾ cups) dashi broth (see p.169)

2 fl oz. (3½ tablespoons) saké

4 tablespoons light soy sauce

Lay a blanched hakusai leaf on a chopping board. Put a slice of bacon on top and roll it up from the white, thicker end of the hakusai leaf. Secure with a toothpick so that the roll cannot open out.

Repeat the process until you have made 12 rolls. Put the rolls in a saucepan and add the dashi broth, saké, and soy sauce. Bring to a boil over medium heat, then immediately reduce the heat to low and simmer for 15 more minutes. Take out the toothpicks and serve.

▲ *Chinese cabbage and bacon rolls.*

ねぎ Negi [SCALLION]

Health benefits Negi has long been considered a healthy vegetable; it has twice the vitamin C content of its bulbous brother and its vitamin B2 content is six times higher. It is believed to calm the nerves, help insomnia, and be good for the stomach. I was always given a cup of hot negi, shredded ginger, and honey if I sneezed more than three times in a row.

Culinary uses Negi's uses in the Japanese kitchen depend on the type: the larger white variety, of which only the white parts are eaten, is an essential ingredient in the famous *sukiyaki*. It is also stir-fried with beef and pork, and is often broiled on skewers with teriyaki chicken. The smaller, greener negi is used as a garnish or herbal condiment in all sorts of Japanese dishes—it is Japan's equivalent of chopped parsley.

Indigenous to western China and Siberia, negi had been introduced to Japan via the Korean peninsula by 493. Although best translated as 'scallion,' negi is quite different from the Western version and has become a uniquely Japanese vegetable. Two main varieties of negi are cultivated in Japan: a long, white, stalk type that is more popular in the eastern part of Japan and a shorter green type which is more widely cultivated in the west of the country.

How it grows Negi prefers a cool climate and has both spring and autumn harvesting varieties, though nowadays it is cultivated all year round. The larger and longer white varieties need to be partially covered with earth to blanch the lower part of the stalk.

Appearance and taste I remember my great excitement when I first saw leeks on sale in London, thinking to myself, thank goodness, at least there are proper Japanese negi in this country! How disappointed I was when I discovered that the Welsh national emblem is not at all the same as the Japanese giant white scallion. The white negi measures 1–2ft, with long stalks ranging in diameter between ⅛ inch–1¼ inches). Only the white part is eaten; it has a mild onion flavor with the fine, delicate texture of young scallions.

▸ A market stallholder weighs a bunch of scallions.
▾ Field workers planting young scallion bulbs.

▸ *Scallion and*
  pork stir-fry.

Negi toro

[MINCED NEGI AND TUNA]

This is one of the most popular fillings and toppings for sushi; it also makes an excellent topping for canapés.

Serves 4 as an appetizer

6 scallions, trimmed

7 oz. fresh tuna

2 teaspoons wasabi powder, mixed to a paste with the same amount of water

1 tablespoon soy sauce

Mince the scallion and tuna on a chopping board. Put them in a mixing bowl, add the wasabi paste and soy sauce and mix well until it becomes slightly elastic. Spoon the mixture on to cheese biscuits or *senbei* (Japanese rice crackers).

Negi to buta-niku no itame

[SCALLION AND PORK STIR-FRY]

This is another quick and easy recipe that can be turned into a one-dish lunch or supper by serving it with either rice or noodles.

Serves 4

2 tablespoons vegetable oil

7 oz. ground pork

4 fresh shiitake mushrooms, stalks removed, finely chopped

8 scallions, finely chopped

2 tablespoons saké

2 tablespoons soy sauce

Heat the oil in a wok over high heat and add the pork and chopped shiitake mushrooms. Stir-fry for 5 minutes before adding the chopped scallions. Add the saké and soy sauce to the wok, stir well and serve.

枝豆 Eda-mame [FRESH GREEN SOYBEANS]

Eda-mame is the young green soybean, harvested before maturity and sold still on the stalk and in the pod. Although the history of soybean cultivation goes back over 3,000 years, its use as a fresh vegetable started some time during the late seventeenth century. Nowadays, when eda-mame start making their appearance alongside cold beer in Japan's beer gardens it's a sign that summer has arrived.

Appearance and taste Eda-mame means 'branch bean,' for they are sold still on their stalks and in their hairy pods. The pods look like flattened peanut shells and each one normally contains two or three beans. They need to be cooked before eating and the most popular way of cooking them is to boil them in salted water and suck the beans out of the pods. They are a subtle green and have a nutty flavor.

Health benefits Eda-mame have the same high nutritional value as ordinary soybeans: they are rich in vegetable protein and vitamins B1, B2, and C, and have a high fiber content. Although the beans are small, they are packed with goodness and the Japanese people eat them as a healthy snack to fend off summer fatigue and heat exhaustion. Their high content of vitamin B1 is particularly good for treating tiredness, stiff shoulders, and headaches. My children are very fond of eda-mame, not only during the summer but throughout the year, which keeps my conscience clear as the beans are a much healthier alternative to potato chips and chocolate.

Buying and storing In the West, eda-mame are most likely to be sold frozen in the pod, ready salted, and needing only a brief boiling.

Culinary uses The best way to cook eda-mame is to boil them in salted water and serve them as a simple appetizer or hors d'oeuvre.

Eda-mame bar-snack style

Eda-mame are hugely popular with beer in Japanese beer gardens in summer and are a much healthier snack than crisps. The recipe below is for frozen eda-mame, which are pre-salted. If you do buy them fresh, separate the pods from the stalks and follow the instructions below, adding 1–2 tablespoons salt to the cooking water.

14 oz. frozen eda-mame

Put the frozen eda-mame in a saucepan and add enough cold water to cover the beans. Bring to a boil over a medium heat without covering. Cook for 3–5 minutes or until the beans are cooked and soft. Drain and rinse under cold running water to preserve the green color. Drain well again and serve.

▸ Green, leafy eda-mame plants ready for harvesting

Eda-mame pasta

Eda-mame are so tasty and nutritious that children and non-drinkers should be allowed to enjoy them too—this is my own invention to let them do just that.

Serves 4

7 oz. (1¾–2 cups) dried penne pasta
2 tablespoons extra virgin olive oil
1 tablespoon butter
1 garlic clove, peeled and gently squashed
1 large ripe beef tomato, blanched, skinned and chopped
4 oz. eda-mame, cooked and shelled
Salt and pepper

Cook the penne in a large saucepan of boiling water. Meanwhile, heat the oil and butter in a skillet over a low heat. When the butter has melted, add the garlic clove and let it infuse slowly. Remove it when it turns golden yellow and discard.

Add the chopped tomato and shelled eda-mame and quickly sauté for 2 minutes. Add a ladleful of cooking water from the pasta pan and let the sauce reduce slightly. Drain the penne and tip into the pan. Stir well, adjust the seasoning if necessary and serve immediately.

▾ *Eda-mame pasta.*

筍 Takenoko [BAMBOO SHOOT]

Bamboo is one of the three most symbolic and auspicious plants in Japan—the other two being pine and plum— and it features in literature, music, architecture, and many other aspects of Japanese life. The young shoots (takenoko or 'child of bamboo') are a key ingredient in the Japanese kitchen. I have a childhood memory of following my grandfather one spring morning into clumps of dew-covered bamboo to dig up a few takenoko. I had to pick my way carefully so as not to tread on the tiny shoots whose tips were just showing above the ground.

How it grows There are some 45 genera and 200 varieties of bamboo growing in Japan but only three varieties are eaten. Although there has been bamboo in Japan since prehistoric times, the three edible varieties were brought over from China some time between the late fifteenth and early eighteenth century. A popular variety called *Mosochiku* can reach over 70ft.

Appearance and taste The most expensive takenoko— *fuyu take* or 'winter bamboo'—is no bigger than a child's fist, but the more popular spring variety is normally 6–18 inches long, and is cone-shaped with a diameter of 2–4 inches. Fresh takenoko is covered with layers of pale brown skin—underneath that skin it is a buttery cream color with narrowly spaced ridges. It

tastes not unlike lightly boiled globe artichoke heart and is similar in texture.

Health benefits Takenoko is low in calories, and relatively high in protein, sugar, and fiber. The high fiber and potassium content relieves constipation, and helps rid the body of waste matter and excess water. Fresh takenoko skins have anti-bacterial properties and are used for wrapping rice balls and sushi.

Buying and storing Freshly dug takenoko can be eaten raw—my personal favorite is thin slices served with wasabi soy sauce. If it's more than a day old, takenoko needs to have all its outer layers peeled off and be boiled in water with a handful of rice bran to remove the tannin and bitterness. Choose takenoko which feel weighty and are still moist.

In the West takenoko is most likely to be found pre-cooked in cans and jars. Unopened cans or jars will keep almost indefinitely but once opened and drained, the contents should be used within a day. There is a dried variety available from Asian and Japanese stores, but personally I don't recommend it, as it can be rather stringy.

Culinary uses The most popular way of cooking takenoko is slow simmering, so not to spoil its delicate flavor. An equally popular method is to cook it with rice: *takenoko gohan*.

Takenoko gohan

[COOKED RICE WITH BAMBOO SHOOTS]

After the early-morning takenoko digging, my grandmother used to go into over-drive, preparing a variety of dishes with the newly harvested takenoko shoots. As a small child I would get excited watching the frantic activity that went on in her kitchen. After all the dishes had been prepared, there was always a bowl of leftover off-cuts that used to be made into this flavorsome rice dish. I sat so far down the table, I never got many of the 'grown-up' dishes but there was always a bowl of *takenoko gohan* to console me.

▸ *Growing bamboo stalks.*

Serves 4

7 oz. skinless, boneless chicken thighs, roughly chopped
3 tablespoons soy sauce
3 tablespoons saké
1 tablespoon mirin
14 oz. (3½ cups) rice, washed and drained
14 fl oz. (1¾ cups) water
1 piece konbu (dried kelp), postcard size
7 oz. (⅔ piece) takenoko, pre-boiled, roughly chopped

Put the chopped chicken pieces in a bowl, add the soy sauce, saké, and mirin, and leave to marinate for at least 1 hour.

Put the washed rice, the water, the konbu, the chicken pieces, and the marinade in a heavy-based saucepan with a tight fitting lid. Bring to a boil slowly over a gentle heat. When you can hear it bubbling, i.e. when it has reached boiling point, remove the konbu and discard it.

Add the chopped takenoko, turn up the heat to medium and cook for 5 more minutes before turning off the heat. Resist the temptation to lift up the lid but let it steam for another 10 minutes. Fluff up the rice with a fork and serve in 4 individual bowls.

▾ *Simmered bamboo shoots.*

Takenoko ni

[SIMMERED BAMBOO SHOOTS]

This dish has a delicate yet sophisticated flavor.

Serves 4

1 piece takenoko, about 10 oz., ready cooked
1 piece konbu (dried kelp), postcard size
15 fl oz. (1¾ cups) water or enough to half-cover the
   takenoko pieces
2 tablespoons granulated sugar
2 tablespoons mirin
2 tablespoons light soy sauce

In the West, takenoko is most likely to be sold pre-boiled in cans or jars. If it comes in one large piece, cut it into bite-size pieces. Put the takenoko in a saucepan with the konbu and half-cover them with water.

Gently bring to a boil over a low heat—make sure that you do not let it boil fast. Cook for 10 minutes or until the piece of konbu is soft and floppy. Remove the konbu and cut it into stamp-size pieces.

Add the sugar and mirin to the takenoko and cook for 10 minutes more. Add the soy sauce, return the chopped konbu to the pan, simmer until the cooking liquid has been reduced by half and serve.

南瓜 Kabocha [PUMPKIN]

Thanks to a series of successful breeding programs during the last century, the Japanese pumpkin has become one of only three recognized breeds of pumpkin grown around the world. The Japanese type has its origin in Central America; it was introduced to Japan in the 1540s by the crew of a Portuguese trading ship that anchored at Kyushu Island and presented a pumpkin grown in Cambodia to a local feudal lord—hence its Japanese name of 'southern squash.' Kabocha and sweet potato were both cultivated extensively during the severe food shortages in the immediate aftermath of the war and they saved Japan from starvation.

How it grows There are many varieties of kabocha grown in Japan and new varieties are added all the time. Japanese varieties are much smaller than Western ones and the plants are creepers.

Appearance and taste The Japanese pumpkin usually has a tough, dark green skin, sometimes with well-marked ridges. The flesh ranges from a rich buttery yellow to bright orange and is dense in texture, similar to that of sweet chestnut or sweet potato. Cooked kabocha tastes sweet and floury and has a chestnut-like aroma.

Health benefits The Japanese pumpkin is rich in vitamin A, which is stored in the liver, and eating kabocha is believed to prevent paralysis and strokes. Every year on July 25th a temple in Kyoto holds a kabocha festival at which people pray for good health.

Buying and storing Choose a dense specimen with unblemished skin. A whole kabocha keeps for several weeks if stored in a cool vegetable rack away from direct sunlight. Once it is cut, keep it in the refrigerator well wrapped with plastic wrap.

Culinary uses Despite its relatively late arrival in the Japanese kitchen, kabocha has made its mark: Japanese people love its fluffy, sweet flavor. The most popular way of cooking kabocha is to simmer it gently with dashi broth to bring out its natural sweetness and floury texture. Thinly sliced kabocha also lends itself very well to deep-frying in tempura dishes. But why not try kabocha risotto?

Kabocha no goma-ni
[SIMMERED PUMPKIN WITH SESAME SEEDS]

This is real comfort food—the sweetness of kabocha goes very well with the nutty flavor of toasted sesame seeds.

Serves 4

1 lb. (2½ cups) kabocha (pumpkin)
7 fl oz. (¾ cup) water
2 tablespoons soy sauce
½ tablespoon mirin
1–3 tablespoons granulated sugar (according to taste)
4 tablespoons toasted sesame seeds, roughly ground

Remove the seeds and cut the pumpkin into bite-size pieces. Put the pumpkin in a saucepan and add all the ingredients except the sesame seeds. Bring to a boil over a medium heat, then reduce the heat to low and simmer until the pumpkin is cooked through. Add the ground sesame seeds and stir gently to coat the pumpkin with the sesame. Turn off the heat and serve.

Kabocha no tempura
[DEEP-FRIED PUMPKIN IN BATTER]

Japanese Zen monks ate vegetarian tempura dishes to give themselves the extra energy they needed to get through their tough training in the hot and humid Japanese summer. But you don't have to be a Buddhist to enjoy the combination of crunchy tempura batter around sweet slices of kabocha.

Serves 4

Vegetable oil, for deep-frying

1 lb. (2½ cups) kabocha (pumpkin), peeled and cut into half-moon slices ⅛ inch thick

For the tempura batter

1 egg, well beaten

Ice water

4 oz. (1 cup) all-purpose flour, sifted

For the dipping sauce

1 piece konbu (dried kelp), postcard size

25 fl oz. (2¾ cups) water

8 fl oz. (1 cup) mirin

8 fl oz. (1 cup) soy sauce

To serve

11 oz. (1¾–2 cups) daikon (Japanese radish), peeled and grated

Put the all the ingredients for the dipping sauce in a saucepan and bring to a boil over a medium heat. Turn off the heat and leave to cool down.

Pour in enough vegetable oil to come halfway up the sides of a wok or shallow saucepan. Heat the oil over medium heat.

Put the beaten egg in a measuring jug, add enough ice water to make the egg up to 3 fl oz. and mix well. Add the sifted flour and mix gently—if you overmix the batter it will become too thick and sticky. Test the temperature of the oil by dropping in half a teaspoonful of batter. If the batter sinks all the way to the bottom then rises to the surface, the oil is about 310°F and is ready. If the batter sinks only halfway and the rises, the oil is too hot for this recipe and you should take the pan off the heat for 5 minutes.

One at a time, dip the kabocha slices in the batter and gently submerge them in the heated oil to deep-fry until the batter becomes crisp. Put the cooked slices to drain on paper towels. Continue until all the slices are done. Serve with the dipping sauce and shredded daikon.

▲ *Deep-fried pumpkin in batter.*

茄子 Nasu/Nasubi [EGGPLANT]

Nasu is yet another imported vegetable—this time from the Indian subcontinent via China—which has made itself at home in Japan. Nasu first appears in records dating back to 750 and crops up frequently after that, in proverbs, legends and, of course, the kitchen.

How it grows There are over 80 varieties of nasu grown in Japan today. An annual, it is easy to grow domestically so like, the dreaded tomato plant, is found in every family vegetable garden! In Japan, it is sown outdoors in spring; some of the earlier varieties can be picked from midsummer onwards. Nasu's best seasons are summer and early autumn.

Appearance and taste The eggplant resembles an elongated purple egg with a firm and beautiful shiny skin. The main difference between Western eggplants and nasu is size—like many other things in Japan, nasu is much smaller. The uncooked flesh is bland and spongy but once cooked, it has a flavor and texture quite unlike any other vegetable: meaty, oily, and very slippery.

Health benefits The Japanese have always considered nasu to be cooling: it brings down fevers, kills pain, and helps to promote healthy circulation.

▼ *Nasu growing en masse in a greenhouse.*

Buying and storing Although the best season for Japanese nasu is between summer and autumn, it is now available all year around both in Japan and in the West. Choose one which feels stiff and weighty, with tight skin and no blemishes. If nasu is bought in prime condition, it should keep fresh for a number of days in the vegetable drawer of the refrigerator.

Culinary uses The flesh of nasu is like a sponge: it absorbs the flavor of whatever it is cooked with—a very useful attribute. It is good in soups, especially miso soup, and in salads. It is great stir-fried with other ingredients, and lends itself very well to tempura. My personal favorite is to bake and skin it, then serve it with soy sauce mixed with shredded ginger.

Yaki nasu

[BAKED EGGPLANT]

This simple dish has become one of my family's most popular dishes. It makes an excellent appetizer, served chilled in wine glasses. I am allowing half an eggplant per person as Western eggplants tend to be much larger than those sold in Japan.

▼ *A barrel of glossy pickled baby eggplants for sale.*

Serves 4
2 eggplants, pricked
2 tablespoons rice vinegar
4 tablespoons soy sauce
1 tablespoon fresh ginger root, shredded

Preheat the oven to 375°F. Put the pricked eggplants on a baking sheet and bake for 15–20 minutes or until they feel soft inside.

Let the eggplant cool for 5 minutes, then peel them with a bamboo skewer: insert the skewer just under the skin at the top of the eggplant and slide it down.

Roughly chop the peeled eggplant and put in a bowl. Add the vinegar and soy sauce and mix gently. Serve with a dab of shredded ginger.

Nasu no dengaku

[DEEP-FRIED EGGPLANT WITH SWEET MISO PASTE]

Here, deep-fried nasu is lightly broiled to get rid of excess oil and crisp the skin. The sweet dengaku miso will keep for a few months refrigerated in an airtight container.

Vegetable oil, for deep-frying
2 eggplants
For the dengaku miso
4 oz. light colored miso paste
4 oz. dark colored miso paste
2 egg yolks
2 tablespoons granulated sugar
2 tablespoons saké
2 tablespoons mirin

Put all the dengaku miso ingredients in a saucepan and stir well with a wooden spoon until it becomes creamy.

Heat a wok of vegetable oil to 310°F and pre-heat the broiler. Prick the aubergines with a toothpick and cut them into rounded chunks 1 inch thick. Deep-fry them in the preheated oil for 3–5 minutes.

Drain on paper towels and let them cool a little, then place the eggplant chunks on a baking sheet and broil them for 5 minutes. Spread a teaspoon of dengaku miso on each chunk. Put them back under the hot broiler for a few minutes and serve warm or at room temperature.

▲ *Deep-fried eggplant with sweet miso paste.*

胡瓜 Kyuri [CUCUMBER]

The cucumber originated in India in the Himalayas, where it has been grown for 3,000 years. It was first introduced to Japan in the sixth century, via China and Korea, but did not gain popularity until the seventeenth century. One of the many things that amazed me when I first came to England was the size of cucumbers: Japanese cucumbers are much smaller. Today, although they are not exactly the same as Japanese ones, one can buy so-called baby cucumbers that are smaller and denser.

How it grows The cucumber is a creeping annual. Whereas once it was harvested in summer and autumn, today it is grown all year around, both inside and outside greenhouses. In Japan there are three basic varieties and many crossbreeds.

Appearance and taste Japanese cucumbers are much smaller and thinner than Western ones. The texture is also different: the Japanese variety is denser and crunchier.

Health benefits Cucumber is 95 percent water and has little nutritional value. It has long been regarded as a cooling vegetable and is often served raw in summer. Valued for its diuretic effects, it is believed to be effective in reducing swelling.

Culinary uses There is an enzyme in cucumbers that destroys vitamin C unless vinegar is present. We can't prove that our Japanese ancestors knew this, but it is interesting that the most popular way to serve cucumbers in the Japanese kitchen is with vinegar dressings. Pickling them in rice bran is also popular. The cucumber is first rolled on a wooden chopping board with a little salt to preserve its bright green color, then gently remove the little stubbles.

Kyuri to wakame no su-nomo
[CUCUMBER AND WAKAME SEAWEED IN VINEGAR]

This is a very refreshing appetizer. It can be turned into a vegetarian dish by omitting the shirasu-boshi (tiny dried sardines, see p.168).

Serves 4
2 baby cucumbers
1 teaspoon salt
4 fl oz. (½ cup) water, combined with 1 teaspoon salt
2 tablespoons dried wakame (seaweed)
½ oz. (1-inch piece) ginger root, peeled and finely chopped
2 tablespoons shirasu-boshi (dried sardines)
For the vinegar dressing
4 tablespoons rice vinegar
1 tablespoon granulated sugar
1 teaspoon light soy sauce
½ teaspoon salt

Roll the cucumbers in the salt on a chopping board and thinly slice them. Soak the slices in the water and salt mixture for 5 minutes and drain well. Meanwhile, reconstitute the dried wakame in hot water, then squeeze out the excess water.

Combine the dressing ingredients. Put the cucumber slices, wakame, chopped ginger, and shirasu-boshi in a mixing bowl, and pour over the vinegar dressing. Mix well, divide between 4 individual dishes, and serve.

↖ *Cucumber cups with wasabi mayonnaise.*
◂ *Cucumbers undercover in the greenhouse.*

Cucumber cups with wasabi mayonnaise

This is a stylish and refreshing canapé that can be prepared in advance.

2 baby cucumbers, cut into chunks 1 inch thick
2 teaspoons wasabi powder, mixed to a paste with water
2 tablespoons good quality mayonnaise
4 teaspoons salmon roe (sold in a small glass jar as savvier)

With a melon-baller (if you don't have one, use a teaspoon instead) scoop out the center of each chunk of cucumber to make cups. Combine the wasabi paste and mayonnaise.

With a teaspoon, fill the cucumber cups with the mayonnaise mixture and top each cup with a small amount of salmon roe. Place on paper towels on a small tray and refrigerate until needed.

Japan is a country of mountains and forests: mountains cover more than three-quarters of the country. Its geography and temperate climate provide ideal conditions for all sorts of mushrooms—of some 10,000 varieties of mushrooms growing in the world, around 3,000 varieties have been identified in Japan.

In Japan, all mushrooms are called *kinoko*, meaning 'children of the trees'—an apt name for these mysterious fungi that grow on and under trees, living and dead—and historical records and drawings show that my Japanese ancestors enjoyed these mystical offerings of nature as much as we do today. *Kinoko gari* (mushroom hunting) was one of the high points of my childhood. I used to forage under every tree and fallen leaf for the highly prized *matsutake* and at the end of an exhausting afternoon I would proudly present my gatherings to the village elders, who would cast their experienced eyes over my findings and expertly sort out what could be eaten. Thank goodness they knew what they were doing! I am pleased that more varieties of Japanese and Asian mushrooms are becoming available so you too can bring the flavor of autumn to the table.

4 Mushrooms

椎茸 Shiitake [SHIITAKE MUSHROOM]

Shiitake is Japan's most famous mushroom but it is as much Chinese as Japanese. Japan cultivates over a staggering 70,000 tons of shiitake a year, of which over 5,000 tons are dried. We don't know when the mushroom was first cultivated, but by the beginning of the seventeenth century it was an important regional produce of Kyushu.

How it grows The modern method for cultivating shiitake mushrooms is to transplant the spores onto cut branches of oak, keep them dark and moist, and harvest the mushrooms twice a year.

Appearance and taste Fresh shiitake mushrooms have a cap with a diameter of 1–3 inches. The caps are meaty, convex, and light brown, with an underside that is pale cream and finely gilled. Fresh shiitake mushrooms have a unique woody aroma and a soft, slippery texture.

Health benefits Shiitake mushrooms have always been associated with long life and are believed to be effective for curing colds, cleansing the blood, and lowering cholesterol. Low in calories, shiitake are rich in fiber, with a high level of vitamins B and D to maintain healthy bones and ward off cancer.

Buying and storing Choose fat juicy caps with the edges curled under. Avoid opened or flattened caps as they quickly become floppy and slimy. In the West, most of the mushrooms on sale in supermarkets are sold prepacked in plastic wrap—make sure that no condensation is visible under the wrapping.

The best quality, dried shiitake is *tenshiro donko*. This variety of shiitake is grown from late winter to early spring especially for drying; its fat meaty caps have characteristic cracks. Cheaper Chinese varieties are available today in the West, but avoid any that are in fragments. Dried shiitake keep almost indefinitely if stored in an airtight container in a cool, dark cupboard, but the flavor deteriorates after a while. The flavor will last longer if the dried shiitake are frozen.

Culinary uses The shiitake mushroom is widely used in Japanese cooking. It is found in soups, salads, sushi, broiled dishes, and tempura—everywhere, in fact. Dried shiitake have a more concentrated flavor than fresh shiitake, so are often used for making dashi broth.

◀ Steamed stuffed shiitake.

Mushi ebi shiitake

[STEAMED STUFFED SHIITAKE]

This easy-to-prepare finger food is delicious.

Serves 4
12 giant shrimp, shelled and de-veined
1 teaspoon salt
2 tablespoons saké
12 fresh shiitake, stems discarded
2 tablespoons cornstarch
12 fresh peas

Put the cleaned shrimp in a bowl and sprinkle with the salt and saké. Set aside. Twist the stems of the shiitake to remove them and cut a deep cross into the outside of each cap. Sprinkle the cornstarch inside each cap, and place a shrimp and a pea in the middle. Steam the stuffed shiitake in a steamer over medium heat for 10 minutes and serve.

▲ Steamed stuffed shiitake.

◀ A couple harvesting shiitake mushrooms and spreading them on racks to dry.

Shiitake no suteki

[SHIITAKE MUSHROOM STEAKS]

There is nothing quite like fresh, plump shiitake mushrooms—cook them simply and let the flavor and texture speak for themselves.

Serves 4
12–20 shiitake mushrooms, stems discarded
4 fl oz. (½ cup) olive oil
2 tablespoons butter
2 garlic cloves, peeled and gently crushed
2 tablespoons saké
1 tablespoon soy sauce
Salt and pepper
To garnish
1 scallion, finely chopped

Cut the stems of the shiitake mushrooms and discard. Put a large skillet over a medium heat and add the oil and butter. Add the garlic cloves and let them infuse for a minute or so before adding the shiitake mushrooms. Remove the garlic cloves and discard.

Add the saké and soy sauce and turn the heat down to low. Shake the pan to toss the mushrooms and coat them with the oil.

Let simmer for 2 minutes. Season with salt and pepper, garnish with the chopped scallion, and serve.

舞茸 Maitake [MAITAKE MUSHROOM]

In Japanese it is called 'dancing' mushroom: an apt name for this spectacular fungus, which grows at the foot of Japanese oak, beech, and chestnut trees. Some claim that maitake moving in a gentle breeze resemble coral dancing in the current. According to another story, a charcoal maker found a maitake, ate it with his rough saké and began dancing in a state of mild intoxication—hence a dancing mushroom. I like both explanations.

How it grows Not until the 1970s was a technique for the cultivation of maitake perfected. Maitake spores are planted on prepared beds of compost or sawdust and over 40–50,000 tons of maitake are cultivated annually.

Appearance and taste There are two varieties of maitake cultivated in Japan: pale white and grey. In terms of flavor, the darker variety is preferred, but white maitake also have their uses in the kitchen, as they do not discolor the soup or sauce they are cooked with. The darker variety has a uniquely subtle woody flavor and a refreshing texture.

Culinary uses Maitake are an essential ingredient in *kiritanpo* (Akita prefecture's famous speciality): hot chicken and vegetable stew eaten with broiled, mashed rice wrapped around bamboo sticks. Maitake lend themselves to almost any method of cooking but are best broiled whole or put in a clear soup so that their full beauty can be appreciated.

Maitake ni

[SIMMERED MAITAKE MUSHROOMS]

This does not have to be made with maitake: you can use any mushrooms of your choice. It will keep for 2–3 days, so it's worth making a large quantity when mushrooms are cheap and serving it as a side dish or with cooked noodles to make a one-bowl meal.

Serves 4

2 tablespoons sesame oil
1 large red chile, seeded and finely chopped
4 oz. shimeji mushrooms, separated and trimmed
4 oz. enokitake mushrooms, separated, the stalk trimmed
4 oz. maitake mushrooms, roughly separated, the stalk trimmed
3 tablespoons saké
3 tablespoons mirin
3 tablespoons soy sauce

Heat the sesame oil in a wok over medium heat and add the chopped chile. Add the shimeji mushrooms first and stir-fry for 1 minute. Then add the enokitake and maitake mushrooms and stir-fry for 2 minutes. Add all the seasonings and cook for 3 minutes more, then turn off the heat and serve.

▸ *A mushroom grower attending the tree barks on which the 'dancing' maitake mushrooms grow.*

Kakitama-jiru

[CLEAR SOUP WITH SWIRLING EGGS]

This is a beautiful-looking soup—frills of maitake floating on a yellow background of swirling eggs. Mitsuba leaves add a dash of green and a subtle aroma.

Serves 4

2 eggs, beaten lightly

1 pint (2½ cups) dashi broth (see p.169)

110g (4oz) maitake mushrooms, broken into bite-size pieces

2 tablespoons saké

2 tablespoons mirin

2 tablespoons light soy sauce

2 teaspoons cornstarch mixed with 2 tablespoons water

Salt

4 sprigs mitsuba, roughly chopped (if unavailable, use flat-leaf parsley)

Mix the eggs with 2 tablespoons of the dashi broth. Put the maitake pieces into a saucepan with the rest of the dashi broth, the saké, mirin, and light soy sauce and place over a medium heat. When the soup reaches boiling point, reduce the heat to low and add the cornstarch solution. Stir well to thicken the soup.

Let the soup return to a boil and add the egg mixture through a small strainer. Move the strainer as you do so to create a swirling effect. Turn off the heat and let the swirling strands of egg rise.

Stir gently, season to taste, add the chopped mitsuba leaves, and serve in 4 individual bowls.

▲ *Clear soup with swirling eggs.*

榎茸 Enokitake [ENOKI MUSHROOM]

wild varieties are light brown, bigger, and squatter. Both wild and cultivated varieties have a very delicate flavor (almost tasteless) but a pleasantly crisp texture. Wild enokitake contain less water, so are crisper than cultivated ones.

Health benefits Enokitake is an ideal diet food as it has no calories but is rich in fiber. Its main medicinal claim is that it wards off cancer: very few cases of cancer are found among enokitake farmers, who eat the mushroom almost every day. It has a surprisingly high vegetable protein of 5 percent.

Buying and storing Enokitake are sold in bundles in plastic bags. Choose firm bundles without any blemishes. Conditions inside the refrigerator are similar to those in which the mushroom is grown, so it will keep fresh for up to a week in a sealed plastic bag in the fridge.

Culinary uses Enokitake has a wide range of uses in the Japanese kitchen and is one of the essential ingredients in *shabu shabu*, the famous Japanese hot-pot dish, and in the equally popular *sukiyaki* (see p.56). Because enokitake has very little flavor of its own but absorbs the flavors of other ingredients, it mixes well with almost anything.

Enoki somen

[ENOKITAKE MUSHROOMS WITH SOMEN NOODLES]

Fine, pale enokitake mushrooms are a perfect partner for the fine strands of somen noodles. This is a subtle noodle dish that should be eaten straight away.

Serves 4
14 oz. (5–6 cups) dry somen noodles
4 oz. fresh enokitake mushrooms
For the soup
17 fl oz. (2 cups) dashi broth (see p.169)
1 teaspoon salt
4 tablespoons light soy sauce
2–3 tablespoons mirin
To garnish
8 strands mitsuba, roughly chopped

Enokitake is also called *yukino shita*, meaning 'under the snow.' In the wild, enokitake grows at the foot of dead broad-leaved trees such as the hackberry and the persimmon. Enoki has recently supplanted shiitake as Japan's most popular mushroom and more than 100,000 tons are grown every year.

How it grows Nagano prefecture is the main producer of the cultivated varieties. Spores are placed in open topped bottles and kept in cool dark rooms.

Appearance and taste Cultivated enokitake, which are the kind most likely to be seen in the West, are anaemic looking: almost white, with long slim stems, their tiny bobble-like caps no more than ½ inch in diameter. The

Bring a large saucepan of water to a boil and add the somen noodles. Add a cup of cold water when the water begins to boil over and bring the water back to a boil before turning off the heat and draining. Run cold water over the cooked noodles and drain well.

Trim and discard the tips of the enokitake stalks and roughly chop the rest of them.

Heat the soup ingredients in a saucepan but do not let boil. Add the noodles and mushrooms to the soup and heat for 2–3 minutes. Transfer the soup to 4 serving bowls, garnish with the chopped mitsuba and serve.

Enoki to shiro-zakana no tsutsumi yaki
[FISH AND ENOKITAKE PARCEL]

In this recipe white fish and enokitake mushrooms are wrapped and steamed in saké and their own juice. When you open the parcel, the delicious aroma envelops you.

Serves 4
2 teaspoons vegetable oil, for oiling the aluminum cooking foil
4 white fish fillets each weighing about 4 oz.
4 tablespoons saké
7 oz. enokitake mushrooms

Preheat the oven to 375°F. Cut 4 rectangles of foil roughly 12 x 8 inches and oil them.

Put one of the fish fillets in the center of 1 of the pieces of foil, drizzle over 1 tablespoon of saké and place a quarter of the enokitake on top.

Fold the 2 longer edges of the foil together, then fold the shorter edges to seal. Repeat this to make 4 parcels. Place the parcels on a baking sheet and bake for 10–15 minutes in the middle of the preheated oven. The foil parcels will expand as the steam rises inside the parcels. Serve unopened.

▾ Fish and enokitake parcel.

しめじ Shimeji [SHIMEJI MUSHROOM]

Shimeji is the third most popular mushroom in Japan. There are many varieties, both wild and farmed. In the wild they grow at the foot of Japanese oaks (*nara*), and red pines. The most popular variety for cultivation is *buna shimeji*, meaning 'beech shimeji,' so-called because in the wild this variety grows on fallen beech or elm trees.

How it grows When cultivated, buna shimeji are grown in bottles in temperature-controlled rooms.

Appearance and taste Buna shimeji grow in tight clusters, joined at the bottom of their stems. They have small, light brown or grey-brown caps, and stems ranging from off-white to pale grey which can be as thick as your middle finger or twice as thin as your little finger. Highly prized for their meaty taste and robust texture, shimeji have almost no aroma.

Culinary uses Like many other Japanese mushrooms, shimeji appear in a wide range of Japanese dishes. They are excellent in soup, in tempura, broiled, or stir-fried with other ingredients. One of my favorite ways of using shimeji is to cook them with rice and make *shimeji gohan*. Here is the recipe.

Shimeji gohan

[RICE WITH SHIMEJI MUSHROOMS]

Serves 4
4 oz. shimeji mushrooms
1 teaspoon salt
14 oz. (1½–2 cups) rice, washed and drained
For the cooking juice
14 fl oz. (1¾ cups) dashi broth (see p.169)
2 tablespoons light soy sauce
2 tablespoons saké
To garnish
A few curls of negi (Japanese scallions, see p.84)

Separate the shimeji and discard the tough bottom parts. Put them in a colander, pour over boiling water and sprinkle on the salt. Then put the mushrooms in a saucepan and add the ingredients for the cooking juice. Bring to a boil over a medium heat, turn the heat down to low and cook for 2 minutes. Take out the mushrooms and set aside, leaving the cooking juice to cook down a little.

Put the washed rice in a heavy-bottomed saucepan with a tight-fitting lid and add the reserved cooking juice. Bring it to a boil over a medium to low heat and when you can hear it bubbling, turn up the heat and cook for 3 minutes more before turning off the heat.

Add the mushrooms, put the lid back on and leave it to steam for another 10 minutes. Stir to combine the rice and mushrooms and serve in individual bowls garnished with curls of negi.

◀ *Slicing off the edible parts of the 'bottled' shimeji.*

Kishi-men noodles with shimeji

Kishi-men noodles are a flat variety of udon noodles from Nagoya (see p.45). You can treat them like pasta except that they are faster to cook.

Serves 4
7 oz. (2½–3 cups) kishi-men noodles
4 fl oz. (½ cup) olive oil
4 garlic cloves, peeled and gently crushed
4 oz. shimeji mushrooms, separated, the base parts
   discarded
2 tablespoons dried porcini mushrooms, soaked in
   hot water—reserve the juice
2 tablespoons soy sauce
2 teaspoons miso paste
Salt and pepper
To garnish
A few sprigs of flat-leaf parsley, chopped

Bring a large saucepan of water to a boil and cook the noodles. Meanwhile, heat the oil in a skillet over a low heat and add the crushed garlic cloves, discarding the garlic when the oil is infused.

Turn up the heat and sauté the shimeji and drained porcini until the mushrooms are soft. Lower the heat and add the reserved porcini juice, a ladleful of cooking water from the noodles, the soy sauce, and the miso paste. Adjust the seasoning with salt and pepper and leave the sauce to simmer.

Drain the noodles and add them to the sauce. Stir well to coat every noodle and serve in 4 individual pasta bowls, garnished with chopped parsley.

▲ *Kishi-men noodles with shimeji.*

滑茸 Nameko [NAMEKO MUSHROOM]

Nameko means 'slippery mushroom' and is a very apt name. Of all the Japanese mushrooms, this is the only one that comes in jars, cans, and plastic packaging even in Japan, so Western cooks need not feel disadvantaged.

How it grows In the wild, nameko grow in the autumn (and in mild winters) on broadleaf trees such as hackberry, oak, and beech in the cooler, northern part of the main island. Today, however, they are mostly grown artificially, in bottles, on beds of woodchips, and also on logs.

Appearance and taste Nameko grow in clusters. A bright orangey-brown, they have a tight little button cap measuring ½–¾ inch across that is covered with gelatinous slime. Nameko have an unmistakable mushroom aroma, but are particularly appreciated for their slipperiness on the tongue, which is unique and worth experiencing.

Buying and storing Fresh nameko have a very limited life once picked; even the wild variety needs to be preserved in brine, which is why nameko are sold in jars or cans or plastic packaging. Preserved nameko keep a very long time but once opened and drained of their brine, they should be used immediately.

Culinary uses One of the most popular ways of using nameko is in soups, especially in miso soup. They also make a delicious yet simple appetizer mixed with shredded daikon (Japanese radish, see p.70) and are often eaten on their own in a seasoned vinegar mixture.

Nameko jiru

[MISO SOUP WITH NAMEKO AND TOFU]

Enjoy the sensation of smooth nameko and silky tofu.

Serves 4
1 piece konbu (dried kelp), postcard size
1 pint (2½ cups) water
4 oz. nameko
3 oz. light colored miso paste
2 oz. silken tofu (soft variety), diced
2 scallions, finely chopped

Put the piece of konbu in a saucepan with the water and gently bring to a boil over a low heat. Take out the konbu when the water reaches boiling point.
  Add the nameko to the soup, and add the miso paste through a small strainer (a tea strainer is ideal). Add the tofu, turn the heat up to medium and bring the soup back to a boil. Sprinkle over the chopped scallion, turn off the heat and serve in 4 separate bowls.

◥ *Nameko with grated daikon.*

Nameko oroshi

[NAMEKO WITH SHREDDED DAIKON]

This is such an easy dish to prepare—you don't even have to turn on the oven. It makes a perfect between-courses palate cleanser.

Serves 4

4 oz. nameko

7 oz. (1 cup) daikon (Japanese radish), peeled and grated

For the vinegar mixture

2 tablespoons rice vinegar

1 tablespoon granulated sugar

1 tablespoon light soy sauce

A pinch of salt (optional)

Mix all the ingredients in a bowl, adjust the seasoning with salt and serve in small wine glasses.

Although most tofu is factory-produced nowadays, I am glad that I am old enough to have experienced the taste of freshly made tofu from small local shops. It was rather like the daily expedition to the bakery in France or the early-morning milk round in Britain. In the morning my mother would walk to a local shop that sold nothing but tofu and its byproducts to buy a block or two (made before dawn) for lunch that day. Then at 5 or 6 o'clock, as she was preparing the dinner, we would hear the familiar sound of the tofu vendor on his bicycle. It was my job to run down the street with a bowl to catch him and buy more freshly made tofu. I always wondered how he managed to keep the tofu intact inside the big, wooden, water-filled box strapped on the back of his bicycle.

5 Tofu & tofu products

豆腐 Tofu [TOFU/BEANCURD]

One of the oldest processed foods of ancient China, tofu has become a major source of vegetable protein throughout southeast Asia, where it is also known as 'field meat' for its high vegetable protein and oil content. Tofu has recently become more popular in the West because of its health benefits and the rise in vegetarianism. It came to Japan from China when Buddhism was first introduced in the middle of the sixth century and has been one of Japan's most important foods ever since. Denigrated as a poor man's food, it was not often included in historical records. The first written record of tofu is as late as 1183— nearly seven centuries after its arrival. Such snobbery did not stop the Japanese embracing tofu, however, refining it to suit Japan's subtle and delicate cuisine.

How it is made The manufacture of tofu is actually quite simple. Tofu is made from soybeans, which in Japan are normally yellow, white or green in color. The beans are soaked overnight, then boiled and crushed to a yogurt-like consistency before being separated into *tonyu* (literally 'bean milk') and *okara* (bean pulp). A coagulant —gypsum—is added to the bean milk, then the warm milk is put in a mold lined with cheesecloth to retain the setting curd and allow the water to drain away. Tofu made this way has a distinctive pattern imprinted on its base and is called *momen-goshi* (cotton-strained tofu) as opposed to the finer, softer, more delicate tofu called *kinu-goshi* (silk-strained tofu), which is made with thicker milk but without the excess water drained off. Once out of the molds, both varieties are suspended in water to continue cooling and firming up.

Appearance and taste Cotton-strained tofu is slightly off-white and firm enough to handle, while the silken type is pure white and very soft and fragile. They are both tasteless without the addition of other flavorings.

Buying and storing Tofu has recently become more widely available not only from Asian/Japanese stores but also from health food or organic food stores. Fresh tofu is normally sold in water-filled plastic containers in rectangular blocks that are 2 inches thick and measure 4 x 3 inches. Tofu is essentially a fresh food that should be eaten within a few days of purchase. It should be kept suspended in a water-filled container in the refrigerator and the water should be changed daily.

Health benefits As tofu's alternative name, 'field meat,' implies, it is highly nutritious. Rich in high-quality vegetable protein, essential amino acids, linoleic acid, vitamins B1 and E, calcium, zinc, and potassium, tofu is an ideal food for preventing hardening of the arteries, high blood pressure, and heart disease. Its rich mineral and calcium content helps to strengthen teeth and bones and slow down the aging process. Easily digested, it is an ideal food for infants, invalids, and elderly people.

Culinary uses Silken tofu is best eaten as it is, either hot or cold, with condiments such as soy sauce, finely chopped scallions, bonito fish flakes, shredded ginger or wasabi. It is also good in soups. Firmer 'cotton' tofu is suited to a wide range of cooking styles: stir-frying, deep-frying, or simmering with other vegetables. Drained and mashed tofu makes an easy base for dips, rather like cream cheese or yogurt.

Agedashi dofu

[DEEP-FRIED TOFU]

This simple dish demands the highest-quality ingredients. The tofu is deep-fried until crisp and golden on the outside and meltingly creamy on the inside, then served with a variety of condiments and a delicious sauce. Serve it immediately before the crispy coating becomes soggy.

Serves 4
2 blocks silken tofu (soft variety), allowing 4–5 oz. per person
3–4 tablespoons vegetable oil, for deep-frying
4 oz. cornstarch
For the sauce
8 fl oz. (1 cup) dashi broth (see p.169)
1 tablespoon saké
1 tablespoon mirin
3 tablespoons light soy sauce
Condiments
4 tablespoons shredded daikon (Japanese radish) mixed with 2 teaspoons red chili paste
2 scallions, finely chopped
4 tablespoons bonito fish flakes

Put all the ingredients for the sauce in a saucepan and heat—do not let boil. Set aside and keep warm. Cut the tofu blocks into 4 equal portions. Wrap each block in a paper towel to allow it to drain. Heat the vegetable oil in a wok to 325–350°F. Coat the tofu blocks with cornstarch and gently slide them into the hot oil. Deep-fry slowly until the tofu starts to become crisp and a light golden color. Drain on paper towels and transfer to 4 individual serving dishes. Arrange the condiments on each block, pour the sauce around the sides and serve while still warm.

Sayaingen no shira-ae

[GREEN BEAN SALAD WITH CREAMY TOFU DRESSING]

This is a modern version of an old Zen Buddhist recipe. Instead of green beans, you can use snow peas, spinach, or bamboo shoots in spring, fava beans, fine beans, or French beans in summer, and persimmon, apples, pears, or sautéed mushrooms in autumn. The tofu dressing is very versatile and can be used with many combinations of fresh vegetables. If made slightly stiffer, it makes a delicious dip.

Serves 4

14 oz. (3–3½ cups) fresh fine beans, cleaned and cut in half

For the tofu dressing

10 oz. (1 block) silken tofu (soft variety)

3 tablespoons sesame seeds, freshly toasted

2 tablespoons granulated sugar

1 teaspoon light soy sauce

1 teaspoon saké

Few drops of truffle oil

A pinch of fine sea salt

To garnish

1 teaspoon toasted sesame seeds

Blanch the tofu in boiling water. Drain and wrap in a paper towel. Sandwich the tofu between 2 chopping boards, tilt the boards slightly and leave to drain for 30 minutes. Steam the green beans for 2–3 minutes. Put under cold running water to freshen up the color and leave to drain.

Grind the sesame seeds with a pestle and mortar until oil appears in the mixture. Press the drained tofu through a fine strainer and add to the ground sesame seeds. Mix well and add the sugar, light soy sauce, saké, and a few drops of truffle oil. Adjust the seasoning with salt and blend well until the dressing is smooth and creamy.

Add the drained beans to the dressing and mix well to ensure that the beans are all coated. Arrange the beans on a large serving dish, sprinkle with more toasted sesame seeds and serve.

▴ *Green bean salad with creamy tofu dressing*

凍豆腐 Kori dofu [FREEZE-DRIED TOFU]

Freeze-dried tofu is also known as Koya dofu (especially in the Kansai region) because it was invented in a Buddhist monastery on Mt Koya, which is over 3,000 feet above sea level with extremely cold winters. According to legend, the idea came to a monk when he discovered an offering of a block of tofu that had frozen overnight on the altar.

How it is made The traditional method was to leave the tofu to freeze overnight then dry in the open air during the coldest part of winter. Today, it is manufactured in freeze-dry chambers.

Appearance and taste Kori dofu has a quite different appearance, texture, and taste from its fresh relatives. It normally comes in blocks 2 x 2 inches and is ¾ inch thick. It is pale cream in color and looks and feels rather like a firm sponge with very fine holes. It smells more strongly of soybean and has a richer flavor than fresh tofu.

Health benefits Kori dofu is made of soybeans, as is fresh tofu, but since it contains virtually no water, the proportion of nutritious elements increases. One slice of Kori dofu is four times as nutritious as fresh tofu.

Buying and storing Kori dofu is usually sold in packets of 5 or 6 pieces with powdered soup broth in which to cook it. It keeps for a long time if stored in a cool, dry cupboard.

Culinary uses The beauty of Kori dofu is that no matter how long it is cooked or how roughly it is handled, it does not fall apart and its spongy texture absorbs the flavor of the broth in which it is cooked. It is often cooked with vegetables in simmered dishes.

Koya dofu no nimono
[SLOW-SIMMERED FREEZE-DRIED TOFU WITH SHIITAKE]

There are many slow-simmered dishes in the Japanese kitchen but what elevates them from average to splendid is the quality of the dashi broth.

Serves 4
4 good-quality, dried shiitake mushrooms
4 blocks Koya dofu (freeze-dried tofu)
32 fl oz. good-quality konbu no tsuke dashi broth
  (vegetarian seaweed broth, see p.121)
4 tablespoons light soy sauce
4 tablespoons mirin
2 tablespoons granulated sugar
1 teaspoon salt

Soak the mushrooms in a bowl of hot water for 15 minutes or until they are soft. Take out, squeeze to extract any excess moisture and reserve the juice. Discard the stalks and cut the caps into quarters.
  Soak the blocks of tofu in hot water, turning them occasionally, until they are soft. Squeeze out the excess water and cut the blocks into bite-size pieces. Put the mushrooms and tofu in a saucepan, add the juice from the mushrooms and the dashi broth. Add all the other seasonings and bring to a boil over a very gentle heat.
  Simmer for 30 minutes or until the cooking juice has been reduced by half. Transfer the tofu and mushrooms to a serving dish and serve hot or warm.

Kori dofu no nimono

[SIMMERED FREEZE-DRIED TOFU]

This is a real store cupboard dish: every Japanese kitchen has some Kori dofu. This dish can be served hot or at room temperature.

Serves 4
4 blocks Kori dofu (freeze-dried tofu)
1½ pints (3⅔ cups) dashi broth (see p.169)
5 tablespoons granulated sugar
2 teaspoons salt
3 tablespoons saké
2 tablespoons light soy sauce
4 eggs
Sansho pepper for sprinkling

◥ Simmered freeze-dried tofu.
◂ Rows of kori dofu drying in the sun.

Place the blocks of tofu in warm water and cover them with a heavy plate to ensure the blocks are immersed. Soak the tofu until soft—the time this takes depends how dry it is to start with or how long it has been kept. Drain the blocks by squeezing them and rinsing them in fresh water. Repeat this process—squeezing, draining, and rinsing—until the water runs clear.

Put the rinsed tofu in a saucepan with the dashi broth, sugar, salt, saké and soy sauce and bring to a boil over a low heat, partially covered. Simmer for 40–60 minutes. Remove the blocks of tofu, reserving the cooking liquor, arrange them in 4 individual dishes and keep warm.

Crack the eggs into the pan of dashi mixture and gently poach. Place an egg on each block of tofu, pour the cooking juice around, sprinkle with sansho and serve.

揚げ豆腐 Age dofu/Abura age [DEEP-FRIED TOFU]

Serves 4

1 sheet deep-fried tofu

1 tablespoon vegetable oil

12 baby turnips, washed, peeled and cut in quarters

16 fl oz. (1¾ cups) dashi broth (see p.169)

2 tablespoons light soy sauce

2 tablespoons mirin

4 tablespoons chirimenjako (dried shrimps, optional)

Salt

Put the deep-fried tofu in a colander and pour boiling water over it to remove the oil. Drain and thinly slice.

Heat a wok over a medium heat and add the oil. Add the quartered turnip and stir-fry for 3–5 minutes. Add the slices of tofu, the dashi broth, soy sauce, and mirin, as well as the dried shrimps, if using. Reduce the heat and let simmer for 10 minutes. Season with salt and serve.

Age-dofu to kyabetsu no miso-shiru
[MISO SOUP WITH DEEP-FRIED TOFU AND CABBAGE]

I love miso soups of all kinds and this one is popular with almost everyone, including my children, who are normally averse to anything called cabbage. The sweetness of the cabbage and distinctive flavor of the deep-fried tofu go well together.

Serves 4

2 sheets deep-fried tofu

32 fl oz. (3⅞ cups) water

8 oz. (2–2½ cups) cabbage, finely sliced

4 tablespoons light colored miso paste

Place the deep-fried tofu in a colander and pour boiling water over it to remove the oil. Drain and thinly slice.

Put the water and shredded cabbage in a saucepan, add the tofu and bring to a boil over a medium heat. When the soup begins to boil, reduce the heat and simmer for 5 minutes before adding the miso paste through a small strainer. Let the soup return to a boil, then take off the heat and serve.

There is nothing mysterious about deep-fried tofu; it is simply fresh tofu, drained and deep-fried in vegetable oil.

Appearance and taste Deep-fried tofu looks like a puffed-up, golden brown envelope covered in oil. In Japanese cooking, deep-fried tofu is often rid of its oil by having boiling water poured over it, which changes its crunchy texture and oily flavor to something much paler, softer, and more absorbant of other flavors.

Buying and storing In Japan deep-fried tofu is—like fresh tofu—made daily by small, local tofu shops, but in the West it is sold prepacked, often frozen. In this form it keeps well for several months.

Culinary uses The best-known use of deep-fried tofu is as a wrapping material for sushi—the sweet, succulent, *inari zushi* (see opposite), which is wonderful for picnics. It is also used in soups, simmered dishes, or rice dishes.

Age dofu to ko-kabu no nimono
[SIMMERED BABY TURNIPS WITH DEEP-FRIED TOFU]

My grandmother often used small, leftover pieces of deep-fried tofu to make a simmered dish of vegetables. I now appreciate her frugality: nothing was ever wasted.

↘ *Stuffed tofu sushi.*

Inari zushi

[STUFFED TOFU SUSHI]

Deep-fried tofu makes a delicious wrapping material for sushi rice. You can mix different vegetables in with the rice and if you keep the parcels bite size, they're ideal finger food for picnics.

Makes 12 parcels
6 sheets deep-fried tofu, each one cut in half
8 fl oz. (1 cup) dashi broth (see p.169)
4 tablespoons granulated sugar
6 tablespoons soy sauce
3 tablespoons saké
3 tablespoons mirin
2 tablespoons toasted white sesame seeds
1 quantity prepared sushi rice (see p.223)

Roll a chopstick over each piece of tofu to make it more malleable, then gently open to make a pouch. Place in a bamboo strainer or colander and pour over boiling water to remove the oil.

Put the tofu pouches in a saucepan and add the dashi broth, sugar, soy sauce, saké, and mirin. Simmer over a low heat until most of the liquid has reduced—this will take 20–30 minutes. Let cool, then drain.

In a bowl, mix the sesame seeds with the sushi rice. Take a heaped tablespoon of the rice mixture and fill a seasoned tofu pouch, making sure you don't overfill the pouch. Carefully fold the edges over to make a neat parcel and repeat until you have 12 parcels and serve warm.

湯葉 Yuba [YUBA]

Yuba is the fine skin that forms on the surface of soybean milk when tofu is being made. Great skill is required to retrieve it: skimmed off in a single swoop with a long bamboo stick, it is then hung up to dry over a charcoal fire.

Appearance and taste Yuba comes in various forms—as flat sheets, thick strips or rolled—but it most commonly comes in slightly crinkled, golden, papery sheets. Yuba acquires a buttery, soybean aroma once cooked in broth or soup but retains its resilient texture.

Storing Yuba keeps well for several months if stored in an airtight container in a cool, dark cupboard.

Culinary uses It is used widely in *Shojin Ryori* (Buddhist vegetarian cooking), in simmered dishes with other vegetables, in soups, and as a wrapping material.

Horenso no yuba maki

[YUBA SPINACH ROLL]

This is a simplified version of a dish I once had at a Zen Buddhist temple in Kyoto. Although yuba is not fragile, it pays to handle it with care.

Serves 4
1 lb. spinach, washed, the roots discarded
2 dried yuba sheets, approximately 12 x 12 inches
For the ohitashi dressing
4 fl oz. (½ cup) dashi broth (see p.169)
1 tablespoon light soy sauce
1 tablespoon mirin
To garnish
1 teaspoon toasted white sesame seeds

First, briefly boil the spinach. Drain and squeeze out excess water. Divide the cooked spinach into 2 portions and shape each portion into a cylinder 6 inches long.

Soak the yuba sheets in warm water for 10–15 minutes to soften. Remove and press each sheet with paper towels to get rid of excess water. Lay them on a flat surface, place a spinach cylinder at the base of each sheet and roll up. Cut each cylinder into 6 equal pieces.

Put all the dressing ingredients in a saucepan and heat over a medium flame. Arrange the pieces of the spinach roll on a serving dish and pour the warm dressing around them. Garnish with sesame seeds and serve.

雁もどき Ganmodoki [DEEP-FRIED TOFU WITH VEGETABLES]

Ganmodoki is deep-fried tofu with vegetables and the name means 'wild goose alike.' It is a strange name for a vegetarian dish that was developed in Zen Buddhist temple kitchens. In the Kansai region it is known by the even more intriguing name of *hiryuzu*, which means 'flying dragon head,' a name believed to be derived from the Portuguese word *filhos*: fruity sweets made from deep-fried flour.

How it is made Drained tofu is mixed with chopped carrots, *gobo* (burdock), shiitake mushrooms, *konbu* (dried kelp), Judas-ear mushrooms, and ginkgo nuts, then deep-fried.

Appearance and taste Ganmodoki has an appetizing, golden color and comes in flat discs 3 inches in diameter or in small egg-shape balls. The unusual name of 'wild goose alike' arises from its texture rather than its taste or appearance.

Buying and storing In the West, ganmodoki is available vacuum-packed or frozen from Japanese stores. It is precooked and ready to eat, though it does benefit from being heated up before serving—microwaving it on low is ideal.

Culinary uses Ganmodoki is delicious on its own and is also good cooked or simmered with other vegetables.

Homemade ganmodoki

Although tofu is recognized as being marvelously healthy, I have to admit it suffers from an image problem and tends to put people off, especially men! But I hope to change all that with this simple and easy-to-make recipe. It makes a deliciously healthy canapé or appetizer and can be served hot or cold.

Serves 4 as an appetizer
1 block 'cotton' tofu (firm variety)
1 piece konbu (dried kelp), 2 x 2 inches
2 dried shiitake mushrooms, softened in hot water
2 oz. (1 small) carrot, peeled and finely chopped
1 tablespoon shredded ginger root
1 egg white, beaten to soft peaks
1 teaspoon light soy sauce
1 teaspoon mirin
½–1 teaspoon salt
Vegetable oil, for deep-frying
For the dipping sauce
4 tablespoons soy sauce
1 tablespoon rice vinegar
1 tablespoon shredded ginger root

Put the block of tofu on a chopping board, place another small chopping board or plate on top, and put a little weight on top of that. Tilt at a slight angle and leave to drain for at least 45 minutes.

Soak the konbu in a bowl of warm water and, when it is soft, chop it into small pieces. Drain the softened shiitake mushrooms, discard the stems and roughly chop. Put the tofu, konbu, shiitake, carrot, ginger, egg white, soy sauce, mirin, and salt in a food processor and whizz for a few seconds.

Preheat a wok of vegetable oil over medium heat to 310°F. Meanwhile, combine the ingredients for the dipping sauce in a serving dish. Shape the tofu mixture into ping-pong balls and deep-fry them in small batches until they are crisp and golden. Drain them on paper towels and serve with the soy vinegar dipping sauce.

No people other than the Japanese regularly incorporate over fifty varieties of seaweed and numerous seaweed products into their diet. The practice dates back to ancient times when my Japanese ancestors burned seaweed to extract salt. Written records show that by the beginning of the eighth century, seaweeds were being harvested and eaten in their own right. As time went by and navigation techniques improved, more and more varieties were being harvested in Hokkaido (the biggest seaweed-producing region in Japan) and brought to the larger cities. Today, seaweed is seen as a 'health food,' not only by the Japanese but also by Westerners. Seaweed is a healthy and tasty gift from the sea. The following are among the most widely used seaweeds in the Japanese kitchen.

6 Seaweed & seaweed products

昆布 Konbu [KELP]

Konbu is one of the most indispensable ingredients in the Japanese kitchen—together with katsuo-bushi (bonito flakes), konbu is used to make the dashi broth that is the fundamental taste of Japan, and is used on its own to make vegetarian dashi. Konbu also occupies a special place culturally, featuring in many celebratory feasts because of a pun on *yorokobu*, the Japanese word for 'rejoice.'

How it grows Konbu's natural habitat is the northern part of the main island of Japan, around Hokkaido and near Sakhalin Island. It grows in relatively shallow water, 6–66 feet deep, clinging on to rock beds. It is a biennial plant that is harvested every second year in the wild, but can be harvested after just one year when cultivated.

Appearance and taste There are many varieties of konbu. It can range in width from 2 to 14 inches and in length from 1 to 60 feet, and is usually about ⅛ inch thick. *Rishiri konbu*, the highest quality konbu, is between 5 to 8 inches wide, 5 to 8 feet long and is ⅛ inch thick. Konbu resembles a wide, dark brown ribbon. It smells distinctively of the sea and has a rich flavor. I love to chew it—it makes a great natural chewing gum.

Buying and storing Konbu is sold in dried form. It is graded according to its quality (reflected in the price) and cut to manageable size. Dried konbu keeps for up to a year if stored in a cool, dry cupboard.

Health benefits Konbu has virtually no protein but is high in calcium, carotene, iron, and dietary fiber. It is also rich in iodine, which aids metabolism and growth. Calcium and other minerals are essential for strong teeth and bones, and can reduce stress and lower blood pressure.

Culinary uses As said earlier, the most important use of konbu in the Japanese kitchen is to make dashi broth. Konbu is also shaved to make wafer-thin ribbons called *oboro konbu* and shreds called *soboro* or *tororo konbu*. *Oboro konbu* is used as a wrapping material for other ingredients and is the essential material for making *battera* (pressed mackerel sushi), while *tororo konbu* is used in clear soup for its special flavor and its distinctive jelly-like texture. A preserved product called *tsukudani*, which is served with plain boiled rice, is made from konbu—sometimes from konbu alone and

↖ *Fisherman harvesting konbu off the coast of Hokkaido.*
↙ *Konbu-marinated flounder.*

sometimes also from other ingredients, such as mushrooms. Konbu is popular, dried and salted, as an accompaniment for plain boiled rice—in this form it is called *shio konbu*. Small pieces of konbu are rolled and tied with kampyo to make *kobu maki*, which is not only a tasty side dish but also an essential ingredient at Japanese New Year. Last but not least, konbu is an essential ingredient of sushi, which requires a postcard-size piece of konbu.

Konbu no tsuke dashi

[VEGETARIAN KELP BROTH]

Strict Buddhist cooking does not allow the consumption of any meat or fish. The most widely used broth—'number one dashi', which is made with bonito flakes—is therefore out of the question. Buddhists use konbu alone to make their stock, and the good news is that this vegetarian version could not be easier to make.

1 piece konbu, postcard size
1¾ pints (4 cups) water

Make some tears in the konbu and leave it in a bowl with the water for 3–4 hours in winter and 2 hours in summer. Simple as that. No cooking required.

Hirame no konbu jime

[KONBU-MARINATED FLOUNDER]

Subtle and sophisticated, this dish is remarkably easy to prepare. The delicate flavor of konbu is transferred to fresh flounder, though any white-flesh fish, such as sea bream, sole, or sea bass, can be used instead—the important thing is that you use the freshest fish.

Serves 4
7 oz. white fish fillet, bones and skin removed
2 sheets konbu, big enough to cover the fish
2 oz. (4 tablespoons) salt
A bowl of water with 8 fl oz. (1 cup) rice vinegar
To serve
Soy sauce
Wasabi paste

Sprinkle a generous amount of salt on both sides of the fish fillet. Cover and refrigerate for 1 hour. Moisten the konbu with a clean damp cloth to soften, then cover the fish with the konbu. Lay it in a non-metallic flat-based container with a little weight on top and chill for 3 hours.

Uncover the fish, wash off the salt in a bowl of cold water and transfer the fish to the bowl of vinegar water. Remove, drain well on paper towels, slice thinly and serve with soy sauce and wasabi paste.

海苔 Nori [DRIED SEAWEED]

An island nation from its earliest history, the Japanese have always enjoyed the fruits of the sea, whether salt, fish, shellfish, or seaweeds. They eat more seaweed, in terms of quantity and variety, and make more products from seaweed than any other nation. Nori is a generic term covering a particular seaweed and its products; it is sometimes called purple laver and is a type of marine algae. There are three types of nori products: *yaki nori* (dry-toasted nori), *ajitsuke nori* (dry-seasoned nori), and *tsukudani nori* (wet seasoned nori). Dry-toasted nori is probably the most famous and popular seaweed of all. Recently, nori has become more familiar as a wrapping material for sushi.

History The earliest mention of nori appears in 689, when it is recorded as an offering at a Shinto shrine. The early Japanese probably ate nori raw, and also used it as a medicine. Later on, nori was used to make seaweed hishio (a fermented, salted mixture of seaweeds). Woodblock prints show that clusters of bamboo poles or branches for collecting seaweed from lagoons around Tokyo Bay were a familiar scene in the eighteenth century. According to historical records, there were 142 nori beds employing 765 people in 1838. Nori had become Tokyo's regional specialty.

How it grows Today, the majority of nori is farmed. Spores are planted in January on nets placed in calm bays or lagoons and harvested in autumn. A young plant resembles a bamboo leaf and is pale red; as it matures the color changes to green and develops pleats around the edge. An average mature plant measures 4 inches wide and 8 inches long.

Manufacture The traditional nori-making process was borrowed from the Japanese paper industry: plants are first washed in fresh water, then thinly spread over mesh sheets and sun-dried on bamboo or wooden frames before being toasted. For dry-seasoned nori, soy sauce and mirin-based flavoring are added. *Tsukudani nori*, or wet seasoned nori, was first devised in the nineteenth century because the sun-drying process sometimes failed and manufacturers were left with wet nori.

Appearance and taste A sheet of dry toasted nori comes in a standard size of 8 x 7 inches and is either near black or dark green in color. A sheet of good nori is thick and has a tight and evenly grained shiny surface. Nori has a crisp dry texture with a pleasant aroma of the sea, and melts in the mouth.

Buying and storing Nori is usually sold in a pack of 10 sheets. The price is a good indication of the quality—avoid thin, flimsy-looking nori. Once opened, nori should be used as soon as possible as it quickly becomes limp and loses its aromatic flavors. Unused sheets of nori should be stored in an airtight container in a dark, dry cupboard. Toast a sheet of nori over a gentle flame before using to revive its crisp texture and flavor.

Health benefits Nori is one of my children's favorite snacks—they all love the taste and crisp texture, and it is good for them, so my conscience is clear. Nori is rich in protein (48 percent of its dry weight), vitamins (especially vitamins A and B1) and minerals such as iron, zinc, and calcium. Nori's high protein and fiber makes it an excellent vegetarian alternative to meat and fish. It is the most easily digested of all the edible seaweeds. Nori's high vitamin and mineral content helps to decrease cholesterol, lower blood pressure, and prevent hair loss. Conversely, mineral deficiencies cause irritability, fatigue, and forgetfulness.

Culinary uses Perhaps the most popular use of nori is as a wrapping material for sushi rolls. In the popular lunch box snack, *onigiri* (rice balls) are wrapped in nori. A packet of dry-seasoned nori is an essential part of the traditional Japanese breakfast, along with a bowl of plain boiled rice. Finely crushed nori is used as a garnish.

▸ *A small-scale nori farm in a secluded bay.*

Onigiri

[RICE BALLS]

Serves 4–6

11 oz. (2½–3cups) Japanese short-grain rice, washed
12 fl oz. (1½ cups) cold water
3 umeboshi (pickled plums), pitted
1 tablespoon toasted sesame seeds
½ teaspoon mirin
2 sheets dry-toasted nori, cut into 6 equal strips
1 teaspoon crushed sea salt

Put the rice in a heavy-based saucepan with a tight-fitting lid and add the water. Bring to the boil over a gentle heat, increase the heat to medium for 5 minutes, then turn it off, leaving the rice to steam with the lid on for 10 minutes more. Drain and set aside to cool.

Meanwhile, mash the umeboshi using the back of a fork and mix with the sesame seeds and mirin to make a rough paste. Set the mixture aside.

Divide the rice into six equal portions. Wet your hands in a bowl of water and sprinkle some salt onto your palms. Spread one of the portions of rice on your left palm and shape it into a firm rounded triangle. Make an indentation in the center of the rice ball and fill with a teaspoonful of the plum paste. Wrap the rice ball with a nori strip just below the plum filling. Repeat with the remaining rice balls and serve.

ワカメ Wakame [SEA MUSTARD]

Of all the varieties of seaweeds that the Japanese eat, wakame is the most popular. The Japanese relationship with wakame is one of the oldest: wakame is listed on a tax record dating from 701 and it features in many of the short poems in Japan's oldest poetry collection, *Manyoshu*. Its nutritional value and ability to keep well have long been recognized in Japan—it is an important item in Shinto religious ceremonies and was used as an emergency food source and field ration during the Civil War period. Today, it is one of the most familiar ingredients in the Japanese kitchen.

How it grows Wakame is found all around coastal Japan, and goes by many different names according to the region. Its favorite habitat is on rock beds 50–66 feet deep in the sea; the best quality wakame grows in rapid currents. A fast growing annual plant, wakame matures in just six months and is harvested between March and June. Although the cultivation of wakame dates back only to 1965, it satisfies almost all the domestic demand (approximately 120,000 tons a year). It is grown mainly in Iwate and Miyagi prefectures, followed by Hyogo prefecture.

Appearance and taste Broadly speaking there are three types of wakame: wakame, hirome, and aowakame. The color of wakame ranges from green to brownish green and deep brown, depending on the variety. The appearances also differ, from the smaller hirome, which measures 12–20 inches wide and 2–3 feet long to the giant, oak leaf-like wakame, measuring 20 inches wide and 6½–10 feet long. Fresh wakame, with its distinctive taste of the sea and silky but resilient texture, is considered a rare seasonal treat—it is mostly sold dried or salted.

Buying and storing Dried wakame should be stored in an airtight container in a cool, dry cupboard. It will keep almost indefinitely.

Health benefits Of all the edible seaweeds, wakame has the highest calcium content. It is also rich in minerals such as zinc and iron and contains a wide range of vitamins, as well as dietary fiber. Historically, growing children and pregnant women were encouraged to eat wakame. It is useful for warding off arteriosclerosis, high blood pressure, constipation, and diabetes.

Culinary uses Fresh wakame is a healthy spring delicacy, eaten lightly blanched with a vinegar dressing. Wakame that is dried or salted needs to be reconstituted. It is widely used in soups, salads, and simmered dishes.

↖ *A woman gathers wakame from a coastal rock bed.*

Wakame no oroshi ae

[WAKAME AND DAIKON SALAD WITH VINEGAR DRESSING]

I love the refreshing taste of daikon and the slippery texture of wakame united by vinegar. The addition of shirasu-boshi adds another dimension and extra calcium.

Serves 4

¾ oz. dried wakame (dry weight)

2 oz. shirasu-boshi (dried sardines)

7 oz. (1 cup) shredded daikon (Japanese radish)

For the vinegar dressing

4 tablespoons rice vinegar

1 tablespoon granulated sugar

1 teaspoon light soy sauce

½ teaspoon salt

Soak the dried wakame in a bowl of hot water. Leave it to stand until the wakame becomes soft and swells up (about 10 minutes). Drain well.

In a separate bowl, soak the shirasu-boshi in hot water, drain and set aside. The shredded daikon should be gently squeezed to get rid of excess water. Mix together the ingredients for the vinegar dressing.

Combine the wakame, shirasu-boshi, and daikon just before serving and add the vinegar mixture. Mix well, then turn into 4 individual dishes and serve.

ひじき Hijiki [HIJIKI]

Hijiki is a curious ingredient, even for the Japanese, who see it and eat it but know little about it.

How it grows Hijiki is native to Japan and grows all around the country on shallow rock beds. It is an annual plant harvested between May and June.

Appearance and taste Hijiki is a twiggy, greeny-brown marine plant 1–3 feet tall with a faint aroma of the sea. Hijiki harvested in May and June is believed to be the most succulent and have the best flavor.

Buying and storing Hijiki is normally sold in dried form and needs to be reconstituted before use. Soak the hijiki in tepid water to let it soften—it will expand to eight to ten times its volume. Dried hijiki will keep for several months if stored in an airtight container in a dry, cool cupboard.

Health benefits Like many other seaweeds, hijiki is rich in calcium, vitamins, and minerals. Unlike other seaweeds, it has a surprisingly high level of carbohydrate—more than 50 percent.

Culinary uses The most popular way of cooking hijiki is to soften it in water, lightly sauté it, then simmer it with other ingredients, such as beans, in a soy sauce-based broth. Seasoned hijiki is a popular side dish at Japanese tables.

Hijiki ni

[SIMMERED HIJIKI]

This is a standard dish at family meals. Highly nutritious, it keeps well for a few days in the refrigerator.

Serves 4 as a side dish
2 oz. hijiki (dry weight)
1 sheet deep-fried tofu
1 small carrot, peeled and cut into matchsticks
2 fl oz. (4 tablespoons) konbu no tsuke dashi
   (vegetarian kelp broth, see p.121)
4 tablespoons soy sauce
3½ tablespoons granulated sugar
2 tablespoons mirin

First, soak the hijiki in a bowl of hot water for 20 minutes, then drain. Put the sheet of tofu in a colander, pour over boiling water to remove the oil, then cut the tofu into thin slices. Put the hijiki, deep-fried tofu slices and carrot sticks in a saucepan. Add the konbu dashi, soy sauce, sugar, and mirin. Cook on low heat until all the juice has evaporated.

Hijiki gohan

[RICE WITH HIJIKI]

As mentioned earlier, a hijiki dish is a regular feature at the Japanese table and there is nearly always some left over. This recipe uses up your leftover hijiki.

Serves 4

7 oz. (¾–1 cup) rice, washed, rinsed and drained
8 fl oz. (1 cup) water
2 tablespoons saké
2 tablespoons soy sauce
2 oz. cooked hijiki

Put the rice, water, sake, and soy sauce in a heavy-based saucepan with a tight-fitting lid, and cook over low heat. When it begins to boil and you can hear it bubbling, turn up the heat to medium and cook for 3 more minutes.

Turn off the heat, add the cooked hijiki, replace the lid and leave to steam for another 10 minutes. Stir and serve.

◀ ◀ Collecting seaweed that has been washed up onto the beach

▾ Simmered hijiki.

寒天 Kanten [KANTEN]

It took me a while to realize that one of my favorite childhood desserts, *mitsumame* (a fruit salad with small cubes of jelly in syrup), was made from kanten, Japan's answer to gelatine or aspic. Kanten is a remarkable ingredient that features in many dishes cooked in the Japanese kitchen.

Habitat, appearance, and taste Kanten is a generic term for a product made from a seaweed called tengusa. Tengusa grows widely around every part of Japan except for Hokkaido, the northernmost island, and is a beautiful, deep purple, lace-like plant 4–12 inches tall. Harvested tengusa is repeatedly washed and dried before being shipped to mountainous regions, such as Nagano prefecture (where the winter is bitterly cold but dry), to be made into kanten. Slightly opaque, kanten has neither flavor nor aroma. It makes a better quality jelly than gelatine, which can be rather rubbery, and kanten does not require refrigeration.

Buying and storing Freeze-dried kanten comes in three forms: as a bar about 10 inches long, as filaments of a similar length, and as a powder. Both bars and filaments need to be soaked and softened before use. Freeze-dried kanten keeps well for several months if stored in a cool, dry place.

Health benefits Kanten has virtually no calories so was not recognized in the past as having any nutritional value. Recently, though, its low calories, absence of fat, and high fiber content have made kanten an ideal slimming food.

Culinary uses Kanten's complete lack of aroma and flavor makes it a perfect setting agent for all kinds of dishes. Kanten is squeezed through a mold to make noodles called *tokoroten*, which are eaten as a snack in the summer with a sweet syrup or savory sauce, and is used as a setting agent for cakes and desserts.

▾ *Making kanten in the mountains of Nagano.*

Kani no kanten yose

[CRABMEAT, FINE BEANS AND CARROT IN KANTEN]

Although it takes a few hours to prepare, this makes a beautiful and sophisticated appetizer that you can make a day in advance. Serve it with vinegar miso.

Serves 4 as an appetizer
⅓ bar kanten
3 fl oz. (⅓ cup) water
3 oz. (½ cup) cooked white crabmeat
2 fine beans, blanched and finely chopped
¼ oz. carrot (1 teaspoon), blanched and finely chopped
For the vinegar miso sauce
2 tablespoons medium colored miso paste
1 tablespoon rice vinegar
1 teaspoon soy sauce
1 teaspoon granulated sugar

Rinse the stick of kanten, then soak it in water for 1 hour or until soft. (A saucer or plate in the top of the bowl will stop the kanten floating up to the surface.) Break the kanten into small pieces and put it in a saucepan with ⅓ cup water. Cook over a medium heat until it has dissolved.

Add the crabmeat, fine beans and carrot to the kanten solution, stir and take off the heat. Moisten the inside of a container or mold and pour in the kanten mixture. Leave it to cool and set while you mix the ingredients for the vinegar miso.

Once set, cover and chill until just before serving, then remove it from the mold and cut it into slices 1 inch thick. Arrange the slices on 4 serving plates and serve with the vinegar miso.

An island nation, the Japanese are the undisputed fish-eating champions of the world and have been eating fish since prehistoric times—archaeologists have found salmon bones dating back 10,000 years. There are fish markets all over Japan and the biggest and most famous market of all is Tsukiji fish market in Tokyo, where over 3,000 varieties of fish and shellfish are sold or auctioned by the 1,000 wholesale stalls. Tsukiji fish market boasts the largest volume and highest cash turnover in the world. There is no doubt that fish and Japanese cuisine are inseparable. Japanese people go shopping every day for the freshest fish and Japanese fishermen travel all over the world to meet the demand back home.

7 Fish & shellfish

鮪 Maguro [TUNA]

There is no doubt that maguro is the heavyweight champion of all the fish used in the Japanese kitchen. Tsukiji fish market alone sees a daily turnover of 3,000 tuna totaling more than 200 tons in weight, and 450 stores out of 1,000 specialize in tuna. Although the Japanese were eating tuna 10,000 years ago, its popularity is, surprisingly, quite recent. Until the beginning of the nineteenth century tuna was considered unappetizing but opinion changed when soy sauce became available to ordinary people. Even so, it was not until the end of the Second World War that the fatty belly of tuna, as opposed to the leaner back part, became the most highly prized cut of all.

Habitat Maguro belongs to the mackerel family and there are seven species of this warm-water fish. Five kinds are found near Japan: the most highly sought after bluefin tuna, and the yellowfin, longtail, albacore (sometimes called longfin) and bigeye tuna; the other two, the blackfin tuna, which lives in the warmer parts of the Atlantic Ocean, and the southern bluefin tuna, are found only in the southern hemisphere. The largest kind, the bluefin tuna, can grow to some 10 feet long, weighing 675–1350 pounds, although the average size is normally something between 3–6½ feet. The main habitat of the bluefin tuna is the north Pacific, north Atlantic and, less commonly, the Mediterranean.

Taste and appearance Tuna is a handsome streamlined fish designed to swim vast distances at high speed. The deep red flesh tastes rich and oily with a sweet flavor and has a dense but smooth texture. Tuna is unique in that the fatty belly part is preferred and fetches a higher price than the leaner back part.

Buying and storing In Japan, tuna is sold already skinned and filleted. Filleting a tuna is a skilled and heavy-duty job performed by a team of two or three men working together. Even busy sushi restaurants in Tokyo do not acquire a whole fish but buy different cuts. The leaner top parts are called *akami*, meaning 'red meat' (the least expensive cut); the next grade up is *chu toro*, meaning 'middle *toro*' (the fatty belly part is known as *toro*); and the most prized and expensive cut is *o toro* meaning 'big *toro*,' which is the lowest part of the belly next to the head. In an ideal situation, tuna that is to be eaten raw should be consumed on the day it is bought, or within two days at most, and should be kept in the coldest part of the refrigerator or in the freezer. In the days before fridges, tuna would have been marinated in a soy sauce and saké mixture.

Health benefits The main health benefit of tuna, especially of fatty *o toro*, is its docosahexaenoic acid (DHA), which slows down the deterioration of brain cells and lowers cholesterol. It is also rich in eicosapentaenoic acid (EPA), which helps to prevent hardening of the arteries. Tuna provides high-quality protein and is a rich source of vitamins, especially vitamin D.

Culinary uses The most popular way of using tuna in the Japanese kitchen is not to cook it but to eat it raw as sashimi or sushi. Marinating tuna is an easy and tasty way of serving it in salad form, and tuna lends itself well to robust methods of cooking such as broiling, pan-frying and stir-frying.

Frozen whole tuna fish for sale at a fishmarket.

Seared tuna with grated daikon and caviar.

Maguro no zuke salada

[MARINATED TUNA SALAD]

In Japan, fish merchants cut tuna lengthways—an operation that resembles the sawing of a sizeable piece of timber and involves two or three skilled fish merchants with big saws and long sword-like knives. It is not a scene for the faint-hearted. After all the prime cuts have been taken out, the leaner trimmings that are left—the *butsu*—are sold relatively cheaply. In the West, most of the fresh tuna sold is what the Japanese regard as lean red meat, which is a perfect cut for this recipe.

Serves 4

14 oz. lean tuna
2 tablespoons rice vinegar
1 teaspoon wasabi powder
2 tablespoons saké
1 tablespoon mirin
4 tablespoons soy sauce
2 scallions, very finely chopped
4 green shiso (perilla) leaves, finely chopped
To garnish
2 teaspoons roasted sesame seeds

Chop the tuna into 1 inch cubes and put them in a bowl. Add the vinegar, wasabi powder, saké, mirin and soy sauce to the bowl and mix well. Add the scallion and shiso leaves, stir well and leave to marinate for 10 minutes before serving garnished with sesame seeds.

Maguro no tataki

[SEARED TUNA WITH SHREDDED DAIKON AND CAVIAR]

This is an adaptation of *tataki*, a traditional treatment for filleted fish or meat which involves searing and briefly marinating it. It is an easy yet highly professional-looking dish, guaranteed to impress your family and friends. Serve it with a dab of shredded daikon and a spoonful of caviar to add a professional touch.

Serves 4

2 teaspoons grapeseed oil
7 oz. tuna fillet, trimmed to make a square
Salt and pepper
1 tablespoon rice vinegar or white balsamic vinegar
1 tablespoon saké
1 tablespoon soy sauce
To garnish
4 tablespoons shredded daikon (Japanese radish)
4 teaspoons caviar
2 green shiso (perilla) leaves, finely sliced
1 teaspoon roasted sesame seeds

Heat a non-stick skillet over a medium heat and add the oil. Season the tuna fillet and sear until the flesh turns white. Take it off the heat and let it cool before cutting it into slices ¼ inch thick.

Put the slices of tuna in a bowl and pour over the vinegar. Add the saké and soy sauce and set aside for 10 minutes. Arrange the tuna on 4 serving plates and spoon the shredded daikon on top.

Spoon on the caviar, top it with the finely sliced shiso leaves and sprinkle with the sesame seeds before serving.

鰹 Katsuo [BONITO/SKIPJACK TUNA]

Katsuo is one of the most important and versatile ingredients in the Japanese kitchen since dashi broth, the fundamental Japanese flavor, is made with dried bonito flakes. Seasonality is extremely important in Japanese cooking, and katsuo symbolizes the beginning of summer: it is a tradition for Japanese gourmets to seek out the first and best katsuo of the season.

Habitat Katsuo is a migratory fish that belongs to the mackerel family. Schools of katsuo travel vast distances in warm water at high speed—they are the bullet trains of the sea. They swim with their mouths open to maximize their oxygen intake and they never stop swimming, even in their sleep. Katsuo are found in warm water all around the world. In Japan, the season starts at the southern tip of Kyushu Island in late March, and the katsuo travel north in the warm currents on the Pacific side of Japan reaching the top

▾ *Fishermen survey their catch of silvery blue bonito.*

of the main island in June. They are called *hatsu gatsuo* (first katsuo) or *nobori gatsuo* (rising katsuo) and command high prices as a seasonal delicacy. Katsuo caught in autumn traveling south are called *modori gatsuo*, meaning 'returning katsuo,' and have a higher fat content, a richer, more buttery flavor and a firmer texture.

Appearance and taste Katsuo is a handsome fish measuring about 3 ft long, weighing about 67–90 lb. when fully grown. Its streamlined body is well suited to high-speed travel. It has a deep blue-mauve back and silver belly, on which darker stripes develop when it is dead. Katsuo flesh is dark red and firm, with a rich taste.

Buying and storing Fresh katsuo is rarely seen outside Japan, as it goes off very quickly. Traditionally, katsuo is caught with a single rod and line, to minimize damage to the fish.

Health benefits Of all the fish in this chapter, katsuo has the highest level of vitamin B12, which is excellent for preventing anemia. Rich in niacin, it is good for the circulation and keeps brain cells healthy. It is also high in both DHA and EPA (see p.132), which lower blood pressure and cleanse the blood.

Culinary uses The most famous way to cook katsuo is *tataki*: searing it over burning straw to rid the fish of its odor and seal in its full, rich flavor. About 30–40 percent of the katsuo catch is made into *katsuo bushi, the* blocks of cooked, dried fish that are shaved to make the dried bonito fish flakes that form the basis of dashi, the all-purpose Japanese broth. Processed and canned skipjack tuna is widely available outside Japan.

Katsuo carpaccio

There is a great similarity between Italian and Japanese cuisine—they both call for fresh products and simple cooking to bring out the best in the ingredients. This dish is inspired by the traditional Japanese cooking method called *tataki*, but it is served with fresh salad just like a carpaccio.

Katsuo is one of the most important and versatile ingredients in the Japanese kitchen since dashi broth, the fundamental Japanese flavor, is made with dried bonito flakes. Seasonality is extremely important in Japanese cooking, and katsuo symbolizes the beginning of summer: it is a tradition for Japanese gourmets to seek out the first and best katsuo of the season.

Habitat Katsuo is a migratory fish that belongs to the mackerel family. Schools of katsuo travel vast distances in warm water at high speed—they are the bullet trains of the sea. They swim with their mouths open to maximize their oxygen intake and they never stop swimming, even in their sleep. Katsuo are found in warm water all around the world. In Japan, the season starts at the southern tip of Kyushu Island in late March, and the katsuo travel north in the warm currents on the Pacific side of Japan reaching the top of the main island in June. They are called *hatsu gatsuo* (first katsuo) or *nobori gatsuo* (rising katsuo) and command high prices as a seasonal delicacy. Katsuo caught in autumn traveling south are called *modori gatsuo*, meaning 'returning katsuo,' and have a higher fat content, a richer, more buttery flavor and a firmer texture.

Appearance and taste Katsuo is a handsome fish

measuring about 3 ft long, weighing about 67–90 lb. when fully grown. Its streamlined body is well suited to high-speed travel. It has a deep blue-mauve back and silver belly, on which darker stripes develop when it is dead. Katsuo flesh is dark red and firm, with a rich taste.

Buying and storing Fresh katsuo is rarely seen outside Japan, as it goes off very quickly. Traditionally, katsuo is caught with a single rod and line, to minimize damage to the fish.

Health benefits Of all the fish in this chapter, katsuo has the highest level of vitamin B12, which is excellent for preventing anemia. Rich in niacin, it is good for the circulation and keeps brain cells healthy. It is also high in both DHA and EPA (see p.132), which lower blood pressure and cleanse the blood.

Culinary uses The most famous way to cook katsuo is *tataki*: searing it over burning straw to rid the fish of its odor and seal in its full, rich flavor. About 30–40 percent of the katsuo catch is made into *katsuo bushi, t*he blocks of cooked, dried fish that are shaved to make the dried bonito fish flakes that form the basis of dashi,

▲ *Katsuo carpaccio.*

鮭 Sake/Shake [SALMON]

Salmon were originally found only in the colder waters of the northern hemisphere but the development of salmon farming means that salmon are now found in the southern hemisphere, too. In Japan, the distinction between salmon and trout is somewhat blurred: while cherry salmon has been classified as a trout and called *sakura masu* or 'cherry trout,' rainbow trout is now a salmon, having been reclassified in 1989, even though its Japanese name remains *nizi masu*, meaning 'rainbow trout.' Salmon has a long history in Japan. The Ainu (the aboriginal inhabitants of the northern island of Hokkaido) believe their gods changed into salmon and by eating them in their entirety, mortal men help the gods to return to their world.

Habitat A young salmon lives in the sea for three to six years before returning to its birthplace upstream to spawn and die. Newly hatched salmon measuring 2 inches travel downstream back to the sea, where they live until they are mature enough to spawn.

Appearance and taste In Japan, sake normally means 'dog salmon' (the most common salmon in the country), 'silver salmon,' and 'red salmon.' The meat of all these salmon is bright orange with white lines across it, and is rich and oily tasting with a buttery texture.

Buying and storing Nowadays salmon is available all year around, yet people seem to forget it is a game fish with a limited season. Salmon farming is a long established practice but I wonder about the environmental costs, and above all what future generations will have to suffer for our greed in wanting to eat salmon all year around. There is something terribly exciting and humbling in waiting for the season as nature intended. I do not condemn fish farming, as it has made fish, especially salmon, available at any time of year at affordable prices. But the taste and flavor of farmed salmon is not comparable to that of wild salmon. As a family, we do not eat half as much as salmon as we would like, but what we eat during the season is truly magnificent and my children love it. I also put two or three whole salmon in my freezer for later. If you have to buy farmed salmon, insist that the fish come from a reputable farm where the fish are kept in decent conditions, not in small, overcrowded cages, and are not fed on steroid-laced foods.

In Japan salmon is usually sold salted or marinated, not completely raw, for fear of parasites.

> *An Ainu prepares a fresh salmon for the annual First Salmon ceremony on the northern island of Hokkaido.*

Health benefits Salmon has high-quality protein that is easy to digest and absorb and its fat contains EPA, which cleans the blood, and DHA, which helps to keep the brain cells active. Salmon is rich in vitamin A, which is excellent for the skin.

Culinary uses There is no part of the salmon that is not edible. A salmon to the Japanese is like a pig to the Chinese: we eat every part of it. Fresh salmon is broiled, fried, steamed, stewed, and used in soup. Salmon is also processed, canned, and smoked. Other salmon products include *sujiko* (salted ovary) and *ikura* (salmon roe).

Salmon fillet wrapped in phyllo pastry

This is an adaptation of a traditional recipe that uses yuba sheets, which are difficult to obtain in the West. I love phyllo pastry as it is so accommodating—it can be refrozen and cut into any shape or size.

Serves 4
12 sheets shop-bought phyllo pastry
1 egg white, beaten to the soft-peak stage
2 oz. (½ stick) unsalted butter, melted
4 salmon fillets, each weighing 4 oz.
4 tablespoons saké
Salt and pepper
4 cilantro leaves

Preheat the oven to 325°F. Put a sheet of phyllo pastry on an oiled baking sheet. Mix the beaten egg white with the melted butter and brush the mixture over the pastry.

Do this with 2 more sheets of pastry, then start again on a new baking sheet, repeating the process until you have 4 piles of phyllo pastry, each containing 3 sheets.

Lay a piece of salmon in the middle of each pile. Pour a tablespoon of saké over each salmon fillet, season, and place a cilantro leaf on top. Wrap the salmon up in the pastry, seal, and brush the surface with the egg and butter mixture. Bake the 4 parcels for 10–15 minutes until the pastry is crisp. Serve immediately.

▸ *Salmon fillet wrapped in phyllo pastry.*

Sake no ama-miso zuke
[BAKED SALMON FILLETS MARINATED IN SWEET MISO]

This is a perfect dish combining the strong, oily taste of salmon with an equally full-flavored miso marinade. Do not marinate the fillets for more than two nights, otherwise they will become hard and too salty.

Serves 4
4 salmon fillets, weighing 4 oz. each
For the sweet miso marinade
1 lb. white miso paste
14 oz. (1¾ cups) granulated sugar
8 fl oz. (1 cup) saké
8 fl oz. (1 cup) mirin

In a bowl, mix together all the ingredients for the miso marinade. Put the pieces of salmon in the marinade and leave overnight. Preheat the oven to 325°F. Wipe clean the salmon fillets and place them on an oiled baking sheet. Bake for 10 minutes or until cooked.

鯖 Saba [MACKEREL]

There is a saying in Japanese: 'Don't let your daughter-in-law eat fall mackerel'—it is simply too good for her in the opinion of a wicked mother-in-law. A kinder interpretation is that pregnant women should abstain from eating saba for fear of parasite infestation. Mackerel has been long appreciated in Japan for its robust full flavor and is universally popular. The biannual practice of exchanging *ochugen* (a summer gift) and *oseibo* (a winter gift) began during the Edo period with the presentation of salted mackerel fillets to the shogun on the eve of the Star Festival on July 6th.

Habitat In Japan there are two types of saba, *ma saba* (Pacific mackerel) and *goma saba* (spotted mackerel), and the generic term, saba, normally means the former. Their territory stretches from the warm parts of the Pacific along the warm current into the Sea of Japan and the East China Sea. They migrate along the coast in large groups.

Appearance and taste Many readers will be familiar with this handsome fish, with its iridescent, greeny-blue back, dark wavy lines and silvery-white belly. Mackerel are usually 12–20 inches long with an average weight of 1½–2 pounds. The succulent flesh is light brown with a rich flavor and a strong, fishy aroma.

Buying and storing Mackerel deteriorate rapidly. They should be eaten on the day they are caught or preserved with salt and a vinegary marinade. Choose fish with bright, clear eyes, shiny skin, and a firm, plump body. Mackerel are at their best in the fall.

Health benefits Saba's 17 percent fat content has high levels of both DHA (docosahexaenoic acid) and EPA (eicosapentaenoic acid). DHA is good for the brain and helps to lower cholesterol while EPA cleans the blood, promotes healthy circulation, and prevents hardening of the arteries.

Culinary uses Even in Japan, saba is rarely eaten raw—it is normally salted and then marinated in vinegar to make *shime saba*, which is one of the most popular ingredients of both sushi and sashimi. Saba also lends itself well to other methods of cooking, such as frying and stewing with miso.

Saba no misoni

[SIMMERED MACKEREL IN MISO]

Get your fish merchant to clean and gut the fish and for this recipe, ask him to cut the fish into steaks 1 inch thick.

Serves 4

1 medium-size mackerel, cleaned and gutted, cut into
  steaks 1 inch thick
2–3 tablespoons salt
1 pint (2½ cups) water
½ pint (1¼ pints) saké
4 tablespoons granulated sugar
2 tablespoons soy sauce
5 oz. white miso paste
1 tablespoon rice vinegar
To garnish
1 oz. (2 inches) ginger root, peeled and finely chopped

◀ *Simmered*
mackerel in miso.

Sprinkle some salt over the mackerel steaks and set them aside. Put the water and saké in a saucepan, add the mackerel and cook over a medium heat. When the mackerel's flesh begins to turn from pink to white, add the sugar, reduce the heat to low and continue to cook.

Skim off any scum and, when the cooking liquid has been reduced by a quarter, add the soy sauce. When the cooking liquid has been reduced to half the original amount, add the miso paste, a little at a time, ensuring it is fully dissolved. Cook for 10 minutes more, add the vinegar and turn off the heat. Arrange the mackerel steaks on a serving dish and top with chopped ginger.

Shime saba no sashimi

[SLICED MACKEREL FILLETS MARINATED IN VINEGAR]

Battera—bars of pressed sushi with marinated mackerel —are the bestselling item at Narita, Tokyo's big international airport. Japanese people traveling abroad sneak a bar or two into their suitcases just in case they get homesick.

Serves 4
2 mackerel fillets, each weighing 4–5 oz.
8 oz. (1 cup) salt

For the marinade
8 fl oz. (1 cup) rice vinegar
2 tablespoons mirin
3 tablespoons granulated sugar
2 teaspoons salt
To serve
4 tablespoons soy sauce
2 tablespoons shredded ginger root

Put the mackerel fillets in a shallow container and cover them with the salt. Place the salt-covered mackerel on a bamboo strainer and set aside for at least 30 minutes, preferably 1 hour, to allow the juices to be drawn out and drained off. Rinse the fillets under cold running water and pat them dry with paper towels.

Mix all the ingredients for the marinade in a shallow dish large enough to hold the fish. Add the fillets and set aside to marinate for 1–2 hours, after which time the flesh should be white.

Take the fillets out of the marinade, pat dry with paper towels, then slowly peel off the filament-like outer skin of the mackerel. (It is very important to get rid of the outer skin as it contains parasitic bacteria.)

Slice the fillets thinly and serve as sashimi with soy sauce mixed with shredded ginger.

鯛 Tai [SEA BREAM, PORGY, RED SNAPPER]

Tai is considered by the Japanese to be the best and most noble of all fish. They love tai's appearance and color and, above all, its taste. A whole broiled tai is one of the essential dishes at the New Year feast, just as a roast turkey is for Thanksgiving or Christmas in the West. Domestic demand far exceeds natural supply, so it is no wonder that the name 'tai' has been added to many non-related species or lookalikes. *Madai* (real tai), wild and farmed, is available only in Japan. However, sea bream, porgy or red snapper are very close substitutes.

Habitat *Madai* live on continental shelves in water 66–666 feet deep. They are found around the Japanese archipelago south of Hokkaido, in the southern part of the Korean peninsula and in the South China Sea—the inland sea of Japan and offshore Kyushu Island are particularly rich in them. They eat prawns and shellfish.

Appearance and taste Tai have a beautiful pale red and pink skin (red has auspicious connotations in Japanese culture), strong jaws, and a pronounced spiky dorsal fin. The largest tai can grow to 3 feet long but they are usually about 12–20 inches. The flesh is a translucent pale pink with darker pink stripes and has a delicately sweet flavor with a firm texture. It is considered one of the best of all fish to eat.

Buying and storing Tai have a thick layer of scales that needs to be thoroughly removed. It is always better to buy a whole fish, if possible, because it is easier to see how fresh it is—choose one with clear eyes and a shiny, firm body, and eat it on the day you buy it, if you're going to eat it raw. The best season for tai is between the Japanese winter and spring; the North American substitute, porgy, comes into season during September and May.

Health benefits Tai contains little fat and has high-quality protein that is easy to digest. Its main health benefit is its high level of vitamin B1, which helps turn sugar into energy.

Culinary uses There is nothing quite like sashimi or sushi of tai. But it is also good broiled, sautéed, or steamed on top of rice.

▸
New sashimi of sea bream.

Tai meshi

[STEAMED RICE WITH PORGY FILLETS]

In Japan, this is a dish for festivals and celebrations. A beautiful whole porgy is laid on a bed of rice, which looks spectacular. In this version, I am using fillets instead, to make it easier to serve and eat.

Serves 4
14 oz. (1½–2 cups) rice, washed, rinsed and drained
18 fl oz. (2 cups) dashi broth (see p.169)
14 oz. tai fillets, weighing 3½ oz. each
1 teaspoon salt
4 tablespoons saké
4 tablespoons light soy sauce
To garnish
4 tablespoons mustard cress

Put the rice and dashi broth in a shallow clay pot or cast iron dish with a tight-fitting lid. Place the tai fillets on top of the rice and sprinkle over the salt.

Pour a tablespoon of saké and light soy sauce over each fillet and put the lid on. Turn the heat on low and when you can hear it bubbling, increase the heat to medium, let it cook for 10 minutes, then turn off the heat.

Resist the temptation to lift up the lid, and leave it to steam for 10–15 minutes more. Serve the fillets on top of the rice, garnished with mustard cress.

New sashimi of porgy

I first came across this dish in a Chinese restaurant—it was quite spectacular to watch smoking hot sesame oil being poured over the plate of thinly sliced tai fillets. The hot oil semi-cooks the fish, hence the name 'new sashimi.' Any other white fish such as sea bass, brill, turbot or sole can be substituted, but of course using tai makes it rather more special.

Serves 4
1 bunch arugula, washed
14 oz. tai fillets, bones and skin removed
4 fl oz. (½ cup) grapeseed or groundnut oil
1 tablespoon sesame oil
2 tablespoons rice vinegar
Salt and pepper
1 teaspoon wasabi powder
1 tablespoon soy sauce

Arrange the arugula leaves on a large serving plate. Slice the fish thinly and put it on top of the salad. Mix both oils in a saucepan and heat until it is smoking.

Meanwhile, mix the vinegar, salt, pepper, wasabi, and soy sauce in a small bowl and set aside. Pour the hot oil mixture over the slices of fish and drizzle the vinegar mixture over the top. Toss and serve immediately.

鱸 Suzuki [SEA BASS]

In Japanese, suzuki is also known as *shusseuo*, meaning 'success fish,' because its name changes as it reaches different milestones. When it begins life in a calm shallow bay or in a river mouth, it is called *koppa*; a year later, by which time it will have grown to 10 inches, it is known as *seigo*; and the two to three year olds, which measure 20 inches, are called *fukko*. It finally earns the name of suzuki when it is about three years old and has grown to more than 2 feet.

Habitat The sea bass is found along the coast of Japan and in the South China Sea. It spawns in shallow water during the winter and the young fry grow up in the relative safety of a bay near their birthplace. The sea bass has a voracious appetite for small fish and crustaceans and grows fast. As it gets bigger, it moves into deeper, more exposed parts of the sea.

Appearance and taste It is a handsome fish with a grey back and silver-white belly. Its flesh is off-white with a pinkish tinge and it has a subtle flavor with a resilient, al dente texture.

Buying and storing In Japan, sea bass comes into season in the summer but nowadays farmed sea bass is available all year round. Buy a whole fish if at all possible because it gives more clues to its freshness. Look for clear full eyes and a firm, shiny silver body, and look into the gills: they should be bright red and not dark blood-red. The fish should have a pleasant smell of the sea, not an unpleasant fishy odor.

Health benefits Although the sea bass is classified as a white-meat fish, the fat content increases as it grows older. The flesh is particularly rich in iron and vitamins A (which helps the body to fend off infectious illnesses), B1, and D.

Culinary uses Sea bass is eaten raw as sashimi during the season. It can also be lightly salted and broiled, or wrapped—whole or filleted—and steamed.

Suzuki no arai

[CHILLED SLICES OF RAW SEA BASS]

Arai means 'to wash' in Japanese: thinly sliced sea bass is doused in icy water to tighten up the flesh and give it an al dente texture. It is a real winner in the hot and humid Japanese summer when many people suffer from a loss of appetite.

Serves 4

14 oz. sea bass fillets, bones and skin removed
A large bowl of cold water with plenty of ice
4 oz. myoga, finely sliced
8 green shiso (perilla) leaves
For the dipping sauce
4 tablespoons light to medium colored miso paste
2 teaspoons granulated sugar
4 tablespoons rice vinegar
½ teaspoon red chili paste

Slice the fish as thinly as possible by holding the knife almost flat against the fillet. Put the slices in the ice-filled bowl of cold water and swirl them—the fish will tighten and shrink in the cold water.

Take the slices of fish out of the water, lay them flat on a bamboo basket if you have one (on paper towels, if not), cover with a plate and refrigerate.

Meanwhile arrange the sliced myoga and shiso leaves on 4 serving plates. Mix all the ingredients for the dipping sauce and divide the sauce between 4 small dishes. Arrange the chilled slices of sea bass on each serving plate and serve with the dipping sauce.

Marinated sea bass with cherry tomatoes

I learnt this dish from an Italian friend of mine. There are two versions of the recipe, depending on how much time you have. If you are short of time, slice the fish as thinly as you can and leave to marinate for 2–3 hours in a cool part of your kitchen. If you have time to begin the night before, leave the whole fillet to marinate overnight in the refrigerator—the marinated fillet is firmer and easier to slice.

Serves 4
14 oz. sea bass fillets, bones and skin removed
Juice of 2 lemons
1 red or white onion, peeled and thinly sliced
1 large red chile, cut into thin rings
For the marinade
½ teaspoon salt
4 tablespoons granulated sugar
4 fl oz. (½ cup) vinegar
To serve
2 scallions, finely chopped
16 cherry tomatoes, halved

Slice the sea bass fillet as thinly as possible. Lay the slices in a large, shallow, flat-bottomed dish and pour the lemon juice over them. Mix together all the ingredients for the marinade and pour over the fish.

Cover the fish with the onion and chile rings, and leave to marinate for 2–3 hours in a cool part of the kitchen.

Lift out the fish slices and arrange them on 4 individual serving plates. Discard the onion but reserve a few chile rings for garnish. Arrange the tomato halves around the fish, sprinkle over the chopped scallion and reserved chile, and serve.

▸ *Sea bass fisherman emptying and watching their nets.*

▾ *Marinated sea bass with cherry tomatoes.*

鰻 Unagi [FRESHWATER EEL/JAPANESE EEL]

It is a Japanese tradition to eat *unadon* (broiled eel on rice) on the Day of the Cow in midsummer. Japanese people believe that it keeps them healthy and wards off summer lethargy. Every year some 1,000 tons of unagi are consumed over this fateful 24-hour period. Japan is the largest consumer of unagi in the world, with an annual consumption of more than 100,000 tons, of which over 70 percent is imported.

Habitat Little is known about the habitat of the Japanese eel: it is only recently that the main place of spawning was found to be west of the Mariana Islands in the northwest Pacific Ocean. The eel begins its life in the sea and travels upstream to live in freshwater lakes and ponds, returning to the sea to spawn after five to ten years.

Appearance and taste The Japanese eel has a unique appearance: it has no ventral fin but its dorsal fin covers the whole length of its back and half of its belly side. Its long stick-like body is smooth and has no scales. A young Japanese eel is semi-transparent and resembles a willow leaf; it darkens to metallic grey once it enters fresh water. The average body length is around 24 inches but some 40–50-year-old eels can grow to over 4 feet, weighing nearly 8 pounds. The flesh of unagi is an opaque pale grey when uncooked and very soft.

Buying and storing Filleting Japanese eels is a highly skilled job that even in Japan is left to trained specialists. In Japan, eel is never eaten raw, as its blood has harmful effects on human red blood cells. In the Kanto area (near Tokyo) the knife is inserted in its back, while in the Kansai region (near Osaka) it is filleted on its belly side. The most popular way of cooking unagi is *kabayaki*, though again the two regions differ: in Kanto, the fillets are steamed before being broiled with sweet soy-based sauce, so the flesh is very soft. Outside Japan, unagi almost always comes filleted and cooked, in vacuum packs or frozen.

Health benefits The fish merchant who first devised the idea of eating unagi on the Day of the Cow was unwittingly quite right: unagi is indeed highly nutritious, being rich in vitamins A, D, and E, which help prevent anemia, fatigue, and night blindness. It is high in fat and contains minerals such as iron and phosphorus.

Culinary uses *Kabayaki*—the most popular way to cook unagi—can be served on its own or on top of plain cooked rice with a sweet, soy-based cooking sauce drizzled over it. The ranking of unagi restaurants is determined by the quality and age of their cooking sauce. Each restaurant has a closely guarded recipe involving soy sauce and mirin slowly cooked with unagi heads and bones. Unagi can also be steamed, smoked, or cooked with vegetables.

Unadon

[BROILED EEL SERVED ON RICE]

This is a bit of a cheat recipe, because even in Japan unagi is almost always sold preprepared as *kabayaki* with ready-made cooking sauce.

Serves 4

7 oz. (¾–1 cup) rice, washed, rinsed and drained
8 fl oz. (1 cup) water
2 packs kabayaki, sold in vacuum packs
2–3 tablespoons ready-made cooking sauce per person
Sansho pepper

Put the rice in a heavy-based saucepan with a tight-fitting lid and add the water. Bring to a boil over a gentle heat, turn up the heat to medium for 5 minutes, then turn the heat off, leaving the rice to steam with the lid on for 10 minutes more.

Take the unagi out of its packaging and cut in half. Put the fish on a microwave-proof plate, cover with plastic wrap and microwave for 30 seconds to 1 minute on medium strength—remember it is already cooked— or until it is warmed through.

Divide the cooked rice between 4 separate bowls and drizzle 2–3 tablespoons of the ready-made cooking sauce over each. Place a piece of unagi on top, sprinkle with a pinch of sansho pepper and serve.

Kabayaki to harusame no salada

[HARUSAME NOODLE SALAD WITH KABAYAKI
AND CUCUMBER]

My mother used to make this dish if she had a leftover piece of kabayaki which was not big enough to serve the whole family. Although this recipe calls for harusame noodles, Thai glass noodles or rice vermicelli noodles can be used instead.

Serves 4
7 oz. (2½–3 cups) dried harusame noodles
4 tablespoons dried wakame seaweed
2 oz. fresh enoki mushrooms, stalks trimmed
1 baby cucumber, peeled and thinly sliced

For the vinegar dressing
4 fl oz. (½ cup) rice vinegar
2 oz. (¼ cup) granulated sugar
4 tablespoons soy sauce
1 teaspoon sesame oil

To garnish
½ piece kabayaki (more if you have it), thinly chopped
2 teaspoons toasted white sesame seeds

Put the noodles in a large bowl and cover with boiling water. Set aside until the noodles are soft, then drain and with a pair of kitchen scissors, chop the noodles into manageable lengths.

Put the wakame in a separate bowl, cover with water, leave until soft, then drain and set aside. Put the enoki mushrooms in a small strainer, pour over boiling water, drain and set aside.

Mix all the ingredients for the vinegar dressing. Put the noodles, seaweed, mushrooms, and cucumber slices in a large bowl, pour the dressing over and toss.

Divide the noodle salad between 4 serving dishes and arrange the chopped kabayaki on top. Sprinkle over the sesame seeds and serve.

▲ *Harusame noodle salad with kabayaki and cucumber.*

烏賊 Ika [SQUID/CUTTLEFISH]

There are some 500 varieties of squid in the world, of which only 130 varieties are found near Japan, yet Japan is the world's largest consumer of squid, eating 60 percent of the world's catch.

Habitat, appearance and taste Most of the squid caught near Japan are *maika* (Japanese common squid), sometimes called *surume ika*. They live at the bottom of the sea, 666 feet deep, and are fished for at night with lights to attract them to the surface. *Maika* have a dark, reddish-brown skin and their bodies are generally about 12 inches long with 8 inches-long tentacles. During the 1960s when the catch fell, Wellington flying squid from New Zealand made an excellent substitute, as they are almost indistinguishable from *maika*.

The second most popular variety is *aori ika* (big fin reef squid). *Aori ika* are relatively large, with a body 16 inches long, and half-moon shaped fins on both sides. They live south of Hokkaido, in the western Pacific and Indian Ocean. This variety has a meltingly sweet flavor and is considered the best for sashimi and sushi.

The other popular variety is *yari ika* (spear squid), which grows to 16 inches and has disproportionately short tentacles. The body has a faintly orangey skin and is slender with a pointed spear-like head. Iridescent and firm, freshly caught squid are among the most beautiful marine creatures of all. The taste of squid varies from one variety to another but they have in common a subtle sweetness and tender yet al dente texture.

Buying and storing Look for a squid that still has its tentacles intact and most of its skin on—these are signs that it has been handled well. Really fresh squid is almost transparent and feels firm—it becomes milky white and limp as it loses its freshness. It is best to buy a whole squid, as any leftover freezes well.

Health benefits Squid is very low in fat, so is also low in calories. Its most notable health benefit is its taurine content: taurine is a kind of amino acid good for the heart, reducing cholesterol and lowering blood pressure.

Culinary uses Ika is a popular ingredient in the Japanese kitchen, and the nation's favorite way of using it is not to cook it but to serve it raw as sashimi. Ika makes a popular topping for sushi and a whole ika is used for making *ika zushi* (ika stuffed with sushi rice). It is used in salads, stewed, stir-fried, broiled, and deep-fried. *Ika no shiokara* is salt-pickled fermented intestines—possibly an acquired taste.

Surume is a whole, gutted, dried ika that goes very well with saké and makes a natural chewing gum. Japanese stores sell it whole or shredded in packets. Ika becomes tough and chewy when overcooked—it is best to cook it very briefly at a high temperature or cook it slowly at a low, simmering temperature.

⌐ *Squids drying in a shop.*

▸ *Deep-fried squid in batter.*

About tempura If I suggest that someone cook a tempura dish at home, the usual reaction ranges from extreme reluctance to sheer panic. There is nothing difficult about cooking tempura at home, provided you understand a few basic principles about the oil temperature and the batter. First of all, always use a vegetable oil such as corn, sunflower, grapeseed, or groundnut. Use a wide, flat-based, shallow saucepan made of thick cast iron. Ideally, filter the oil with paper towels after each use and exchange about a third of the used oil for fresh oil. As for the mysterious batter, the most important thing is to avoid making it sticky and elastic, so always use ice-cold water, mix small quantities of batter just before use and do not stir it too much—a few lumps will not harm it. Below is a basic guide for the perfect batter.

Thin batter mix for white fish, shellfish, and vegetables
4 oz. (1 cup) sifted all-purpose flour mixed with one egg, made up to 4 fl oz. (½ cup) with ice-cold water

Thick batter mix for oily fish, such as sardines, mackerel, horse mackerel, squid, and mixed vegetables
4 oz. (1 cup) sifted all-purpose flour mixed with one egg, made up to 3 fl oz. (⅓ cup) with ice-cold water

Ika no ikura ae

[SQUID WITH SALMON ROE]

A stylish accompaniment to saké.

Serves 4
7 oz. fresh squid, cleaned and skin removed
1 teaspoon salt
2 tablespoons saké
2 lemons, halved
4 tablespoons salmon roe

With a very sharp knife, thinly slice the squid. Put the slices in a bowl, sprinkle with the salt and saké and leave to stand for 10 minutes.

Squeeze and reserve the juice from the halved lemons and scoop out the flesh to make 4 lemon cups. Sprinkle 2 teaspoons of lemon juice over the slices of squid, add the salmon roe and mix. Divide the squid mixture between the 4 lemon cups and serve.

Ika no tempura

[DEEP-FRIED SQUID IN BATTER]

8 oz. fresh squid
7 fl oz. (¾ cup) thick tempura batter (see left)
Vegetable oil, for deep-frying
4 oz. (1 cup) all-purpose flour spread out on a plate

Detach the head and tentacles by pulling them firmly from the body. Pull the translucent, quill-shaped piece of cartilage out of the body and discard. Insert a sharp knife into the body and carefully slit it open. Pressing down on the flat body, pull the two triangular fins away. With a clean, damp cloth, pull the skin off and discard. Turn the body over and wipe away the mucous lining on the inside. With the tip of a sharp knife, make a criss-cross pattern across the body and cut it into pieces (1 x 2 inches).

Mix the batter and keep it cold in the refrigerator. Preheat the oil to 325–350°F. To test the temperature, drop a globule of batter into the oil. If it sinks halfway then rises to the surface, it is ready.

Turn a piece of squid in the flour to coat it, then dip it in the batter and gently put it in the hot oil. Cook only 3 or 4 pieces at one time, so that the temperature remains stable. Drain over paper towels and serve.

蛸 Tako [OCTOPUS]

Tako has long occupied a rather special place in Japanese food culture, with its extraordinary appearance and bright red skin when it is cooked. There are many folk tales and legends featuring tako, some funny, others scary. Of the 250 varieties of octopus found around the world, about 60 varieties are caught near Japan, of which only a handful are considered edible. The Japanese consume around 160,000 tons every year or nearly two-thirds of the world's catch.

Habitat, appearance, and taste In the Japanese kitchen, *madako* (common octopus) is the variety most commonly eaten, and most of Japan's *madako* is imported from Africa. *Madako* grows to 2 feet long and can weigh 11½ pounds. Other common varieties include the relatively small *iidako* (webfoot octopus), which measures 10 inches and is found around Japan, the Korean peninsula, and in the east China Sea. Octopus is rarely eaten raw in Japan as it is too chewy, and is most often sold ready-boiled. Once boiled, the skin becomes bright red and the flesh changes from opaque grey to white. Tender and succulent, octopus has a faintly sweet taste.

Buying and preparing Ready-boiled tentacles are available from Japanese stores or fish merchants but if you are buying a whole fresh octopus, it needs to be first cleaned and rubbed with salt to tenderise it before being boiled in plenty of water with shredded daikon (Japanese radish) for 20–30 minutes. Boiled tentacles keep for a few days in the refrigerator.

Health benefits Tako is 16 percent high-quality protein. But, like squid, its most notable health benefit is its taurine, which lowers cholesterol and blood pressure and prevents gallstones.

Culinary uses Tako has numerous uses in the Japanese kitchen. It is a popular topping for sushi; it is mixed with vinegar and other ingredients to make a refreshing salad; and the tentacles are used in a simmered dish called *oden*. One of the nation's favorite street snacks is *tako yaki* (small dumpling balls), which have small pieces of boiled tako in the center.

Spicy octopus salad

Here boiled octopus is served as a salad with a spicy citrus dressing—a refreshing appetizer or stylish lunch dish.

Serves 4
7 oz. octopus tentacles, boiled
4 oz. mixed salad greens
For the spicy citrus dressing
2 teaspoons shredded ginger
2 teaspoons Tabasco sauce
2 teaspoons soy sauce
2 teaspoons lime juice
4 tablespoons extra virgin olive oil
Salt and pepper (optional)

▸ *Broiled octopus with sweet miso sauce.*

Put all the ingredients for the dressing in a lidded jar and shake vigorously. Season with salt and pepper if required.

Cut the octopus tentacles into thick slices. Divide the salad greens between 4 serving plates and arrange the slices of octopus on top. Drizzle over the dressing and serve.

Tako no ama-miso ae

[BROILED OCTOPUS WITH SWEET MISO SAUCE]

This is based on a dish served by Nobu, the famous Japanese restaurant in London. There is no doubt that founder and proprietor Nobu (after whom the restaurant is named) has put Japanese cuisine on the world culinary map. He is my mentor and I am so happy to pass on his wisdom, adapting and simplifying his recipes for the domestic kitchen, so that we can all enjoy the essence of Japanese cuisine.

◂ ◂ *Trays of vinegar-marinated sliced octopus for sale.*

Serves 4

1 lb. fresh octopus tentacles, cleaned, rubbed with salt and rinsed
2 tablespoons olive oil
Salt and pepper
For the sauce
2 tablespoons light colored miso paste
2 tablespoons saké
1 tablespoon mirin
2 tablespoons oyster sauce
2 teaspoons soy sauce
1 teaspoon red chili sauce

Preheat the broiler to the highest setting. Bring a saucepan of water to a boil and blanch the octopus tentacles for 5 minutes. Drain, hold briefly under cold running water to preserve the bright red color, then coat the boiled tentacles with olive oil and season. Mix all the sauce ingredients in a saucepan and bring to a boil over a medium heat. Boil for 2 minutes, then take off the heat and leave to cool. Broil the octopus under the preheated broiler for 3 minutes on each side. Chop the broiled octopus into small chunks, drizzle over the sauce and serve.

平目 Hirame & Karei [FLAT FISH]

Habitat There are 85 known species of *hirame* in the world, 10 of which are found around Japan, and 93 of so-called *karei* in the world, with 39 varieties around Japan. In other words, there are nearly 50 varieties of flat fish caught and eaten in Japan, some of which live in warm waters, others in temperate or cooler waters.

Taste and appearance Whether a fish is *hirame* or *karei*, all flat fish share a 'flat' body shape, with darker skin on the top side and paler skin on the underside. The color of its meat is always a translucent white, with a subtle, delicate taste. A delicacy often reserved for valued customers in sushi bars, the comb-like edges of the fish are called *engawa*.

Buying and storing Buying a whole fish or at least seeing the whole fish is always preferable to buying ready-cut pieces because you have more clues as to its freshness. Choosing a fish is no different from assessing a person. Look the fish in the eye and avoid ones with sunken, bloodshot eyes or eyes that are murky and dull. Use your nose: avoid those that smell fishy and unpleasant—fresh fish should smell of the open sea. The skin should be shiny and feel springy. Always buy your fish from a reputable fish merchant, and get to know your local fish merchant's. Fish should be eaten on the day of purchase; generally flat fish tend to stay fresh longer than oily fish such as mackerel and sardines.

Health benefits Like all white colored fish, flat fish are low in fat and calories, yet are a rich source of vitamins. Easy to digest, they provide high-quality protein that is supposed to be good for lowering blood pressure and maintaining healthy skin.

Culinary uses The delicate flavor and texture of *hirame* and *karei* have earned them a special place in Japanese cuisine. Flat fish are used for sashimi and, of course, for sushi, and are also simmered, broiled, steamed, and deep-fried (as tempura).

There is no direct translation for 'flat fish' in Japanese. The fish that is classified as 'flat fish' in the West, because of its flat body shape, belongs to either the *hirame* or *karei* groups, according to where its eyes are located. Those fish which have their eyes on the left of their heads, such as flounder, turbot, and brill, are called *hirame* while those with their eyes on the right, such as halibut, flounder, and sole, are grouped together as *karei*. But the Japanese classification is by no means definitive and can be extremely confusing, since fish are also classified according to the color of their flesh—red or white—regardless of their body shape.

Hirame no tsutusmi-yakii

[PARCELS OF SOLE]

Wrapping in aluminum foil is an ideal way of cooking delicate flavored sole. Make the inside as attractive as possible as the whole parcels will be served.

Serves 4

4 fillets of sole, each weighing about 4 oz.

½ teaspoon salt

4 tablespoons saké

4 fresh shiitake mushrooms, cleaned, the stalks removed

4 fresh mitsuba or cilantro leaves

To serve

1 lime or lemon, cut into 4 wedges

Preheat the oven to 325°F. Cut 4 sheets of aluminum foil large enough to envelop the pieces of fish. Place a fillet in the center of the foil.

Sprinkle salt and saké over the fish and place a shiitake cap and mitsuba leaf on top. Bring up the edges of the foil to make a parcel. Repeat the process until you have made 4 parcels.

Put the parcels on a baking sheet and place in the middle of the oven to cook for 10 minutes. Lay each parcel unopened on a plate and serve with a lime or lemon wedge.

秋刀魚 Sanma [PACIFIC SAURY]

The fall is the season of plenty and the Japanese fall is particularly generous. One of the highlights of the season is sanma, a particular favorite of mine, which heralds the arrival of the fall. In Japan, sanma fishing opens on August 15 near Hokkaido and from the end of September in the rest of the country.

Habitat Found in tropical and temperate seas around the world, sanma are migratory fish that travel in summer up to Russia in large shoals, then head south again down the Pacific coast of Japan. The southbound sanma caught in the fall off the coast of Sanriku (the northwest part of the main island) are considered the best as they are very high in fat—the fish mature fast in just 12 months.

Appearance and taste The Japanese name of sanma is very descriptive: it means 'fall swordfish.' The mature fish are about 18 inches long and weigh about 1½ pounds. They have long slim bodies with a dark blue-grey back and shiny silver-white belly. The meat is pale orange and very oily (especially between September and October) with a rich flavor.

Buying and storing Like other blue-backed fish, sanma deteriorate rapidly after they are caught and should be eaten on the day you buy them. Choose shiny plump fish that feel firm to the touch.

Health benefits Sanma is at its best in the fall, when its fat content reaches as high as 20 percent. The DHA and EPA (see p.132) in the fat help to prevent hardening of the arteries and cerebrovascular accidents; they also lower blood pressure and are good for the brain cells. High in vitamin D, which strengthens bones and teeth, it is an ideal food for growing children as well as for adults.

Culinary uses The most popular way to cook sanma—available ready seasoned in cans—is to broil it over a charcoal fire with a sprinkling of salt. Salted and dried sanma is also popular. Very fresh sanma is delicious in both sushi and sashimi.

Sanma no shio-yaki
[BROILED SALTED SANMA]

I used to be an investment banker with an English merchant bank and it was during one of my business trips to Japan that I smelt the tempting aroma of broiled sanma wafting out of the Japanese equivalent of a transport café. Following my nose I dived in. The young Japanese stockbroker with a Harvard MBA who was accompanying me was utterly horrified by my choice of lunch venue but 20 minutes later we both came out fully satisfied.

Serves 4
4 fresh sanma, cut in half and lightly salted
4 tablespoons shredded daikon (Japanese radish)
4 teaspoons shredded ginger root
4 teaspoons soy sauce

Preheat the broiler. Place the sanma halves on the rack and broil for 5–7 minutes or until the skin begins to bubble and turn a golden color. Turn over to cook the other side.

Meanwhile mix the shredded daikon and ginger, then lightly squeeze the mixture to remove the excess liquid. Make 4 small mounds and place 1 on the edge of each serving plate. Put the shredded sanma on the serving plates, drizzle the daikon mound with soy sauce.

Pan-fried sanma with mushrooms

This is an autumnal dish using shimeji and shiitake mushrooms to accompany sanma. Ask your fish merchant to fillet the fish if you can't do it yourself.

Serves 4
4 fresh sanma, filleted and cut into pieces
   2 inches long
Salt and pepper
3 tablespoons olive oil
1 garlic clove, peeled and thinly sliced
8 shiitake mushrooms, stalks removed, cut into quarters
2 oz. shimeji mushrooms, separated, stalks trimmed
2 tablespoons saké
1 tablespoon soy sauce

To garnish
1 tablespoon chopped flat-leaf parsley

Season the sanma with salt and pepper. Heat the oil in a skillet over a medium heat. Add the pieces of fish, skin side down, and cook for 3 minutes, then turn them over to cook the other side.

Add the sliced garlic and cook for 2 minutes before adding the mushrooms. Sauté the mushrooms for 3 minutes, then add the saké and soy sauce. Adjust the seasoning with salt and pepper and serve garnished with the chopped parsley.

海老 Ebi [SHRIMP]

The Japanese are the largest consumer of shellfish of all kinds and they are particularly fond of ebi, a term that includes *kuruma ebi,* generally known as tiger shrimp in the West, the smaller *ko ebi* (shrimp) and *ise ebi (*lobster).

Kuruma ebi (Giant shrimp) Although there are only 28 species known in the world, this group is the most important to the shrimp-fishing industry. They live at the bottom of shallow seas across the world and can grow to 10 inches long but usually measure less than 8 inches. The giant shrimp has a pale grey, reddish-tinged shell with characteristic dark brown stripes. In Japan, between 4,000 and 5,000 tons are eaten every year, about half of which are farmed. All varieties of giant shrimp live for only one year.

The sweet and succulent flavor of *kuruma ebi* means that they are widely used in Japanese cooking—perhaps the most popular way being to deep-fry them in tempura batter or coated with breadcrumbs. They are also broiled, simmered, stir-fried, marinated, and used to make the famous *odori* ('dancing') sushi: freshly shelled shrimp with its tail still twitching.

Ko ebi (Shrimp) The main difference between giant shrimp and other shrimps, apart from size, is the way in which the female shrimp carries her eggs under her belly to protect them until they hatch, whereas the giant shrimp simply ejects her eggs into the water. The most widespread variety of shrimp is *ama ebi* (northern shrimp or pink shrimp), which is found in large areas of the northern Pacific Ocean. *Ama ebi* are all male until they are 2 or 3 years old and measure over 4 inches, then they all become female. Another important variety of shrimp, found mainly on the Pacific side of Japan, is called *sakura ebi,* because it turns a beautiful cherry-blossom pink when it is dried. Shrimp are sweet and succulent and are often eaten whole.

Ise ebi **(Spiny lobsters)** While shrimp are suited to swimming, the body of *ise ebi* and its relatives is better suited for walking on the sea bed. Spiny lobsters have ten well-developed legs and their body is covered by a deep reddish-brown, hard protective shell with spiny thorns. *Ise ebi* is the largest and most valuable variety of all shrimps, averaging 12 inches in length. The breeding period is between June and September and the female lays a staggering 600,000 eggs that hatch within 35–50 days. The young fry float near the surface of the sea for a year before they go down to live on the sea bed and start to look like *ise ebi.* The handsome and delicious spiny lobster is always part of the New Year feast. Successful farming methods have yet to be developed, so much of the domestic demand has to be satisfied with imports from Europe, North America and Australia.

Health benefits The average protein content of shrimp and lobsters is about 20 percent. They are low in fat, and their shells contain chitin, which lowers blood pressure and cholesterol, and is known to be an anti-carcinogen.

Buying Shrimps are good during the autumn; and lobsters are in season in the fall and winter. When buying ebi with the shell on, choose ones that have a transparent appearance and feel firm. When buying shelled ebi, pick ones that are plump and, again, feel firm.

Culinary uses I rather dreaded writing this entry, because ebi are used in almost every aspect of Japanese cooking. They appear in soups, simmered dishes, salads, hot-pots, tempura, broiled dishes and steamed dishes—in other words, everywhere, in fresh and dried form.

Ebi no tempura

[DEEP-FRIED PRAWNS IN BATTER]

Tempura is a perfect way to enjoy the juicy flavor of giant shrimp—just follow the instructions for tempura in the section on squid (see p.147). Try to buy unshelled shrimp as the crispy fried legs add an exciting new texture.

Serves 4
12 unshelled giant shrimp
8 fresh shiitake mushrooms
8 fresh green shiso (perilla) leaves
4 oz. (1 cup) all-purpose flour for coating
2 batches thin tempura batter (see p.147), about 7 fl oz. (¾ cup) each batch
Vegetable oil, for deep frying

For the dipping sauce
½ oz. bonito fish flakes
8 fl oz. (1 cup) water
2 fl oz. (3½ tablespoons) mirin
2 fl oz. (3½ tablespoons) light soy sauce
To serve
7 oz. (1 cup) shredded daikon (Japanese radish)
4 teaspoons shredded ginger root

Prepare the dipping sauce first. Place all the ingredients in a saucepan and bring to a boil over a medium heat. Remove from the heat and let cool before straining.

Remove the shrimp heads and shell them, putting the legs to one side for later and keeping the tails intact. Make a shallow insertion along the back to remove the dark vein and make 2–3 cuts on the undersides of the shrimp to prevent them from curling up during frying. Cut off the stalks of the shiitake mushrooms and discard. Wash the shiso leaves and dry with paper towels.

Make two batches of batter, each in a separate bowl. Make sure you mix the egg and cold water well and add all the sifted flour at once, folding it in lightly with a fork no more than 3 times. Refrigerate until needed. Heat the oil and test its temperature by dropping in a globule of batter. When it sinks halfway then rises to the surface, the oil is ready.

Dip a shrimp in the flour and dust off the excess. Holding the tail, dip the shrimp in the batter and slide it gently into the hot oil. Do not cook more than 3 or 4 at a time. When the shrimp have turned crisp and golden, put them to drain on a rack and keep warm while you cook the rest. Deep-fry the reserved legs on their own, without batter, until crisp. Drain and keep warm.

Turn off the heat for 5 minutes to allow the temperature of the oil to fall slightly to about 325°F. Turn the heat back on. Take out the second bowl of batter and deep-fry the mushrooms in the same way as the shrimp. Lower the heat slightly, dust the shiso leaves in flour, dip the back of the shiso leaves in the batter and deep-fry until crisp. Arrange the tempura on four separate serving plates. On the edge of each plate, make a small mound of shredded daikon and top each mound with shredded ginger. Divide the dipping sauce between 4 serving bowls. Give each person a bowl of dipping sauce, in which they may like to mix their daikon and ginger.

Kuruma ebi no amazu zuke

[MARINATED GIANT SHRIMP IN SWEET GINGER MARINADE]

2–3 cooked giant shrimp per person
For the marinade
4 fl oz. (½ cup) rice vinegar
2 tablespoons granulated sugar
2 tablespoons juice from shredded ginger root
½ onion, peeled and shredded
6 tablespoons soy sauce
2 teaspoons red chili paste
To garnish
8 fresh green shiso (perilla) leaves
6 baby vine tomatoes, halved

If the shrimp are not shelled, pull off the heads and shell them, leaving their handsome tails intact. Run the tip of your knife down the back of each shrimp to take out the dark vein that runs from head to tail. Place the peeled shrimp in a shallow plastic or glass dish, mix together the marinade ingredients and pour over the shrimp. Leave to marinate for 8 hours or overnight. Garnish with the shiso leaves and halved baby tomatoes and serve.

▼ *Marinated giant shrimp in sweet ginger marinade.*

蟹 Kani [CRABS]

There are over 5,000 varieties of crab in the world, of which 1,000 are found near Japan, but in the context of the Japanese kitchen only a handful of varieties are relevant. The Japanese have a long association with crabs and there are many folktales and legends in which they feature.

Watari gani/gazami (Swimming crab) This is a commonly found variety on the coast of Japan, the northern coast of China and near Korea. They are known to be great swimmers as both the Japanese and English names suggest, and indeed the lower parts of the back legs look like flippers. They mate between mid September and mid October and lay eggs between April and June and, for a second time, between July and August. The pregnant female crabs are considered a delicacy in the winter, while the best season for crabmeat is the summer.

Kegani (Horsehair crab) This hairy crab is relatively slow growing and takes five years to reach maturity. It is a regional delicacy of Hokkaido, especially in winter, but it is also found in the Sea of Japan, the northern part of the Pacific coast, and from the eastern coast of Russia across to Alaska. Unlike shrimp farming, crab farming has proved to be uneconomical and a shortfall in domestic supply is met by a growing import market.

Zuwai gani (Snow crab/queen crab) Known as 'the winter taste of the Sea of Japan,' snow crabs come mainly from the coast of the Sea of Japan. They are distinguished by their long and tasty legs—the leg of a mature male can measure 32 inches long—and are fished for a limited period in winter. It takes about ten years for a zuwai gani to mature, so it is not economically viable to farm them. Once again, the shortfall is met by imports.

Taraba gani (Alaskan king crab) The Japanese name means 'cod fishery crab': about 100 years ago a careless fisherman let a cod fishing net sink to the bottom of the sea and accidentally caught magnificent large crabs. It is the most important of all the crabs fished in Japan, although strictly speaking it is not part of the main crab family but belongs to the hermit crab group. Large males can weigh over 22 pounds and can have bodies that measure 12 inches across, with a span from leg to leg of more than 3 feet. They live in relatively cool waters (less than 50°F), from the northern part of the Sea of Japan, the island of Hokkaido and the Bering Sea across to Alaska and the Canadian coast. Slow to mature like other crabs, they take ten years before they are ready to breed, and the average life expectancy is around thirty years.

Buying and storing In the West, crabs are normally sold ready-boiled—choose one that feels heavy and solid and look out for unblemished joints. Increasingly, crab is sold ready-dressed or frozen, which make it easier to handle. Crabmeat is also sold in cans.

Health benefits Crabmeat is low in calories but has plenty of high-quality protein. It is also rich in calcium, vital for healthy bones and teeth and good for combating stress.

Culinary uses One of the nation's favorite ways of eating crabmeat is to dress it with a sweet vinegar mixture and serve it as a refreshing salad. Crab hot-pot is a favorite in winter.

◄ *A crab seller at a morning market.*

Kani su salad

[CRAB SALAD WITH SWEET VINEGAR]

Kani su is such a simple dish that the freshness and flavor of the crab you buy determines its success. I have turned this traditional dish into a salad by adding blanched shungiku and enoki mushrooms—if you can't get hold of these ingredients, use fresh salad greens instead.

Serves 4
7 oz. (2–2½ cups) shungiku (chrysanthemum greens)
2 oz. enoki mushrooms, the stalks trimmed
4 oz. (¾ cup) dressed crabmeat
For the sweet vinegar dressing
8 fl oz. (1 cup) dashi broth (see p.169)
4 fl oz. (½ cup) rice vinegar
3 fl oz. (5 tablespoons) mirin
2 tablespoons light soy sauce
Salt

Mix together in a bowl all the ingredients for the sweet vinegar dressing and set aside.

Blanch the shungiku in boiling water for 2–3 minutes, then quickly transfer to a colander and run cold water over. Drain well and chop roughly. Blanch the enoki mushrooms for 1–2 minutes, drain and leave to cool.

Put the crabmeat, shungiku, and enoki in the bowl with the dressing and mix. Divide the salad between 4 serving dishes and serve.

Crabmeat, chile, and lime sushi

This is my own fusion sushi, combining the Thai flavors of lime and chiles with crabmeat—a rather spur of the moment invention, it has become one of my family's favorite sushi. By all means vary the amount of chile to suit your taste and use frozen white crabmeat if you want to economize.

1 quantity prepared sushi rice (see p.223)
6 oz. (1–1¼ cups) white crabmeat
1–2 large red chiles, seeded and finely chopped
Juice of 1 lime
4 sheets nori (dried seaweed)
To garnish
Fresh cilantro leaves
Slices of lime

Combine the prepared sushi rice, crabmeat, and chopped chiles in a bowl and pour in the lime juice to loosen the rice.

Cut each sheet of nori to fit your plates and lay a sheet on each plate. Divide the rice mixture into 4 and pile a quarter on each of the squares of nori.

Garnish with the cilantro leaves and slices of lime and serve.

▲ *Crabmeat, chile, and lime sushi.*

蛤 Hamaguri [HARD CLAM]

Clams are one of the oldest foods eaten by the ancient Japanese, as archaeological evidence reveals. Hamaguri, meaning 'beach chestnut,' has a special place in Japanese cultural and food history. A traditional toy called a *kai awase* is made of a set of hamaguri shells, the object of the game being to match pairs of shells. Because of its association with 'matching pairs,' hamaguri features in Japanese wedding ceremonies and feasts. My own memories of hamaguri are of gathering shellfish on shallow, sandy beaches in spring – armed with a rake and a bucket, I would dig around the low tide mark. I was never one for bucket and spade holidays, but I loved gathering shellfish and eating my delicious finds.

▶ *Edo-period woodblock print of women and children gathering clams.*

Habitat Tokyo Bay was once a major source of clams, but hamaguri are highly sensitive to pollution and have moved away, so there are very few there now. Hard clams are still found in sandy parts of Japan's coast, especially in the south, but many of the clams sold in Japan are imported from China and Korea.

Appearance and taste A pair of hard shells with darker markings protects the delicate and sweetish meat.

Buying and storing The season for clams is from the late fall through to spring. Choose ones that are tightly closed and feel solid, and that make a clear sound when you tap them. Always cook them on the day of purchase and discard any that don't open.

Health benefits Clams provide high-quality protein and have a high level of amino acids. Rich in minerals and calcium, clams are particularly good for women as they are low in calories and help to maintain healthy skin.

Culinary uses Clams are used widely in the Japanese kitchen, steamed with saké, served in clear soups and broiled. Dried clams are cooked with rice and in simmered dishes.

Hamaguri no suimono

[CLEAR CLAM SOUP]

This is a delicately flavored, clear soup made from konbu broth. In Japan, it would be eaten at the start of a meal, while more robust miso soups are served at the end.

Serves 4
8–12 clams, depending on their size
A bowl of tepid water with a teaspoon of salt added
1 piece of konbu, postcard size
16 fl oz. (1¾ cups) water
1 tablespoon saké
½ teaspoon salt
To garnish
4 sprigs mitsuba, roughly chopped

Soak the clams in the tepid salted water to make them expel any sand. Scrub them clean under cold running water. Put the konbu and the clams with the water in a saucepan and bring to a boil over low heat.

Remove the konbu and let the clams simmer for 3 minutes or until their shells are open, skimming off any scum. Take the saucepan off the heat, scoop out the clams and transfer them to 4 soup bowls.

Strain the soup through a fine strainer lined with paper towels. Return the soup to the saucepan, add the saké and salt, and reheat. Gently ladle the soup over the clams, garnish with the mitsuba and serve.

Fried clams with somen noodles

This is the Japanese equivalent of spaghetti alle vongole. Pairing fine somen noodles with delicately flavored clams gives a perfect match.

Serves 4
4 bundles somen noodles
20–24 clams, soaked in a bowl of tepid water with a teaspoon of salt added
4 tablespoons saké
8 fl oz. (1 cup) dashi broth (see p.169)
8 sprigs mitsuba, roughly chopped
Salt
Sansho pepper

Bring a saucepan of water to a boil, add the noodles and stir. When the water comes back to a boil, add a cup of cold water. The noodles are ready when the water begins to bubble up again. Drain the noodles and set aside.

Put the soaked clams in a large sauté pan with a tight fitting lid and add the saké and dashi broth. Bring to a boil over a high heat with the lid on. When all the clams are open, add the noodles and mitsuba and stir.

Add salt if needed and divide between 4 serving dishes. Sprinkle over some sansho pepper and serve.

▲ *Fried clams with somen noodles.*

牡蠣 Kaki [OYSTER]

Oysters in Japan go back a long way: archaeologists have found remains of oysters all over the coastal regions of Japan and oyster farming dates back to the seventeenth century when fishermen noticed that oysters adhered to bamboos or branches stuck into the sea bed.

Habitat In Japan, the most widely eaten variety is the giant Pacific oyster. Oyster farms are found mainly along the shore of the Pacific Ocean, around the northernmost island of Hokkaido and in the calm Seto Inland Sea.

Appearance and taste Giant Pacific oysters are rectangular, about 3 inches long and 1½ inches wide. The variety found in Hokkaido can grow as long as 12 inches.

Buying and storing In Japan, people are advised not to eat oysters after the cherry blossom is finished—in other words, to eat oysters only between October and March. Oysters spawn during the summer period and not only does their flavor deteriorate but they may cause food poisoning. There is a specie called 'rock oyster' or 'summer oyster,' however, that is larger than the giant Pacific oyster and its season is summer.

Always buy oysters from a reputable fish merchant. Choose ones that are tightly closed and feel heavy, and eat them the same day.

Health benefits Oysters have a high level of minerals and are rich in vitamins B1 and B2, which are particularly good for your liver.

Culinary uses As in the West, the most popular way of eating oysters is raw. Oysters become hard and shrink if cooked too long, so deep-fried oyster is another popular dish.

Kaki zosui

[RICE CONGEE WITH OYSTERS]

My mother used to make this for me when I had to stay up late revising for yet another exam. She used cold, ready-cooked rice, which makes it very easy to prepare, very gentle and nutritious and, above all, very comforting.

Serves 4
1 lb. (6–7 cups) cooked rice
12 oysters, shelled
1½–2½ pints (4–6 cups) dashi broth (see p.169)
2 tablespoons soy sauce
2 eggs, lightly beaten
To garnish
2 scallions, finely chopped

Put the cooked rice in a strainer, rinse under cold water and drain. Refresh the shelled oysters in a bowl of cold salt water and drain.

Put the rice and dashi broth in a saucepan and slowly bring to a boil. Add the soy sauce and oysters and cook for 3 minutes before adding the beaten eggs.

Stir gently, turn off the heat, put on the lid and leave to stand for 3 minutes. Divide between 4 serving bowls, garnish with the chopped scallions and serve.

↘ *Fresh oysters with grated daikon salsa.*
◂ *Oyster beds.*

Nama-gaki no oroshi ae

[FRESH OYSTERS WITH SHREDDED DAIKON SALSA]

Why not try raw oysters served with a refreshingly spicy
daikon salsa?

Serves 4
12 fresh oysters in the shell
For the daikon salsa
4 oz. (½–¾ cup) shredded daikon (Japanese radish)
1 shallot, peeled and shredded
1 tablespoon light soy sauce

1 teaspoons yuzu (or lime) juice
2 teaspoons rice vinegar
2 teaspoons Tabasco sauce

Allow 3 oysters per person. Make a bed of crushed ice
on a large serving plate and place the oysters on top.

Mix together all the ingredients for the daikon salsa
and, with a teaspoon, spoon the salsa over each oyster
and serve.

In the Japanese kitchen, almost every part of the fish is eaten, including the roes. Fish roe is rarely eaten raw but is preserved in salt or dried to make it keep longer. It is a valuable source of protein and in many cases considered a rare delicacy. Fish products, such as flakes and paste, epitomize the Japanese fondness for fish! No fish of any kind, big or small, escapes the cooking pot.

8 Fish roes, products, & pastes

海胆 Uni [SEA URCHIN]

The rich, golden, melt-on-the-tongue sensation of fresh sea urchin makes it one of the choicest of toppings for sushi.

Habitat Uni is a spiky round creature which lives on the sea bed in shallow water and in rockpools.

Appearance and taste The size and color varies from one variety to another but the *murasaki uni* (Japanese purple sea urchin), commonly found around Japan, measures 2 inches in diameter and is—as the name suggests—deep purple. The spherical body is covered with strong spikes, like a marine version of a prickly chestnut bur. Only the ovaries, which have a rich bittersweet taste and smooth, buttery texture, are eaten. Uni has a distinctive ammoniacal aroma that may not appeal to everyone, though the fresher it is, the less strongly it smells.

▲ *A basket of freshly caught sea urchins.*

Buying and storing Fresh uni is washed in salt water and sold in small boxes—it should be eaten within two days of purchase. You can also buy jars of seasoned uni in alcohol.

Health benefits Raw uni has long being used as an aphrodisiac—what could be a more delicious pick-me-up? Its high vitamin A content is good for the eyes.

Culinary uses Sea urchin is eaten raw in sushi, and salted or mixed with alcohol to make it keep longer. It makes a rich dressing or sauce.

Soba no karashi uni ae
[SOBA NOODLES WITH SPICY SEA URCHIN SAUCE]

Fresh sea urchins are expensive but this recipe makes a little go a long way.

Serves 4
14 oz. (5 cups) dried soba noodles
For the sauce
7 oz. fresh sea urchin ovary, mashed
1 tablespoon Chinese chili bean sauce
1 tablespoon light soy sauce
2 tablespoons sake
To garnish
2 scallions, finely chopped

Mix together all the ingredients for the sauce and set aside. Bring a saucepan of water to a boil over high heat. Add the noodles and stir to stop them sticking.

When the water begins to rise, add a cup of cold water and let it return to the boil again. You may have to repeat this once more depending on how dry the noodles are. Drain well. Return the noodles to the saucepan you have been using, add the sauce and stir well.

Divide the noodles between 4 serving plates, garnish with the chopped scallion and serve.

数の子 Kazunoko [HERRING ROE]

Kazunoko, once so plentiful and cheap, used to be considered poor man's food or, worse still, used as fertilizer. Nowadays it is also known as 'yellow diamond,' because it is an expensive, rare delicacy reserved for special occasions such as New Year.

Appearance and taste Kazunoko is salted herring ovary; it is an opaque yellow and looks like a small flattened banana with a semi-divided underside. It has a crunchy texture.

Buying and storing Kazunoko needs to be soaked in water overnight before you use it, to soften it and remove the excess salt.

Culinary uses An essential ingredient at the Japanese New Year feast, kazunoko is seasoned with soy sauce and bonito fish flakes and is also used for sushi topping. It is rarely available in the West but good sushi bars serve it.

Kazunoko to kyuri no chirashi zushi

[KAZUNOKO AND CUCUMBER SALAD ON
A BED OF SUSHI RICE]

This makes an easy to prepare but spectacular-looking sushi dish. Both the salad and sushi rice can be prepared in advance and assembled just before serving.

Serves 4
4 kazunoko, soaked in water overnight
4 teaspoons mirin
4 teaspoons soy sauce
4 tablespoons bonito flakes
2 baby cucumbers, peeled and cut into matchsticks
5 oz. (2 cups) prepared sushi rice (see p.228)
½ teaspoon wasabi powder mixed with 1 teaspoon water
2 tablespoons good-quality mayonnaise

Slice the kazunoko, following the natural rifts in its underside. Mix together the kazunoko, mirin, soy sauce, and bonito flakes and set aside.

Prepare the cucumber and leave it to soak in a bowl of cold water.

Divide the prepared sushi rice into 4 equal portions and, with a moistened ramekin, make 4 rice cakes and put one on the center of each serving plate.

Divide the kazunoko mixture into 4 and put a portion on top of each rice cake. Drain the cucumber and make an attractive peak on the top of each mound of kazunoko.

Mix the runny wasabi paste with the mayonnaise, drizzle around each mound and serve.

イクラ Ikura [SALMON ROE]

The name *ikura* is derived from the Russian word for fish eggs. A whole salmon ovary (*suziko*) is washed in warm salt water to separate each egg; each egg is then coated with olive oil to prevent oxidation and to preserve its glossiness.

Buying and storing In the West, ikura is normally sold as 'red caviar' or 'saviar' in small glass jars that will keep for a week in the refrigerator.

Health benefits Ikura is richer than its parent in both fat and protein.

Culinary uses In Japanese cooking, ikura is used as a topping for sushi, an accompaniment to saké, a garnish, and an ingredient in hors d'oeuvres.

Chilled soba noodles with salmon roe and avocado

I have always liked the combination of buttery avocado and salmon roe with fiery wasabi sauce. This is a noodle dish with a difference.

▼ *Salmon roes drying in the sun on a riverbank.*
◥ *Ikura and smoked salmon rice sushi.*

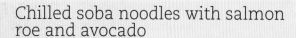

14 oz. (5 cups) dried soba noodles
1 tablespoon saké
4 oz. salmon roe
1 ripe avocado, pit removed, flesh diced
2 teaspoons wasabi powder, mixed with water to heavy cream consistency
1 tablespoon light soy sauce

Bring a saucepan of water to a boil and add the noodles. When the water begins to boil again, add a cup of cold water and bring back to a boil. Drain the noodles, rinse under cold running water and set aside to drain again.

Sprinkle the saké over the salmon roe—this will separate the eggs and make it easier to handle—and mix the avocado with the salmon roe in a bowl.

Add the wasabi and soy sauce. Divide the noodles between 4 serving dishes and arrange them in nests. Top with the avocado and salmon roe mixture and serve.

Ikura and smoked salmon rice sushi

This is another invented sushi of mine, using both 'parent' and egg parts of the salmon. It's easy to make, visually beautiful and delicious—what more can one ask?

Serves 4
1 quantity prepared sushi rice (see p.223)

For the scrambled eggs

2 eggs, beaten

1 teaspoon granulated sugar

½ teaspoon salt

1 teaspoon vegetable oil

1 tablespoon saké

2 oz. salmon roe

2 oz. smoked salmon, roughly chopped

2 tablespoons capers, drained and chopped

First, make the scrambled eggs. Mix together the beaten eggs, sugar, and salt. Heat a non-stick skillet over medium heat and add the oil. Pour in the egg mixture and cook, stirring continuously with chopsticks or a whisk. Set aside.

Add the saké to the salmon roe to separate the eggs. In a large bowl, mix together the prepared sushi rice, the salmon roe, the smoked salmon, and the capers.

Transfer the sushi mixture to a large serving dish, top with the scrambled eggs and serve.

煮干し Niboshi [DRIED SARDINES]

Niboshi means simply 'cooked and dried' and while many different ingredients, such as shrimps and scallops, can be used, the most common ingredient is sardines. Small sardines less than 2 inches long are first boiled, then dried. The resulting niboshi is boiled for 5 minutes to make a strong-tasting dashi broth that is quite different from the dashi broth made from kelp and bonito flakes. This stronger dashi broth is used as the base for fuller-flavored soups such as miso, simmered dishes and noodle broth.

How to make niboshi dashi Put 1¾ pints (4 cups) water with 2 oz. of niboshi in a saucepan. Bring to a boil over a medium heat, skimming off any scum that rises to the surface. Reduce the heat and let it simmer for 5 minutes before taking off the heat and straining.

Shirasu-boshi/Chirimen-jako Shirasu-boshi (or chirimen-jako, depending on which part of Japan you come from) are tiny white sardines less than 1 inch long, salted and dried. In Kanto region near Tokyo, they are called shirasu-boshi, while in the Kansai region near Osaka they are known as chirimen-jako. Kansai's chirimen-jako are drier and harder than their Tokyo counterpart. They are eaten mixed with shredded daikon (Japanese radish), used in salad to give an extra texture or cooked in tempura. The easiest way to serve them is on top of a bowl of hot, plain boiled rice.

Oroshi daikon to shirasu-boshi
[DRIED SARDINE AND RADISH SALSA]

I always knew when my grandfather had lost his appetite: he would ask for this dish and eat it with a bowl of plain boiled rice. I like to eat this when I feel I've eaten too much meat.

1 lb. (2½–2¾ cups) shredded daikon (Japanese radish)
2 oz. shirasu-boshi (dried sardines)
3 tablespoons soy sauce

Simply mix the 3 ingredients in a bowl and serve with boiled rice.

◂ *Dried sardine and radish salsa.*

◂ *From left to right: shirasu-boshi (or chirimen-jako) and niboshi.*

鰹節 Katsuo-bushi [BONITO FLAKES]

The rasping sound of katsuo-bushi being made is like the overture to a grand opera: in this case, it signals the imminent arrival of good food. My own grandmother always started cooking by shaving a handful of katsuo-bushi on a shaving box (an upside-down plane with a box underneath to collect the shavings). Katsuo-bushi is one of the most important seasoning ingredients in the Japanese kitchen. It is combined with dried konbu (kelp) to make dashi, the Japanese broth.

How it is made Making katsuo-bushi is a lengthy process: a fresh bonito weighing less than 6 lb. is filleted, cooked, dried, and shaped before being stored to develop mold.

Appearance and taste As the name implies (*bushi* is the knot you find on trees) a bar of katsuo-bushi resembles a dense, dried piece of wood. It has a distinctive smoky aroma and tastes of skipjack tuna.

Buying and storing Today, most katsuo-bushi is sold ready-shaved as *kezuri-bushi* or *hanagatsuo*, making it easier and quicker to use. The shavings are graded according to quality—in general, broader shavings are of better quality. Ready-shaved katsuo-bushi is sold in small sachets or larger bags; once opened, the bags should be resealed and keep in a dry, cool cupboard.

Health benefits In the old days, katsuo-bushi made a useful field ration and storecupboard ingredient. It is packed with high-quality protein and minerals.

Hundreds of bonito fillets drying in the sun before being flaked.

Culinary uses The single most important use for bonito flakes is in dashi. Fine shavings of katsuo-bushi are sprinkled over other dishes as a garnish and, mixed with soy sauce, katsuo-bushi makes a tasty filling.

Ichiban dashi
[NUMBER ONE JAPANESE BROTH]

In the Japanese kitchen, *ichiban dashi* (meaning 'number one broth') is often the first thing to be prepared each day—it should be used the day it is made as it quickly loses its aroma and flavor. There are different varieties and this is the most widely used one. The whole process should take no more than 20 minutes from start to end.

Makes 1¾ pints (4 cups)
1 piece dried konbu (kelp), postcard size
1¾ pints (4 cups) water
¾ oz. bonito flakes (about a handful)

Put the konbu with the water in a saucepan. Heat gently and take out the konbu when it begins to float. When the water comes to a boil, take off the heat. Add the bonito flakes and let them settle at the bottom. Strain the broth through a fine strainer lined with paper towels.

Niban dashi
[NUMBER TWO JAPANESE BROTH]

This is a stronger and more robust broth than number one. In some ways it is easier to make as both the konbu and katsuo-bushi are added to the water at the beginning.

Makes 1¾ pints (4 cups)
1 piece dried konbu (kelp), postcard size
1¾ pints (4 cups) water
¾ oz. bonito flakes (about a handful)

Put the konbu, water and bonito flakes in a saucepan and bring to a boil over a medium heat. When the water begins to boil, reduce the heat to low and continue to cook for 5 minutes more. Turn off the heat and strain the broth through a fine strainer lined with paper towels.

練物 Neri-mono [FISH PASTES]

A wide range of puréed fish products is used in Japanese cooking, and they come in a variety of shapes, sizes, and colors. The origin of neri-mono (fish paste products) is not entirely clear, but the first written record, describing how puréed catfish was molded around thin bamboo sticks that were cooked over a fire, dates back to the early sixteenth century. The following are the fish pastes most commonly used in the Japanese kitchen.

Kamaboko Kamaboko is made of puréed white fish such as sea bream, flounder, and plaice. The flesh is ground and puréed, then mixed with salt, sugar, and other seasonings. The mixture is shaped into various forms, then steamed, boiled, and some broiled. The standard version is called *ita kamaboko*, which is shaped over a small, rectangular wooden board. Those from the Kansai region tend to be flatter and have a broiled, brown surface, while those from Odawara are steamed and have a smooth surface. They are generally an opaque white but some come in pink. Kamaboko is mildly fishy with virtually no aroma and it has a resilient, gelatinous texture (it needs to be cut off the board on which it is stuck). It can be served thinly sliced with soy sauce and wasabi paste or cooked with other ingredients in simmered dishes.

Chikuwa *Chikuw*a means 'bamboo ring.' It is fish paste that is molded around a bamboo stick, then steamed and broiled; when the bamboo stick is taken off it leaves a tube of fish paste with a hole down the middle. A normal sized chikuwa is about 6 inches long with a hole running the length of it. The outer skin is broiled, giving it a bubbly, golden brown surface. Like kamaboko, chikuwa can be eaten sliced with soy sauce and wasabi paste or shredded ginger root, or simmered with vegetables in hot-pot dishes.

Satsuma-age This is a deep-fried version of kamaboko. It comes in various shapes, colors and flavors—the plain ones are normally flattish discs 2 inches in diameter. Satsuma-age can be eaten as it is with soy sauce and shredded ginger root, or used in simmering dishes such as *oden* (see p.182), soups, and noodle dishes. Pour boiling water over it before you use it to remove the excess oil. Two of the most popular flavored versions are *ika-maki*, which is deep-fried kamaboko roll with squid stuffing, and *gobo-maki*, which has burdock stuffing and is normally served with shredded ginger root and soy sauce.

Hanpen Made of puréed shark's meat mixed with shredded yam and egg whites, hanpen normally comes in 3 inches white squares. It has a light fluffy texture and can be eaten as it is or broiled with soy sauce and wasabi or mustard. It is also used in soups and simmering dishes.

Chikuwa to wakame no sunomono
[CHIKUWA WITH WAKAME SEAWEED IN VINEGAR]

This is a store cupboard dish that can be prepared in 5 minutes.

1 chikuwa (bamboo-ring fish paste)
1 baby cucumber, thinly sliced
¾ oz. dried wakame, reconstituted in water
1 teaspoon shredded ginger root
For the vinegar dressing
4 tablespoons rice vinegar
1–2 tablespoons granulated sugar
1 teaspoon light soy sauce
½ teaspoon salt

Cut the chikuwa on the diagonal to make attractive rings. Mix together all the ingredients for the vinegar dressing, add the chikuwa rings, cucumber slices, softened wakame, and shredded ginger, and stir.

Satsuma-age to wasabi mayonnaise

[DEEP-FRIED FISH PASTE WITH WASABI MAYONNAISE]

This makes an easy to prepare party canapé dish with a Japanese twist.

Makes about 24 canapés
4 satsuma-age, reheated in a warm oven
2 teaspoons wasabi powder, mixed with water to a paste
2 tablespoons good quality, ready-made mayonnaise
2 teaspoons light soy sauce

Cut the satsuma-age into bite-size pieces and spear with cocktail sticks to make them easier to eat. Mix the wasabi paste, mayonnaise, and soy sauce in a small dish. Put the dipping sauce in the center of a large serving platter and arrange the pieces of satusma-age around it.

▾ *Sliced white fish paste with salmon roe and wasabi.*

Kamaboko to ikura

[SLICED WHITE FISH PASTE WITH SALMON ROE AND WASABI]

This is another easy to prepare yet stylish canapé.

Makes about 24 canapés
1 block kamaboko (white fish paste)
1 teaspoon saké
2 tablespoons ikura (salmon roe)
1 tablespoon wasabi powder, mixed with the same amount of water to cream cheese consistency

Cut the kamaboko block from its board and slice it ¼ inch thick. Mix the saké in with the salmon roe to separate the eggs. Put a pinhead-size dab of wasabi paste on each slice of kamaboko and lay 2–3 eggs on top of that.

Japanese cuisine is not renowned for its use of meat and poultry, although there is some evidence to suggest that my prehistoric ancestors ate a wide range of game and that meat continued to be eaten even after rice began to be cultivated in the thirteenth century BC. Meat-eating was banned when the Yamato Imperial court established a new government in the seventh century AD and embraced the teaching of Buddhism, but the first ban in 676 was not entirely successful, and many more bans were to follow, applying not just to beef and poultry but also to game and even fish.

We can probably assume that the ruling Imperial family, high-ranking aristocratic courtiers and Buddhist priests observed a strict vegetarian diet until the twilight years of the Heian period in the tenth century. But as the imperial and aristocratic hold on political power waned, giving way to military rule, the country descended into centuries of political unrest, and ordinary Japanese people once again started to eat whatever was available. Nevertheless, animal husbandry for meat was never practiced: animals were kept by farmers and samurai as beasts of burden and for transport. Only in the mid nineteenth century did meat and poultry became an acceptable sight on the Japanese table.

9 Meat & poultry

鶏肉 Tori-niku [CHICKEN]

The history of chicken goes back a long way in Japan—many terracotta chickens dating from the prehistoric Jomon period have been found. At first chickens were kept not just for eating but also for ornamental and religious purposes, and later on for fighting and as an indication of the hours. Eating chicken was banned in the seventh century and after that there is little evidence to suggest that the Japanese were eating even chicken eggs, let alone the bird. The eating of chicken and eggs began again after the Meiji Restoration in the mid nineteenth century and today both chicken and eggs are popular ingredients in the Japanese kitchen—more than beef or pork, as the leanness and mild flavor of chicken suits the Japanese palate and the Japanese style of cooking.

My grandparents always kept chickens in their orchard—I grew up with them, chasing them around the garden, as a naughty child would do. One of my earliest jobs was to collect newly laid eggs that were still warm and bring them to my grandmother, who would make sweet, succulent rolled omelets.

Shoga gayu
[GINGER AND CHICKEN CONGEE]

Warming and comforting, this soupy rice dish was one of my grandmother's specialities. She used to make this whenever someone showed the slightest sign of being under the weather.

Serves 4

7 oz. (¾–1 cup) rice, rinsed and drained

2 oz. (4-inch piece) ginger root, peeled and finely ground

4 oz. skinless chicken thigh fillet, flesh roughly chopped

1¾ pints (4 cups) water

Salt to taste

To garnish

A few sprigs of mitsuba or scallions, chopped

Put all the ingredients in a heavy-based saucepan with a tight-fitting lid and slowly bring to a boil over a low heat. Skim off any scum that rises to the surface and continue to cook over a low heat for 20 minutes. Season with salt, garnish with chopped mitsuba or scallions and serve.

Tori no teriyaki
[CHICKEN TERIYAKI]

This must be one of the most popular Japanese dishes of all time. It is certainly my children's favorite.

Serves 4

14 oz. skinless chicken thigh fillets, chopped into bite-size pieces

3 tablespoons cornflour

1 tablespoon vegetable oil

For the teriyaki sauce

3 tablespoons soy sauce

3 tablespoons saké

3 tablespoons sugar

2 tablespoons mirin

Coat the chicken with the cornflour. Heat the oil in a skillet over medium heat. Cook the chicken until browned, shaking the pan gently, and use a piece of rolled-up paper towel to soak up the excess fat. Mix together all the ingredients for the teriyaki sauce and pour over the chicken. Reduce the heat to low and cook for 3 more minutes. The dish is ready once the sauce has thickened and the chicken is glazed. Transfer to 4 serving plates and serve.

◀ *A yakitori street vendor; the delicious aromas travel for miles.*

Yakitori

[CHICKEN AND LEEK KABOBS]

This is a popular accompaniment to saké, but you don't have to be over 18 to enjoy these mouth-watering mini kabobs basted in a rich aromatic sauce. I prefer to use pre-steamed chicken, so that the chicken doesn't burn or dry out and the aroma of the basting sauce is not lost.

Serves 4

450g (1lb.) skinless, boneless chicken thighs, chopped in small pieces

12 bamboo skewers

4 baby leeks, cut into 1-inch lengths

For the basting sauce

3 tablespoons mirin

2 tablespoons soy sauce

2 heaped tablespoons sugar

To serve

Shichimi togarashi

Put the chicken on a plate and steam it in a steamer for 10 minutes or until it is almost cooked through. Meanwhile, soak the bamboo skewers in water to prevent them burning. Thread alternate pieces of chicken and leek onto the skewers, beginning and ending with chicken.

Mix together all the ingredients for the sauce and put in a tall jar. Preheat the oven to 425°F and line a baking sheet with a piece of aluminum foil. Dip every kabob in the basting sauce before laying them on the sheet, covering the ends of the skewers with foil to prevent them from burning.

Cook for 5 minutes, then remove from the oven to baste with the sauce again. Return to the oven for another 3 minutes. Remove from the oven and dip each kabob in the basting sauce before serving. Sprinkle with shichimi togarashi to taste.

鴨 Kamo [DUCK]

The culinary history of duck in Japan dates back to prehistoric times. Even after the Buddhist ban on eating meat and poultry, wild birds such as pheasants and ducks were considered a delicacy by the ruling aristocracy and formed an important part of a banquet, though duck has never gained widespread popularity in Japan as it has in China. Duck is for special occasions and not often seen in the domestic kitchen.

Kamo no yunan-zuke

[MARINATED DUCK BREAST]

This is an easy to prepare dish that can be made in advance and served as a substantial main course or a light one-dish lunch. You can reuse the marinade on noodles or as a salad dressing.

Serves 4
2 duck breasts, skin side pricked with a fork
1 teaspoon vegetable oil
For the yunan marinade
8 fl oz. (1 cup) soy sauce
4 tablespoons saké
2 tablespoons mirin
2 tablespoons yuzu (or lime) juice

Cut off the excess skin and fat from the duck. Heat the oil in a skillet and cook the duck skin side down over medium heat for 5–7 minutes or until the skin is golden brown. Turn over and cook the other side for 3 minutes. Place the duck in a colander and pour boiling water over both sides to wash off the excess fat.

Mix together all the ingredients for the marinade and put the duck in immediately. Leave to marinate overnight. Thinly slice the breast and serve with wasabi paste or on a bed of soba noodles with the marinade.

Kamo nanban

[NOODLE SOUP WITH DUCK BREAST]

Nanban literally means 'southern barbarian'; it was a derogatory term referring to the foreigners who came to southern Japan in the sixteenth century. Today, the term refers to dishes that contain non-traditional ingredients.

Serves 4
14 oz. (5–6 cups) dried udon noodles
1 teaspoon vegetable oil
2 duck breasts, trimmed of excess fat and skin scored
4 baby leeks, cut into 1-inch lengths
Shichimi-t garashi (optional)
For the broth
1¾ pints (4 cups) niban dashi broth (see p.169)
4 tablespoons saké
4 tablespoons sugar
4 tablespoons mirin
4 tablespoons soy sauce
1 teaspoon salt

Bring a saucepan of water to a boil and add the udon noodles. When the water returns to a boil, tip in a cup of cold water and bring back to a boil. Drain the noodles, rinse them under cold running water and drain again.

Meanwhile, heat all the ingredients for the broth in a separate saucepan. Heat the oil in a skillet and fry the duck skin-side down until golden, then turn over and cook the other side. Remove from the pan and slice. Sauté the leeks in the same skillet for 2 minutes.

Add the duck and leeks to the broth, bring back to a boil and add the noodles. Divide the soup between 4 serving bowls and offer round the shichimi togarashi.

◀ *Noodle soup with duck breast.*

豚肉 Buta-niku [PORK]

The first ban on meat eating in 676 referred to beef, horsemeat, chicken, and monkey. Later bans also covered game, including wild boar, venison, pheasant, and even fish, but curiously there was no mention of pork. This is because pigs were kept purely for eating and played no agricultural or religious role. The Japanese continued to eat pork until the Edo period in the seventeenth century, when the powerful feudal regime of the Tokugawa reintroduced the ban on eating meat. Pork did not regain popularity until the Meiji Restoration. Today, most of the pigs reared in Japan are pure foreign breeds, mainly from Britain or America, or are crossbreeds.

Tonkatsu

[CRISPY DEEP-FRIED PORK CUTLETS]

This succulent pork cutlet in a crispy breadcrumb coating is always served with tonkatsu sauce (available from Japanese stores) and finely sliced cabbage.

Serves 4
1 lb. pork tenderloin
Salt and pepper
Vegetable oil, for deep-frying
8 cabbage leaves, finely shredded
To coat
7 oz. (1¾ cups) all-purpose flour
2 eggs, beaten
14 oz. (2½ cups) breadcrumbs
To serve
Tonkatsu sauce

Cut the pork into 1-inch cubes and sprinkle with salt and pepper. Roll the pork in the flour to coat, dust off the excess, then dip in the beaten egg and roll in the breadcrumbs. Refrigerate for 30 minutes. Meanwhile, heat the oil to 350°F.

Cut out the hard stalk of the cabbage leaves and cut them in half. Layer 3 or 4 pieces together, roll them up tightly and shred finely. Leave to soak in cold water.

Deep-fry the cubes of pork in small batches until they are golden brown, turning them to ensure even cooking. Drain well over paper towels. Drain the cabbage, put a generous heap on each plate and arrange the pork next to it. Serve with tonkatsu sauce.

Buta niku no umeboshi mushi

[STEAMED PORK WITH PLUM PASTE]

This recipe requires thinly sliced shoulder of pork—ask your butcher to use his bacon slicer—and you may have to substitute white onions for Japanese giant scallions. The steaming keeps the pork tender and succulent and the mild, sweet flavor of the pork goes perfectly with the sour umeboshi.

Serves 4
7 oz. shoulder of pork, thinly sliced
2 white onions, peeled and thinly sliced
For the umeboshi paste
6 umeboshi (pickled plums), pitted and mashed
1 tablespoon soy sauce
1 tablespoon mirin
1 tablespoon saké

Mix together all the ingredients for the umeboshi paste. Coat each pork slice with the paste and pile them up in layers. Put the stack of pork on a plate and steam in a steamer for 15–20 minutes.

Meanwhile, soak the onion in cold water. Drain well and heap on the serving plate. Put the steamed pork on top of the bed of onion and serve.

◂ *Steamed pork with plum paste.*

牛肉 Gyu-niku [BEEF]

After more than 1,200 years of a meatless diet, the Japanese had to make a complete culinary U-turn in 1868 when a new imperial government replaced the feudal Tokugawa shogunate and began a rapid modernization of the country. The Japanese people absorbed every aspect of Western culture, including Western food, and fashionable men flocked to *gyunabe-ya*, restaurants specializing in beef dishes. Although Japan's history of beef rearing goes back little more than a hundred years, Kobe beef (also known as Matsuzaka beef) has earned an international reputation for quality and high price.

Breeds Breeding from a small number of native cattle, the beef farmers of Japan developed 4 types of *wagyu* (Japanese beef cattle). The most popular, which accounts for 90 percent of beef consumed, is the black-haired *kuroge-washu,* a crossbreed of native and imported cattle. The reddish-brown *katsumo-washu* is the second most popular breed and is found in warmer southern regions. The short-horned *nihon tankakushu* is a cross between the native cattle and English Shorthorns, and there is also a hornless crossbreed called *mukakushu,* which is part Aberdeen Angus.

Appearance and taste Top-quality Japanese beef is pink, rather than red, with white fat. This is because the cattle are massaged with beer to distribute the fat throughout the meat to produce sweet, succulent, meltingly tender, and very rich flavored meat. Japanese beef is sold thinly sliced, which suits the Japanese style of cooking.

Buying and storing Japanese beef is not available outside Japan, but it is possible to use thinly sliced sirloin or fillet steak as a substitute.

Culinary uses In Japanese cooking, beef is rarely eaten on its own, except in the case of steaks. As the oven is a relatively new arrival in the Japanese kitchen, most beef dishes are cooked on the stove.

Niku jaga
[SIMMERED BEEF WITH POTATOES]

This is a curious dish because it is a typical example of home cooking, passed down from mother to daughter, yet it is made with two most un-Japanese ingredients.

Serves 4
1 tablespoon vegetable oil
1 white onion, peeled and cut into wedges
4 medium-size potatoes, peeled and quartered
7 oz. lean rump beef, thinly sliced
To season
8 fl oz. (1 cup) dashi broth (see p.169)
2 tablespoons granulated sugar
2 tablespoons saké
2 tablespoons mirin
2 tablespoons soy sauce

Heat the oil in a saucepan over medium heat. Add the onion and sauté for 3 minutes, then add the potatoes and cook for 5 minutes more. Add the slices of beef and cook for 2 minutes. Add all the seasoning ingredients and bring to a boil, removing any scum that comes to the surface. Reduce the heat and simmer for 15–20 minutes or until the cooking liquid is reduced by half.

Wafu steki
[JAPANESE-STYLE STEAK]

This is steak with a difference, both in its seasoning and service. In Japan, everything is eaten with chopsticks so even a steak has to be served in small bite-sized pieces.

Serves 4
1 lb. sirloin or fillet steak
Salt and pepper
1 tablespoon beef fat
2 tablespoons saké
2 tablespoons soy sauce

▶ *Sliced, seared fillet of beef.*

◀ *A farmer proudly shows off his Kobe beef cow.*

To garnish

4 tablespoons shredded daikon
1 teaspoon shredded ginger root
4 mitsuba leaves

Sprinkle the steak with salt and pepper and gently pat it all over. Heat a skillet and melt the beef fat over a medium heat. Turn the heat up to high, add the steak and sear one side. Turn it over and cook the other side as you like it.

Remove the steak and reduce the heat to low. Add the saké and soy sauce and cook for 1 minute. Cut the steak into bite-size pieces and arrange them on 4 serving plates. Pour the juices over the steak. Mix the shredded daikon and ginger and make a small mound on the side of each plate. Garnish with the mitsuba leaves and serve.

Gyu no tataki

[SLICED, SEARED FILLET OF BEEF]

This cooking method is called *tataki*, which means to 'beat' or 'slap': hitting the slices of beef with the palm of your hand helps to tenderize the meat. A perfect piece of beef *tataki* is seared on the outside and rare in the middle.

Instead of cress and cucumber, you could use chives or some shredded carrot for color. The dish can be prepared several hours in advance up to the wrapping stage, and should be served at room temperature.

Serves 4

1 lb. beef fillet
2 teaspoons vegetable oil
Salt and pepper
4 tablespoons rice vinegar
½ cucumber, peeled and sliced into matchsticks
1 garlic clove, finely shredded
1 piece of ginger root, thumb-size, peeled and finely shredded
1 container fresh cress
4 tablespoons soy sauce
1 teaspoon roasted sesame seeds

Coat the beef with the oil, season with salt and pepper and make ready a large bowl of ice water. Heat a griddle or skillet over high heat. Sear the fillet on one side for 1 minute or 2 or until just the outside is browned, then turn the fillet over and brown the other side.

Turn off the heat, pour over the rice vinegar (this helps to tenderize the meat) and plunge the beef into the bowl of water for a few seconds to stop it from cooking further. Wipe the beef dry with paper towels. With a very sharp knife, slice the beef as thinly as possible—¼ inch thick. Place each slice on a chopping board and give it a firm slap with the palm of your hand.

Wrap a few cucumber sticks in each slice of beef, and arrange on a serving plate. Put a dot of shredded garlic, ginger and cress on each piece of beef and drizzle with soy sauce. Sprinkle with the sesame seeds and serve.

Here are some traditional, if rather curious-sounding, ingredients that feature in many aspects of Japanese cooking. They are unrelated in every way and don't really 'belong' to any of the other chapters in this book. They have therefore been labelled 'store-cupboard products' since the only thing they have in common is that they keep well and are often on-hand to lend a little extra to a soup or snack.

10 The store cupboard

こんにゃく Konnyaku [DEVIL'S TONGUE]

Konnyaku is yet another curiously named ingredient from the Japanese kitchen and its strange name matches its equally strange appearance and texture. Although it originated in China (the technique for making it was introduced to Japan at the same time as Buddhism), it has become a uniquely Japanese ingredient.

How it is made Konnyaku is made from the root of the konnyaku plant, a kind of yam. The root is boiled, peeled and mashed to a sticky paste. The paste is then mixed with lime water, which acts as a coagulant, and is shaped in a box before being boiled to harden.

Appearance and taste There is no doubt about it, konnyaku seems very strange to those who have not being brought up with it. It comes in many different shapes and colors: green, thinly sliced *sashimi konnyaku*, ball-shaped konnyaku, flavored konnyaku

and *ito-konnyaku*, named for its translucent white strings. In the West, the standard *ita konnyaku* (meaning 'board konnyaku') is the one most likely to be sold in Japanese stores. *Ita konnyaku* is normally grey with dark speckles, though there is a less common white variety; it has a slippery, rubbery texture with no aroma or taste of its own.

Health benefits Konnyaku has no calories; it is 97 percent water, so is an ideal diet food. It has a trace of calcium and potassium but the remaining 3 percent is mainly an indigestible fiber that works as a wonderful cleansing agent for the intestines, so helps to prevent constipation.

Buying and storing The standard *ita konnyaku* is about 6 x 3 inches—⅜ inch thick—and is sold in a water-filled packet. Once the packet is opened keep the *ita konnyaku* in the fridge in plenty of water, which should be changed daily. It should keep for up to two weeks this way.

Culinary uses Fresh konnyaku—an essential ingredient for *oden*, a simmered hot-pot dish with fish cakes—is eaten raw like sashimi with soy sauce and wasabi. It is also cooked with other ingredients in soups, rice dishes and stir-fried dishes.

Oden

[SLOW COOKED VEGETABLES WITH KONNYAKU AND FISH CAKES]

There is nothing pretentious about *oden*—it is warming yet easy to prepare, as you can buy assorted ready-made fish cake balls from Japanese stores. There is no definitive list of ingredients—it's open to improvization. The following quantities will serve 4.

Suggested ingredients:
1 piece konbu (kelp), postcard size
1 lb. (2½–3 cups) daikon, peeled and cut into chunks
1 konnyaku (devil's tongue), cut into 2 squares, then cut diagonally into triangles
2 medium potatoes, peeled and cut in half
4 eggs, hard-cooked and shelled

2 chikuwa (see p.170), cut diagonally in half

2 Satsuma-age (see p.170), cut in half

1 thick, deep-fried tofu block, cut in 4 square pieces

4 fresh shiitake mushrooms, stalks removed

For the soup broth

3½ pints (8 cups) niboshi dashi (see p.168)

4 fl oz. (½ cup) saké

2 tablespoons soy sauce

1 tablespoon salt

To serve

English mustard

Wrap the konbu in a wet dish towel for 5–10 minutes or until soft enough to handle. Cut it into thick ribbons and tie each ribbon in a knot.

Put all the ingredients for the soup broth in a large, heat-resistant clay pot or cast-iron saucepan. Add the konbu, daikon, konnyaku, potatoes, and eggs.

Bring to a boil over a medium heat and skim off any scum that rises to the surface. Turn down the heat and add the chikuwa, satsuma-age, deep-fried tofu, and mushrooms. Simmer for at least 1 hour before serving with a dab of English mustard and the cooking juices.

乾瓢 Kampyo [DRIED GOURD STRIPS]

Kampyo has a unique role in the Japanese kitchen in that it is used to tie food together and looks more like a piece of string than something edible. It was first used in the Zen Buddhist cuisine of *Shojin ryori* in the twelfth century and became more widespread during the late seventeenth century.

How it is made The flesh of the gourd is thinly sliced into a long ribbon over 7 feet long. The ribbon is smoked in sulphate to whiten it, then dried.

Appearance and taste Kampyo looks like an off-white, slightly creased ribbon with a gentle, sweet and sour aroma. It has hardly any taste of its own; its main attribute is its resilient but malleable texture, which makes it ideal for tying up other food.

Buying and storing Kampyo is sold in packets of 1½–2 ounces from Japanese or Asian grocery stores. Good-quality kampyo should keep for up to a year if stored in a cool, dry cupboard.

Culinary uses Apart from tying food together, kampyo is also used as a popular filling in sushi rolls after it is has been softened and seasoned in soy-based stock.

Kampyo maki zushi

[THINLY ROLLED SUSHI WITH SEASONED STRIPS OF GOURD]

Sushi does not have to use raw fish, as this recipe proves. In the Japanese kitchen, there is always a packet of kampyo ready to be turned into a delicious high-fiber filling.

Makes 6 rolls
1 oz. dried kampyo
2 tablespoons salt
16 fl oz. (1¾ cups) dashi broth (see p.169)
2 tablespoons granulated sugar
2 tablespoons soy sauce
1 sheet dried nori (dried seaweed), cut in half
1 quantity prepared sushi rice (see p.223)

Wash the dried kampyo in cold water using a scrubbing action. Add the salt and rub the kampyo together with your hands. Rinse and soak in water for 2 hours (or according to the packet instructions). Drain and put the kampyo in a saucepan with the dashi broth, sugar and soy sauce. Bring to a boil and simmer for 10 minutes or until it is soft and golden. Let it cool down in the broth before cutting it to the desired length.

Now put half a nori sheet, lengthways, on top of a bamboo rolling mat, with the shiny smooth side down. Place a handful of the sushi rice on the nori and spread it evenly to cover, leaving a 1-inch margin at the top. Take a few strips of drained kampyo and place them along the center of the rice. Lift up the edge of the mat closest to you, and slowly roll it away from you. Let the near edge meet the far side of the rice—you will need to exert gentle pressure on the roll to keep it neatly compacted. Lift the mat slightly and push the roll forward a little so that the uncovered strip of nori seals the roll (the moisture from the rice acts as an adhesive).

Push in any stray grains of rice at both ends to tidy it up. Put the roll on a clean chopping board. Dip your knife in water and cut the roll into 6 bite-size pieces, moistening the knife between each cutting. Serve immediately with a dipping sauce of your choice.

麩 Fu [GLUTEN SPONGE CAKE]

The history of fu goes back a long way. It was first developed in China and resembles bread in that it uses wheat flour and baking powder, but the Japanese have developed ultra-light dried fu in many different colors, sizes and shapes to use as a decoration. It was most probably brought over to Japan with Buddhism in the middle of the sixth century. Despite its long history, fu has not received the recognition it deserves—in fact, it has long been denigrated as fish food for goldfish and Japan's famous koi carp.

How it is made Making fu is quite a lengthy process. Wheat flour is mixed with water and salt and kneaded until it becomes elastic. The mixture is then washed in plenty of water in a fine mesh bag to get rid of the unwanted starch, keeping only the gluten. The gluten mixture is then washed some more and steamed to make 'fresh fu', which is rarely seen in the domestic kitchen nowadays: *yaki fu*, meaning 'baked fu' is more commonly used.

Appearance and taste *Yaki fu* comes in all kinds of shapes, sizes, and colors—it is made to look like flowers, leaves, and even fish—but it always looks like finely textured sponge cakes or dry bread. It has no taste or aroma of its own; it absorbs the flavor of the broths or juices in which it is cooked.

Buying and storing Different varieties of *yaki fu* are available from Japanese grocery shops. Stored in a cool, dry cupboard away from direct sunlight, it should keep for several months.

Health benefits Fu is high in carbohydrate (around 60 percent) and is 25 percent protein.

Culinary uses The main use of fu is as a decorative garnish in clear soups or simmered vegetable dishes. It's used like croutons.

Fu to shiitake no suimono

[CLEAR SOUP WITH FU, SHIITAKE MUSHROOMS AND SPINACH]

This soup can be very decorative if you get hold of colored fu pieces in pretty shapes.

1 piece dried konbu (kelp), postcard size
1 pint (2½ cups) water
4 dried shiitake mushrooms
12 small pieces fu, shaped like flowers
2 oz. (1½ cups) spinach, washed and roughly chopped

Put the piece of konbu in a saucepan with the water and bring to a boil over a low heat.

Meanwhile, soak the mushrooms in a cup of hot water until they become soft. Drain (reserving the soaking liquor), discard the stems and slice thinly.

Add the sliced mushrooms and the reserved liquid to the soup. Just before the soup reaches boiling point, take out the konbu, add the fu and chopped spinach and bring it to a boil. Turn off the heat and serve.

漬物 Tsukemono [PICKLES]

Pickling is one of the oldest methods of preserving food, especially vegetables, known to mankind. Chinese records show that as long ago as 1058 BC—more than 3,000 years ago—the Chinese were already making pickles. In Japan, where there is no salt bed and salt making was in the early stages, ancient Japanese soaked vegetables in seawater, then dried them to make *shio juke*, salted pickles. When Buddhism was introduced from China some 1,500 years ago, new techniques came with it, and the Japanese learnt different methods of pickling based on fermentation. Japan's first recorded pickles were made using *hishio* (see p.11), fermented salt.

Pickles and a bowl of rice are the Japanese equivalent of bread and butter—the two are inseparable. There are many different types of pickles and pickling agents in the Japanese kitchen, and different regions have their own speciality. The first and the most important type of pickle—*shio juke*—uses salt; this is closely followed by the uniquely Japanese *nuka juke*, which uses rice bran. The third most popular pickling method requires a kind of vinegar called *su juke*. Other pickling agents include miso, wasabi, soy sauce, and various by-products from saké brewing and soy sauce making, such as *koji* (starter mold), *moromi* (the fermented rice malt present before saké is filtered) and *kasu* (the mildly alcoholic pulp left after filtering).

The importance of pickling in Japanese housekeeping is captured by a saying 'soko no tsuma.' *Soko* means 'saké pulp and rice bran' (both of which are cheap but effective pickling materials) and *tsuma* means 'wife'; the whole expression means a frugal and supportive wife. My maternal grandmother was a particularly keen pickle-maker and kept many pickling barrels. When my mother married and left home, my grandmother gave her a small quantity of well-seasoned rice bran so that she could start her own pickling barrel. Sadly, making pickles at home is now a dying practice in Japan, but the nation remains very fond of its diverse range of pickles. A bowl of hot miso soup and rice accompanied by a small dish of tsukemono is the quintessential Japanese meal. The following are some of the more popular pickles sold in the West.

Shio juke (Salted pickles) Pickling using salt is the oldest and most popular method. Vegetables such as cucumbers, eggplant, daikon (Japanese radish), and hakusai (Chinese cabbage) are first covered in salt, with or without other seasoning ingredients like seaweeds and red chiles, and left to stand with a weight on top. It is a relatively quick and easy method, so is good for doing at home. I regularly clear the little bits of vegetables left nestling in the corner of my refrigerator—carrots, cucumbers, cabbages, and cauliflower—and chop them up into small pieces before rubbing them with salt, squeezing them a little to soften them and packing them into a plastic container. I use a plate to cover the vegetables (often mixing in some shredded konbu and chopped red chiles for extra flavor), then put a weight on top to compress them. By the following morning, I have juicy and crunchy pickles for breakfast.

Umeboshi (Salt-pickled plums) Botanically, ume belongs to the rose family. It has always been loved by the Japanese for its late-winter blossom, especially by the samurai class, who saw it as a symbol of resilience—one of the largest clans even incorporated the blossom in its family crest during the Edo period. It is not entirely clear when umeboshi were first made but *ume-su* (plum vinegar) predates rice vinegar and soy sauce, and was used as an important seasoning. Plums are salted and sun-dried before being pickled with purple perilla

▸ *Slicing turnips for senmai juke.*

▸ *Umeboshi.*

▸ ▸ *Rakkyo.*

leaves, which give a deep red color. Umeboshi are a natural antiseptic, preservative, and digestive aid, but as one umeboshi contains about 10 percent of the recommended daily salt intake, anyone who suffers from high blood pressure should restrict their consumption of them.

Nuka juke (Rice bran pickles) Nuka juke is made using a unique pickling method found only in Japan. Nuka (rice bran that is made from ground husks) is mixed with water and salt to make *nuka doko*, a bran pickling bed in which all manner of vegetables are buried for several days or weeks. As the *nuka doko* ages and ferments, it develops complex flavors and an aroma with which the vegetables buried in it are imbued. There is a real skill to maintaining a *nuka doko*: it needs to be turned over thoroughly every day to keep the pickling bacteria alive and healthy so that the bed does not become moldy and start to reek. To me, the smell of a rice bran pickling bed conjures up my grandmother— who kept dozens of pickling barrels of all different sizes —and my entirely secure childhood. Her gentle

caressing hands, which served all kinds of deliciously crunchy pickles at every meal, always had a faint smell of nuka—how I loved the smell of her hands.

Takuan (rice bran-pickled daikon) Takuan is one of the most popular pickles in Japan. In late fall the newly harvested daikon (see p.70) is hung to dry for a few weeks before being salted and pickled in rice bran for two to three months. The end result is slightly salty with a touch of sweetness: a soft yet crunchy yellow daikon. Takuan (1573–1645), a Buddhist monk from Tokyo, is believed to be the inventor of the pickle. The traditional method uses a natural food dye while commercially produced takuan is often colored bright yellow with artificial food coloring. In the West, takuan is normally sold vacuum-packed, sometimes ready-sliced, with and without seasonings such as bonito flakes.

Su juke (Vinegar pickles) Some books say that pickling with vinegar does not exist in Japan—they are entirely wrong. Pickling with vinegar has of course existed

since ancient times, as vinegar is one of the most ancient Japanese ingredients. The Japanese method is different than that used in the West: the Japanese allow the vinegar (most often rice vinegar) to ferment and develop lactic acid, which has a rather sweet flavor. Two of the most famous vinegar pickles are *rakkyo* and *senmai juke*.

Rakkyo [example of vinegar pickle] Rakkyo's origin in Japan is not entirely clear—it was probably introduced from China some time after the mid sixth century, more as a Chinese herbal medicine than as a food. Rakkyo is a small perennial vegetable which looks like baby shallots and tastes like garlic. It is far too pungent to eat raw and so is normally pickled in sweet vinegar, which gives it a more palatable sweet flavor. Pickled rakkyo is served as a nibble with drinks or as a condiment for many meat dishes and curries.

Senmai juke [example of vinegar pickle] Literally translated, senmai juke are 'thousand slice pickles.' Kyokabu (large turnips harvested near Kyoto) are peeled and thinly sliced before being salted and marinated in a sweet vinegar mixture which ferments and gives them their distinctive sweet flavor.

Cabbage and radish salt pickle

1 lb. (4½ cups) spring cabbage
4–6 radishes (round Japanese radishes—not daikon), thinly sliced into rings
1 piece fresh ginger root, thumb size, peeled and cut into thin matchsticks
2 teaspoons sea salt

Separate the cabbage leaves, remove the hard core and, with your hand, tear the leaves into small pieces.

Put the cabbage, the slices of radish, and the ginger in a large bowl and sprinkle with the salt. Using your hands mix and massage lightly.

Cover the bowl with a plate that is small enough to sit on the contents. Put a little weight on top (a tin of tomatoes is ideal) and leave for at least 2 hours. Drain the juice and serve.

Stir-fried takuan with sesame seeds

Try this recipe if you have any leftover takuan and are tired of eating it on its own.

Serves 4
4 oz. takuan
1 tablespoon sesame oil
1 piece fresh ginger root, thumb size, peeled and cut into thin matchsticks
1 tablespoon soy sauce
1 tablespoon toasted sesame seeds
2 tablespoons bonito flakes

Cut the takuan into thin slices. Heat a wok or skillet over medium heat and add the oil. Add the takuan and ginger and stir-fry for 2–3 minutes.

Season with soy sauce and turn off the heat. Add the sesame seeds and bonito flakes, stir to mix well and serve.

◥ *Stir-fried chicken mince with rakkyo.*
◀ *A shop counter showing the wide variety of pickles on offer.*

Rakkyo to tori-niku soboro

[STIR-FRIED CHICKEN MINCE WITH RAKKYO]

Soboro is a unique term for cooked mince made from ingredients such as meat, fish, and shellfish. It is often served on top of plain boiled rice.

Serves 4

4 oz. rakkyo
3 tablespoons rakkyo's sweet pickling vinegar
1 tablespoon vegetable oil
10 oz. ground chicken
1 red chile, seeded and finely chopped
1 tablespoon saké
2 tablespoons mirin
3 tablespoons soy sauce
4 bowls plain boiled rice

Take the rakkyo out of its bottle and reserve the vinegar. Chop very finely. Heat a wok or skillet over medium heat and add the oil. Cook the ground chicken for 5 minutes and reduce the heat to low.

Add the chopped chile, saké, mirin, soy sauce, and 3 tablespoons of the reserved vinegar, and mix well. Turn off the heat, add the chopped rakkyo and stir to mix. Serve on a bowl of boiled rice.

The Japanese archipelago stretches from the northern tip of Hokkaido (the equivalent latitude to Seattle or Milan) to the southernmost edge of Okinawa (the same latitude as Havana or the Canary Islands), and is sandwiched between the cold currents of the Sea of Japan on the west and the warm currents of the Pacific on the east. In addition to this climatic range, Japan has four well-defined seasons and a varied geography (three-quarters of the country is mountainous and covered with forest, while the rest is lowland and coastal), so is blessed with a variety of fruit and nuts, ranging from the apples of Aomori prefecture to the sub-tropical fruit, such as pineapples and coconuts, grown on the island of Okinawa. In the Japanese kitchen, fruit is eaten either fresh as a dessert or used to make traditional Japanese confectionery called wagashi.

11 Fruit & nuts

柿 Kaki [PERSIMMON]

The persimmon tree is thought to be native to Japan and, having grown there since prehistoric times, it features in many Japanese folk tales. Its naked branches laden with bright orange fruit against the background of a clear blue sky is a typical autumn scene in the Japanese countryside and the persimmon symbolizes the fall in many religious festivals. As a child, I remember climbing persimmon trees to get the biggest and ripest fruit, which always seemed to grow at the top.

How it grows Some 1,000 varieties are found in eastern Asia, and the persimmon is grown both commercially and domestically almost throughout Japan, although the sweet varieties tend to prefer the slightly warmer climate in the south. The fruit is harvested from October to December.

Appearance and taste There are two basic types: sweet and bitter. Both varieties contain bitter tannin when the fruit are unripe, and in the bitter varieties this remains the case even when they are ripe, making them inedible without processing. The persimmon looks almost identical to the Sharon fruit, measuring about 4 inches in diameter with a hard, shiny, deep orange skin. Some varieties are egg-shaped while the most common is slightly flattened and cuboid. The flesh is dense and sometimes crunchy, pale to bright orange in color, with or without several flat brown stones inside. In the West, you are most likely to find the variety called Jiro or Fuyo.

Health benefits Kaki is rich in vitamin A (carotene), which helps to ward off cancer, and vitamin C, which lowers blood pressure and works as an antidote for hangovers.

Culinary uses The sweet varieties are eaten fresh, while the bitter varieties are often dried and eaten like figs. The tannin of the bitter varieties is extracted and used in saké brewing.

Kaki no shiro ae
[WHITE HARMONY OF PERSIMMON]

You may wonder what I mean by 'white harmony.' In the Japanese kitchen, when something is being coated with another ingredient, we do not say we are 'mixing' them but use the word *aeru*, which means 'to unite.' In other words, we harmonize the two ingredients. In this recipe, three autumnal ingredients—persimmon, shungiku, and shimeji mushrooms—are harmonized with white tofu.

Serves 4
1 block 'cotton' tofu (firm variety), drained
2 oz. shimeji mushrooms, separated, stalks removed
8 fl oz. (1 cup) dashi broth (see p.169)
1 tablespoon light soy sauce
1 tablespoon saké
4 oz. shungiku mushrooms
1 tablespoon granulated sugar
1 teaspoon light soy sauce
1 tablespoon light cream
1 persimmon, peeled and chopped, any pits removed

Start by draining the tofu. Sandwich it between two small chopping boards or plates with a little weight on top and let it drain for at least 30 minutes.

Put the shimeji mushrooms in a saucepan with the dashi broth, soy sauce, and saké and cook until the mushrooms are soft. Let cool and drain well.

Blanch the shungiku, drain well and chop into 1-inch lengths. Put the drained tofu in a bowl and mash it with a fork. Add the sugar, soy sauce, and cream and mix well to a creamy consistency. Combine the chopped persimmon and the mushrooms with the tofu mixture, divide between 4 dishes and serve.

梨 Nashi [JAPANESE PEAR]

Nashi probably originated in China. The oldest record of it dates back to the early tenth century but it was almost certainly grown in Japan before then.

How it grows Nashi is grown throughout Japan. The trees tend to be kept to about 6 feet to protect them from typhoons and strong winds and have beautiful pure white blossom in spring. They fruit between July and October. There are some 10 varieties and crossbreeds grown in Japan, of which the most popular ones are Nijuseiki meaning 'twentieth century,' Chojuro and Kosui.

Appearance and taste Japanese pears are round, resembling large apples with pale yellow, greenish-yellow, or golden skins, and weigh around 10 ounces, depending on the variety. The crunchy flesh is off-white and grainy in texture, and very juicy.

Health benefits In Chinese herbal medicine, nashi is used to treat respiratory diseases and sore throats. It is also used to bring down high fevers.

Culinary uses Nashi is sometimes used to make jam or fermented to make an alcoholic drink, but it is mostly eaten raw as an hors d'oeuvre or dessert.

▲ *A nashi orchard.*

Nashi no aka wine ni

[JAPANESE PEARS IN RED WINE]

This is inspired by Western poached pears. It is better prepared the night before to let the flavors develop.

Serves 4
1 bottle red wine
10 oz. (1¼ cups) sugar
2 lemons, sliced
4 nashi, peeled
To decorate
4 mint leaves

Heat the wine in a saucepan and add the sugar, stirring until it dissolves. Next add the lemon slices.

Place the peeled pears in the saucepan and simmer gently for 30 minutes. Turn off the heat and leave the pears in the saucepan to cool down overnight.

Serve the pears with a little of the liquid in which they were cooked and decorate with mint leaves.

梅 Ume [JAPANESE PLUM]

Ume is one of Japan's oldest fruits. It originated in China, and spread no further than China, Korea, Taiwan, and Japan. Ume has an important place in Japanese culture—it is one of the three auspicious plants, along with pine and bamboo—and its beautiful blossom has long been loved by the Japanese, as countless poems and paintings testify.

How it grows Botanically, the Japanese plum belongs to the rose family. There are some 300 varieties, which are broadly categorized as ornamental or fruit-bearing. Ume blossoms in late winter and early spring and the fruit ripen any time between late May and July.

Appearance and taste The fruit are about the size of golf balls, weighing around ¾–1¼ ounces, depending on the variety. Like apricots, ume change from green to yellow with reddish patterns as they ripen but unlike apricots they are never eaten fresh. Not only do they taste too sharp to eat but their cores contain prussic acid, which can cause stomach upsets. Ume are pickled or made into jellies, and the juice is used in confectionery or made into an alcoholic drink. The most popular use by far is to make umeboshi (dried, salted, pickled plums). Umeboshi are red and slightly squashy, with a salty, citric taste.

Buying and storing In the West, ume are most

commonly found as umeboshi (pickled ume). They are sold in plastic packs or vacuum packs. Once opened, umeboshi will keep for up to several months in the refridgerator.

Health benefits Umeboshi make a powerful antiseptic and are good for the digestion—one umeboshi is traditionally eaten at breakfast as a pick-me-up.

Culinary uses The most basic form of Japanese packed lunch is called *hinomaru bento*: plain boiled rice with an umeboshi in the middle, to stop the rice from spoiling. It looks like the Japanese flag. Umeboshi are often served as a side dish to accompany plain boiled rice.

Umeboshi dressing

This refreshing salad dressing is a beautiful red color. I like serving it with a salad of canned tuna, hard-cooked eggs, and salad greens.

4 umeboshi, pitted and mashed
2 tablespoons rice vinegar or red wine vinegar
1 tablespoon granulated sugar
1 teaspoon soy sauce
4 tablespoons grapeseed oil

Put all the ingredients in a blender or food processor and combine. The dressing will keep for 1 week in the refridgerator.

蜜柑 Mikan [TANGERINE/SATSUMA/MANDARIN]

Mikan has become a popular winter fruit in the West, where it is known as a tangerine, satsuma, or mandarin. Believed to have originated in India, the mikan came to Japan from China at the same time as Buddhism. Today, Japan ranks as the world's third largest producer of mikan after China and Spain. Mikan is one of my favorite fruits: it keeps me happy and healthy throughout the winter with its shiny orange skin and juicy fruit packed with vitamin C.

How it grows One of mikan's English names—satsuma—comes from the old name for the coastal region of southwest Japan from where it was first exported. Mikan grow in the warmer parts of Japan, especially in the southwest coastal region that borders the Pacific Ocean and the sheltered Inland Sea. Many varieties and crossbreeds have been developed in Japan, but in general the trees are not dissimilar to orange trees. They flower in April or May, depending on the variety, and bear fruit from December until March.

Appearance and taste The average fruit weighs around 2 ounces with a glossy, bright orange skin. Mikan taste not dissimilar to oranges—refreshing and juicy with a citric flavor—but are easier to peel. The fruit is in segments with or without pips.

Health benefits Mikan are rich in minerals and vitamins —they are particularly high in vitamin C, which wards off colds in winter. Their juice is good for healthy skin.

Culinary uses Mikan is mostly eaten raw as a snack or dessert, although there is a demand for its juice. About 10 percent of domestic production is canned in syrup, while a very small amount is made into jellies and preserves.

Tangerine and watercress salad with sweet vinegar

I came up with this recipe one time when I had run out of oranges in my fruit basket and substituted mikan. Although I don't normally like mixing fruit with vegetables, I do think that the combination of mikan and watercress works very well.

Serves 4
4 mikan (tangerines)
½ white onion, peeled and finely sliced
7 oz. (1 bunch) watercress, trimmed
For the mikan dressing
Juice of 2 mikan
1 tablespoon granulated sugar
1 tablespoon rice vinegar
1 teaspoon light soy sauce

Peel the 4 mikan and separate their segments, peeling off the pith. Put the finely sliced onion in a bowl of cold water for 5 minutes and drain.

Mix all the ingredients for the dressing and set aside. Put the mikan, watercress, and onion in a large salad bowl, coat with the mikan dressing and serve.

林檎 Ringo [APPLE]

of apple is a regular feature in the Japanese lunch box. The rest are made into juice, or canned or preserved.

Japanese-style apple sauce

This is another of my invented recipes—fear not, it has been tested and I use it often with pork chops, soaked in a marinade of sake, soy sauce, and mirin for 30 minutes and then broiled or barbecued.

Serves 4
2 medium fuji apples, peeled and cored
1 teaspoon granulated sugar
2 tablespoons soy sauce
1 tablespoon cider vinegar
½ teaspoon sesame oil

Shred the apples, add all the other ingredients and mix well. Serve the apple sauce next to the cooked pork chops.

Ringo no filo zutsumi

[APPLE IN A PHYLLO ROLL]

This is an easier version of apple strudel using versatile, tissue-thin phyllo pastry sheets.

2 average sized apples, peeled and cored
4 tablespoons unsalted butter, melted
2 oz. (¼ cup) sugar
4 walnuts, lightly toasted and chopped
8 phyllo pastry sheets

Preheat the oven to 275°F. Cut the apples vertically into thin slices. Add half the melted butter to a skillet and sauté the apple for 2–3 minutes before adding the sugar. Cook until the slices are soft and lightly browned. Turn off the heat, add the chopped walnuts and set aside.

Lay out one phyllo sheet, brush it with melted butter and lay another sheet on top. Place a quarter of the apple on the lower edge and roll towards the top. Repeat the process to make 4 rolls.

Brush the outside with more melted butter and bake on a baking tray for 10 minutes or until the apple rolls are golden.

Apples are one of the most commonly grown fruits in the world: there are some 10,000 varieties in existence. Botanically apples belong to the rose family and are believed to have originated in central Asia, making their way from China to Japan in the twelfth century. Today, there are nearly 1,500 varieties grown in the country though only 20 varieties are grown commercially. Most of the varieties grown now in Japan were introduced from America in the nineteenth century. The Meiji government actively encouraged the cultivation of apples and many crossbreeds have been developed since. Apples are grown all over the country (except on Okinawa Island in the south) but the larger producers are concentrated in the cooler regions, with Aomori prefecture, the northernmost county on the main island, producing half the domestic supply.

Health benefits Apples help maintain a healthy digestive system and can fight fatigue. They are also effective against constipation if eaten raw with the skin on.

Culinary uses About 80 percent of apples grown in Japan are eaten raw, as a dessert or snack—a slice

柚 Yuzu [YUZU]

There is a saying in Japanese: 'Peaches and sweet chestnuts take three years, persimmon takes eight years but silly yuzu takes eighteen years to bear fruit.' Although it originated in China, yuzu is the most famous and popular of the citrus fruits used in Japanese cooking.

How it grows Yuzu trees tolerate cold conditions. They resemble tangerine trees and have similar fruit, which ripen in November.

Appearance and taste The fruit are bright yellow, weigh about 4 ounces, have a thick, firm skin and are in season throughout the winter. Yuzu have a unique, penetrating aroma with a clean citrus flavor. Although the juice is widely used in Japanese cooking, the fruit are too sharp to eat.

Buying and storing In the West, fresh yuzu are difficult to come by, but the juice is sold in bottles in Japanese stores. A citrus flavoring called *ponzu*, which resembles yuzu juice, is also sold. Both pure juice and *ponzu* keep well in the refrigerator; but once opened they slowly lose their flavor, so you should use them within a few months.

Health benefits Yuzu is rich in vitamin C and helps to smooth the skin. Try putting a whole yuzu in a hot bath: it is good for your skin, soothes stiff shoulders, eases back pain, and warms up the whole body.

Culinary uses Although the fruit is not edible, both its rind and juice are used extensively in Japanese cooking. Small pieces of skin are sliced thinly or shredded and used to garnish soups, simmered dishes, salads, pickles, relishes, and Japanese candies. The juice is used to make salad dressings and brings an extra flavor to clear soups and dipping sauces. A whole fruit cut in half with the flesh scooped out makes an attractive serving cup. The shredded skin and juice are made into a paste called *yuzu kosho*, which is used as a condiment for many dishes, especially udon noodle dishes.

Yuzu dressing

Yuzu has achieved international acclaim and these days it is used in many different cuisines, even French and Italian. Yuzu's level of acidity is not as high as that of lemon but the fragrance is far superior. It makes an excellent salad dressing.

4 tablespoons bottled yuzu juice
2 tablespoons soy sauce
1 teaspoon granulated sugar
½ teaspoon freshly ground black pepper
4 tablespoons grapeseed oil

Mix all the ingredients in a lidded jar and shake well. It will keep for 2 weeks in the refrigerator.

栗 Kuri [SWEET CHESTNUT]

There are four basic varieties of sweet chestnuts in the world: Japanese, Chinese, American, and European. The history of the Japanese using sweet chestnuts goes back to prehistoric times, when, according to archaeological evidence, my early Japanese ancestors gathered and ate kuri.

How it grows Kuri belongs to the Japanese beech family and is relatively fast growing. In Japan, many varieties have been developed from the native *shiba guri*. The trees flower between June and July and the nuts are harvested from September until late October.

Appearance and taste Kuri come in sets of two or three, inside a prickly protective shell. A ripe kuri has a hard brown husk, inside which there is another thin but rather bitter skin. The flesh of kuri is ivory and the sweetness increases with cooking.

Health benefits Sweet chestnuts are nearly 40 percent carbohydrate, which makes it a good source of energy. It has a high content of vitamin B1, so is good for anyone suffering from beriberi or general fatigue.

Buying and storing Choose kuri that look glossy and feel solid. If refrigerated in plastic bags, they should keep for up to a month. Peeled kuri are available in cans, both cooked and uncooked.

Culinary uses Kuri is one of the most useful ingredients in the Japanese kitchen. It can be eaten broiled, roasted or boiled as a snack and is widely used as a filling in traditional Japanese candies. Often used as a symbol of the fall in *kaiseki ryori* (see p.18), kuri also appears with a sweet glaze as *kuri kinton*, one of the traditional dishes eaten at Japanese New Year. *Kuri gohan* (kuri cooked with rice) is a popular fall dish.

Kuri gohan

[BOILED RICE WITH SWEET CHESTNUTS]

This brings back many happy memories of my childhood. My mother and grandmother would spend hours peeling the kuri—peeling sweet chestnuts is not the easiest job—so I have cheated a little here by using ready peeled ones.

Serves 4
5 oz. (¾ cup) rice, washed, rinsed and drained
2 oz. (¼ cup) glutinous rice, washed, rinsed and drained
8 fl oz. (1 cup) water
12 ready peeled sweet chestnuts
½ teaspoon salt
2 tablespoons mirin

Put the two kinds of rice with the water in a heavy-based saucepan with a tight-fitting lid over a low heat.

Let the water come to a boil, then quickly add the chestnuts, salt, and mirin, and put the lid back on.

Increase the heat to medium for 5 minutes, then turn off and let steam for 10 minutes more before serving.

銀杏 Ginnan [GINGKO NUTS]

Gingko trees originated in south China and are believed to have come to Japan before the Ice Age, when the Japanese archipelago was still joined to the Asian landmass. Gingko trees are tough, largely invulnerable to pests and, most amazingly, fire-resistant. It is not uncommon to find huge, blackened gingko trees growing in temple grounds in Japan; in fact, many of those old giants were planted as fire barriers to protect the temple buildings. One famous tree even survived the atomic blast in Hiroshima.

How it grows Gingko trees are either male or female, blossoming in spring and bearing fruit in late September and October.

Appearance and taste A gingko nut is about the size of a fingertip, green when fresh, with a rather unpleasant odor. When cooked it has a distinctive milky flavor with a faint touch of bitterness that is appreciated by connoisseurs. The nut has a hard, off-white, protective shell and can irritate the skin.

Buying and storing Gingko nuts are sold uncooked in their shells or peeled and blanched in vacuum packs or cans. Whole gingko nuts in their shells keep for up to a month in a cool, dry place out of direct sunlight. Once peeled, they must be used within a few days.

Health benefits Gingko nuts are high in sugar, fat, and protein but, unusually for nuts, are also rich in vitamin B, C and carotene. They are known to be effective in lowering blood pressure, and have energizing and aphrodisiac qualities. More unusually, toasted gingko nuts are given to people suffering from an over-active bladder and children with bed-wetting problems.

Culinary uses Salted, roasted gingko nuts are a popular accompaniment to saké. They are often used to give extra flavor and texture to hot-pot dishes and *chawanmushi* (savory steamed egg dishes).

Iri ginnan
[TOASTED GINGKO NUTS WITH SALT]

I have a wonderful memory of gingko nuts. A group of us were firing our pots in an ancient pottery kiln up a mountain. We worked in shifts, manning the kiln for several days and nights, feeding it with a large pile of logs. One night, between 2 and 6 am, during one of my shifts, the master potter brought out a large bottle of saké, and as we sat drinking we got rather peckish. Fortunately he had an ancient gingko tree in his garden full of nuts. You can probably guess what happened to those gingko nuts and the large bottle of saké!

20 gingko nuts
8 oz. (1 cup) salt

Gently shell each nut with a pair of nutcrackers or pliers. Boil the shelled nuts for 3 minutes, then drain. Add the salt to the saucepan and keep shaking over a high heat until the salt becomes dry. Serve on a bed of salt—this will help to keep the nuts warm.

In the Japanese kitchen, herbs and spices are used in quite different ways from the European kitchen, where they are cooked with the main ingredients or in sauces. Japanese herbs and spices are more often used uncooked and are served separately or as garnishes to give an additional aroma, flavor, texture, or color to a dish.

12 Herbs & spices

紫蘇 Shiso [PERILLA LEAVES]

Many Westerners' first encounter with shiso is a little strange or inconsequential: a leaf of shiso is placed delicately on the corner of a plate of sashimi or shredded shiso is laid on top of a salad. It is one of the most commonly used herbs in Japan.

How it grows Shiso is a tender annual. A bushy plant, it comes in two main varieties—red leaved and green leaved—but there are many crossbreeds that have speckles of one color or the other.

Appearance and taste Shiso leaves, whether red or green, bear a close resemblance to stinging nettles, with the leaves of the red variety ranging from pink to deep red to rich copper. The size of the plant depends on the growing conditions and the climate but the red varieties tend to be taller: 18–36 inches. The flavor of shiso is distinctive and unique—hard, in fact, to describe. It is peppery, minty, and citrussy, a cross between lemon, basil, and cilantro.

Health benefits The medicinal value of shiso has been long appreciated in Japan. Its unique, pungent fragrance has antiseptic and preservative properties. It also increases appetite and stimulates digestion, and works as a natural antidote to food poisoning from fish and shellfish. It is rich in vitamins B, C, and E, as well as calcium, iron, and other minerals. Shiso-flavored shochu is a natural remedy for anemia. Anyone who suffers from poor blood circulation, irregular periods, neuralgia or back pain may want to try putting a few shiso leaves in the bath.

Buying and storing Shiso leaves are delicate and easily discolor. Store them covered in the refrigerator and use within a few days.

Culinary uses Shiso's main use in the Japanese kitchen is as a seasoning herb and garnish for dishes such as sashimi, tempura, salads, and broiled fish. All parts of the plant—seeds, sprouted seeds, tiny seedlings, mature leaves and flowering spikes—are used. The red leaves not only add color to salads or vinegary starters, they also turn juices a beautiful pink. Red shiso leaves and seeds are widely used in making pickles, while green leaves are often used as an edible wrapping for other ingredients such as beef, pork or fish. Leaves, seeds, and other parts are also dried, ground, and mixed with salt to make *furikake*, a flavoring sprinkled on rice.

Ao-ziso no dressing
[GREEN SHISO DRESSING]

In Japan, one can buy many kinds of ready-made dressings but there is nothing quite as good as a freshly made salad dressing.

10 leaves fresh green shiso, finely chopped
4 tablespoons soy sauce
4 tablespoons rice vinegar
1 tablespoon granulated sugar
½ teaspoon salt
½ teaspoon freshly ground black pepper
4 tablespoons grapeseed oil

Put all the ingredients in a lidded jar and shake vigorously to mix. The dressing will keep for a few days in the refrigerator before the shiso leaves discolor.

Aka jiso gohan

[RICE WITH PURPLE PERILLA]

Both my grandmothers and mother successfully grew green and purple varieties of shiso in their gardens—I have tried and failed many times. In the West, however, crushed dried perilla leaves are available from Japanese stores. This is an easy dish to prepare using the purple variety.

1 lb. (6–7 cups) cooked rice
2 tablespoons saké
4 tablespoons crushed dried purple shiso
2 tablespoons toasted sesame seeds
4 tablespoons chirimen-jako (dried sardines)

Wet a large mixing bowl with water to stop the rice sticking to the bowl. Add the rice and drizzle in the saké. Then add the shiso, sesame seeds, and chirimen-jako and mix well. Divide between 4 rice bowls and serve.

◄ *Rice with purple perilla.*

三つ葉 Mitsuba [MITSUBA]

Mitsuba means 'three leaves' and is found in the wild across China, Japan, and North America. It is closely related to honeworth, a North American wild plant that was used by the Native Americans as a medicinal herb and vegetable. In Japan, it is regarded as one of the most important native vegetables and features in a wide range of traditional Japanese cooking.

How it grows Mitsuba is essentially a cool-climate hardy perennial which prefers damp, lightly shaded conditions. In Japan, there are three basic varieties: young green-stem mitsuba, root mitsuba, and blanched mitsuba. The young green-stems are sown from spring to the early fall and are harvested just 60 days after sowing. Nowadays, they are usually grown in greenhouses. The root variety is sown in spring and harvested early in its second year. Commercial growers in Japan use various methods to tenderize or blanch mitsuba, the traditional method being to sow it in spring, then lift and move it into darkened beds. It can also be earthed up during winter and harvested the following spring.

Appearance and taste The average height of a mature mitsuba plant is 12 inches. The saw-toothed leaves range from light to dark green, are slightly heart-shaped and about 3 inches wide. They grow in pretty groups of three at the end of long stems and have a delightful flavor not unlike a mixture of mild celery, parsley, and angelica.

Health benefits Mitsuba has a particularly high vitamin C content and is rich in carotene, which the liver converts to vitamin A. Its refreshing aroma stimulates the appetite and helps digestion.

Buying and storing Mitsuba is sold in small bunches with trimmed roots. If you keep the roots moist with wet tissue and store it in a plastic bag in the refrigerator, it will last for a few days.

Culinary uses Mitsuba's main attraction is its unique and strong aroma; only a small amount needs to be added to clear soups or tempura dishes. The stalk makes a very elegant tie for food—plunging it into boiling water softens it and makes it more flexible.

Mitsuba to buta-niku no itame-mono

[STIR-FRIED MITSUBA WITH PORK]

This is my adaptation of what my mother used to make with her home-grown mitsuba and the very thin slices of pork that are available only in Japan.

4 oz. ground pork
1 tablespoon saké
1 tablespoon sesame oil
2 tablespoons rice vinegar
3 tablespoons soy sauce
1 bunch mitsuba, trimmed and roughly chopped
Salt and pepper to taste

Sprinkle the pork with the saké and set aside. Heat the oil in a skillet over a medium heat and cook the pork for 3 minutes. Season with the vinegar and soy sauce, add the chopped mitsuba and stir-fry for 1 minute. Turn off the heat and adjust the seasoning with salt and pepper.

茗荷 Myoga [MYOGA]

Myoga belongs to the ginger family and is a perennial plant believed to originate in either tropical Asia or Japan. There is an endearing legend about one of the ten disciples of Buddha who was so forgetful that he had to carry a paper tag bearing his name around his neck. He was diligent, however, and dutifully learnt all the teachings of Buddha. When he died, strange looking plants grew around his grave and, according to the legend, people named these plants myoga (meaning 'carrying name'). I was forbidden to eat this delicious and aromatic vegetable when I was a child, as my parents feared that I might become more forgetful than I was already!

How it grows Myoga prefers warm, shady conditions, and in Japan it is found in the south, down to the island of Okinawa. Although it was cultivated in ancient China, it has now become a uniquely Japanese vegetable. The part eaten is actually the bud of the plant, which grows directly from the root stem. The cultivated varieties are allowed only brief exposure to the sunlight to protect their pretty pale pink coloring.

Appearance and taste Myoga looks not dissimilar to an unopened gladiolus bud. Very pale pink, it smells and tastes quite unique, more like a medicinal herb than a vegetable, with its distinctive, almost antiseptic aroma. It has a crunchy texture and—too bitter to eat raw—normally comes pickled, which gives it a milder taste and refreshing scent.

Health benefits Myoga is a stimulant: it keeps one alert and stimulates the appetite and metabolism. My grandmother used to put chopped up myoga in an old sock in her bath to relieve her stiff shoulder.

Buying and storing If you are fortunate enough to come across fresh myoga in a specialist Japanese store, treat it like ginger root. Do not refrigerate it and use it within a few days before it loses its precious aroma.

Culinary uses Myoga is used in dipping sauces, tempura, and as a garnish for sashimi and other fish dishes.

Myoga in avocado

The familar smoothness of avocado is given a new twist by the refreshing flavor of myoga.

Serves 4
2 ripe avocados, halved, pit removed
2 teaspoons rice vinegar
8 myoga, very finely sliced
4 teaspoons soy sauce
2 teaspoons wasabi powder, mixed with the same
   amount of water

Put half an avocado in each serving dish and drizzle with the vinegar to prevent any discoloration. Put the myoga in a bowl of cold water and leave to stand for 10 minutes to refresh it and wash out the bitterness.

Drain, divide into 4 equal portions and put a portion in the center of each avocado half. Drizzle with the soy sauce, top with a small mound of wasabi paste and serve.

山葵 Wasabi [JAPANESE GREEN HORSERADISH]

Wasabi is otherwise known as *namida*, meaning tears—an apt name for Japan's most famously pungent spice. Although *wasabi* translates as 'mountain hollyhock' it is not related to the hollyhock: its English name is Japanese green horseradish. It is to be used with caution—in small quantities only—and should never be eaten as a dare.

How it grows Wasabi is a perennial aquatic plant that grows wild across temperate regions of Asia. In Japan it is found in shallow parts of remote mountain streams, but nowadays tends to be commercially cultivated using pure, clean water from the mountains with the temperature kept at a constant 53–55°F.

Appearance and taste Wasabi plants grow 12–16 inches tall and have glossy, heart-shaped, coarse-toothed leaves. The rhizomes (the size of an average carrot) are green and knobbly. Although the whole plant has a pungent horseradish-like smell, it is the root part that is used in the Japanese kitchen. The taste and aroma increases when the root is shredded.

Health benefits The unique tear-jerking fumes of wasabi stimulate the appetite, aid digestion and are a natural diuretic. Wasabi is a powerful antibacterial agent and neutralizes fishy smells.

Buying and storing Fresh wasabi roots are expensive and hard to obtain in the West. If you do get hold of some, they will keep for up to a week if you wrap them in damp paper towels and put them in the refrigerator in a plastic bag. Outside Japan, wasabi is most likely to be found as a dry powder or in plastic tubes ready-mixed. Although the tube form is easier to use, it starts to lose its aroma and pungency as soon as it is opened and very often contains artificial colorings. Once opened, the tube should be kept refrigerated and used as soon as possible. Personally, I recommend that you buy dry, powdered wasabi in small cans or sachets. It lasts almost indefinitely if stored in a cool, dry cupboard. Make up only what you need at the time, mixing it with an equal amount of tepid water to make a cream cheese-like paste, and leave it to stand for at least 10 minutes so that the full flavor and aroma have time to develop. Once mixed, it should be used the same day.

Culinary uses Wasabi and raw fish are inseparable. A small amount of wasabi paste is always used for sashimi and sushi. It is also used for pickling vegetables and to make refreshing salad dressings.

◤ *Fresh wasabi roots.*
▼ *An aquatic wasabi farm.*

Wasabi no dressing

[WASABI SALAD DRESSING]

This is a refreshing dressing for seafood salads, broiled fish, or indeed almost any fish and shellfish dishes. It contains dashi broth so does not keep long—make a fresh batch each time you need it, in small quantities.

Makes about ½ pint (1¼ cups)
3 tablespoons wasabi powder
4 fl oz. (½ cup) dashi broth (see p.169)
2 tablespoons saké
2 tablespoons mirin
4 tablespoons soy sauce

First, dissolve the wasabi powder in the dashi broth. Put the broth with the rest of the ingredients in a lidded jar and shake well to mix.

Wasabi and avocado dip

This is a simple combination of mayonnaise, wasabi and ripe avocado. You may vary the amount of wasabi according to your heat tolerance.

1 very ripe avocado
2 tablespoons good quality mayonnaise
2 tablespoons wasabi powder, mixed with the same
    amount of water
1 teaspoon light soy sauce
Salt

Peel the avocado and remove the pit. Roughly mash and put in a food processor. Add the rest of the ingredients and process until the mixture is smooth and creamy. Season with salt if necessary.

▲ *Wasabi and avocado dip.*

生姜 Shoga [GINGER ROOT]

Appearance and taste Fresh ginger roots have a golden skin. The rhizomes vary in size and grow in a haphazard manner, rather like a child's drawing of a cloud, with many knobbly extensions growing out of the main rhizome. Ginger has a refreshingly clean and pungent aroma. Young ginger roots are tender and juicy, while older roots tend to be fibrous and hotter in taste.

Health benefits Ginger has powerful, natural antibacterial properties and is always served with sushi, sashimi, and other fish dishes. Ginger also aids digestion—a tablespoonful of ginger juice is an effective home remedy for diarrhoea and stomach ache. My grandmother often used to ease her rheumatism or backaches with a pack containing shredded ginger and flour, and would ward off colds with a cup of hot ginger tea with a drop of honey. Ginger is also known to stimulate the circulation.

Buying and storing Nowadays, fresh ginger is available all year round. Choose firm, smooth skinned roots that feel weighty; avoid ones with dry wrinkled skin that feel floppy. Stored in a cool, dry place, ginger bought in prime condition should last for up to two weeks.

An indispensable ingredient in the Japanese kitchen, ginger is a perennial plant indigenous to the Indian subcontinent and Malaysia. It has long been cultivated in Asia and has become of the most important herbal vegetables in the world. It was introduced to Japan from China in the third century or earlier and has been valued ever since as a medicinal and seasoning vegetable.

How it grows Ginger is a curious plant that rarely flowers. It is cultivated by the propagation of its rhizomes. The plant grows to about 2 feet tall and has long, narrow, pointed leaves. Young ginger is harvested in summer after 3–4 months' growth, while the plants are still green; more mature ginger, 7–10 months old, is harvested in the fall, when the skin on the rhizome has set and it will store well. In addition to root ginger, Japan boasts a variety called *ha-shoga* (leaf ginger), which is harvested with its green leaves in early summer and pickled with the short stalks still attached. A third variety is called *me-shoga* (sprout ginger) or *nanka-shoga* (tenderized ginger). This is also pickled and used to garnish fish dishes.

Culinary uses Ginger is often pickled on its own or with other ingredients. Pickled ginger is an essential accompaniment to sushi, sashimi, and many other fish dishes. Shredded ginger is used to make dipping sauces for broiled meat, tempura and many hot pot-dishes, such as *shabu-shabu*.

Shoga gohan
[BOILED RICE WITH GINGER]

In Japan, in early summer, ginger comes into season. New ginger is pale cream with pinkish tips and, like new potatoes, has virtually no skin. The taste is not as hot as older ginger. Mildly sweet and very juicy, it is just what you want on a hot and humid summer's day.

Serves 4
2 sheets deep-fried tofu
14 oz. (2 cups) rice, washed, rinsed and drained
17 fl oz. (2 cups) water

4 oz. (8-inch piece) fresh ginger root, peeled and finely ground

4 tablespoons saké

2 tablespoons light soy sauce

1 teaspoon salt

4 oz. (¾–1 cup) eda-mame (fresh green soybeans) or fresh peas, boiled and shelled

Put the sheets of deep-fried tofu in a colander and pour boiling water over them to remove the oil.

Put the rice, water, ginger, tofu, saké, and soy sauce in a heavy clay pot or cast iron saucepan with a tight-fitting lid. Cook over low heat.

When you can hear the water bubbling, remove the lid, turn the heat up to high for 3 minutes and add the salt and shelled eda-mame.

Turn off the heat, put the lid back on and leave to steam for 10 minutes more. Stir and serve.

Spicy sushi ginger and miso pesto

I don't know where the recipe for this pesto came from but there is always a jar of it in my refrigerator. It keeps for a few weeks. It is great to have these homemade, ready to use sauces so that you can prepare a lunch or supper at a moment's notice.

4 tablespoons pickled sushi ginger, drained

1 tablespoon light colored miso paste

1 tablespoon saké

1 teaspoon light soy sauce

1 teaspoon granulated sugar

Put all the ingredients in a food processor and whizz until smooth. A favorite use for this pesto is to dress finely sliced, poached chicken breast served on a bed of watercress. It is also good drizzled over pan-fried tofu.

▸ *Boiled rice with ginger.*

Shoga-joyu

[GINGER DIPPING SAUCE]

This spicy sauce is good with any deep-fried dishes—try it with *satsuma-age* or *hanpen* (see p.170). It will keep for about a week if refrigerated.

4 tablespoons soy sauce

4 tablespoons rice vinegar

2 tablespoons finely shredded ginger root

2 teaspoons granulated sugar

1 teaspoon dry chili flakes

Put all the ingredients in a jar, shake to combine and keep in the refrigerator until needed.

七味唐辛子 Shichimi togarashi

[JAPANESE SEVEN-SPICE CHILI PEPPER]

I had a little difficulty deciding in which category to place this ingredient. Shichimi togarashi literally means 'seven flavor Chinese chili pepper.' Originally imported, it has become an integral part of the traditional Japanese kitchen yet still retains its foreign identity—a classic example of how the Japanese adopt foreign ingredients and modify them to suite their taste. Red chiles originated in Central America, where they were discovered by Christopher Columbus. They were introduced to both Europe and Asia in the sixteenth century and were soon being cultivated all over Asia. The Portuguese brought red peppers to China, from where they made their way to Japan in the sixteenth century.

How it is made As the name implies, shichimi togarashi contains seven different ingredients—usually dried red chili powder, pepper, dried ground tangerine skin, poppy seeds, hemp seeds, dried seaweed, and roasted white and black sesame seeds—but the combination varies from one blender to another. Sometimes it contains other ingredients, such as dried ginger or shiso powder, so the flavor and, above all, how hot it is, can vary greatly. I have memories of my parents sampling different blends, going from one stall to another in the grounds of a temple at one of Japan's many festivals. The mixture was sold in a short bamboo container.

Buying and storing Nowadays it is sold in small glass bottles and will keep for up to a year if stored in a cool, dry cupboard.

Culinary uses In Japan, shichimi togarashi is used like salt and pepper. A small pot of shichimi togarashi is found on every table in noodle houses all around Japan.

Karashi joyu

[SPICY SOY GLAZE]

This is a handy glaze to have ready in your kitchen— brush this on chicken, meat, or oily fish such as mackerel and sardines. It will certainly spice up your barbecues.

4 tablespoons soy sauce
4 tablespoons mirin
2 tablespoons saké
2–4 teaspoons shichimi togarashi (adjust the amount according to taste)

Mix all the ingredients together in a lidded jar. It will keep for 2 weeks if refrigerated.

▲ *Women shopping at a street market in a hot spring resort.*

胡麻 Goma [SESAME SEEDS]

Sesame is believed to have originated in either India or Egypt and has been cultivated in Japan since prehistoric times. Large quantities of sesame seeds have been found in 10,000-year-old archaeological sites.

How it grows Sesame is an attractive tropical and sub-tropical annual that grows 2–3 feet tall. It has pale pink/purple flowers and needs a long hot growing season. The oval pods have either 4 or 8 compartments, with each compartment containing between 9 and 20 seeds.

Appearance and taste Tear-shaped and very small, sesame seeds measure only ⅟₁₆-inch long. Although the outside of the seeds varies from white to golden brown to black, the inside is always white. Both the flavor and aroma are intensified when the seeds are heated or crushed. Rich and crunchy, they have an intensely nutty smell.

Health benefits Sesame seeds ensure long life. Rich in high-quality vegetable protein and cholesterol-free fat, they also have a high vitamin, mineral, and fiber content.

Buying and storing Ready toasted sesame seeds can be bought in Japanese stores. The seeds keep very well for several months if stored in an airtight container in a cool, dry cupboard.

Culinary uses Sesame oil is used extensively in Japanese cooking: in tempura and other deep-fried dishes, and in stir-fries too. Black sesame seeds are mixed with salt to make *goma shio*, which is sprinkled over plain boiled rice. Crushed white sesame seeds make an excellent paste with which to dress cooked vegetables and make *goma dofu* (sesame seed tofu). Both black and white seeds are also used to make Japanese candies but they are more widely encountered as a spice and garnish.

Goma dare
[SESAME DRESSING FOR COOKED VEGETABLES]

This dressing is quick and easy to put together and makes any cooked vegetable, such as fine beans or French beans, a little more exciting. I often use this recipe when my family is tiring of a glut of home-grown vegetables.

3 tablespoons toasted sesame seeds
½ garlic clove, crushed (optional)
2 tablespoons mirin
3 tablespoons soy sauce

Put the sesame seeds in a mortar and grind them with a pestle until you have a paste. Add the garlic, mirin, and soy sauce and continue to grind until the ingredients are well blended.

山椒 Sansho [JAPANESE PEPPER]

According to a Japanese proverb, sansho describes someone who is small but highly effective.

How it grows Sansho is a low-growing deciduous tree that belongs to the tangerine family. Short prickly bushes of it grow in the wild all over Japan, China, and along the Korean peninsula and, thanks to its dual roles as home medicine and spice, it is found in many Japanese gardens too.

Appearance and taste There is a use for almost every part of the plant. The young leaf shoots that appear in spring are called *kinome*, meaning 'shoots of trees.' No longer than 2 inches, the middle stems have 6–10 pairs of small leaves with one leaf at the end, which taste refreshingly peppery with citrus and mint undertones. Tiny greenish-yellow flowers called *hana sansho* are borne in the spring, and, like the *kinome*, smell faintly minty. Bitterly pungent little berries called *sansho no mi* or *tsubu sansho* appear in early summer. When these bitter berries ripen in autumn, they are discarded but the seedpods are dried and ground to make sansho powder, which is light brown with a soothing minty aroma, not nearly as pungent as black or red pepper.

Buying and storing Outside Japan, sansho is most easily obtained in powder form, in small bottles or cans. If you store it in a cool, dry cupboard, it won't go off, though it slowly loses its pungency once opened and should be used within a few months.

Health benefits Sansho has long been considered an effective home remedy for digestive problems, diarrhoea, stomach cramps, and even the common cold. Sansho powder relieves toothache and sore gums, while the juice from sansho leaves makes a soothing lotion for insect bites.

Culinary uses Powdered sansho is used in much the same way as pepper in the West, most famously with broiled eel fillets. It is also a vital ingredient in shichimi togarashi (Japanese seven-spice chili pepper, see p.210). Fresh *kinome* (sansho shoots) and *hana sansho* (sansho flowers) are used to garnish simmered dishes, clear soups, sashimi, and broiled fish.

▼ *A well-stocked herb, spice and grocery store.*

Boiled quails' eggs with salt and sansho

Quails' eggs are an ideal size for picnics and canapés. Here is a Japanese alternative to the traditional accompaniment of celery salt.

12 quails' eggs
1 tablespoon salt
1 teaspoon sansho pepper

Place the eggs in a saucepan and add enough water to cover. Heat the water over a medium heat and take the saucepan off the heat when the water begins to boil. Leave the saucepan covered for 2 minutes, then add cold water to bring down the temperature.

Gently roll the eggs on the worktop and peel. Mix salt and sansho pepper in a small dish and offer it with the peeled eggs.

In the Japanese kitchen salt and miso are the two oldest and most important seasonings, closely followed by world-famous soy sauce. Many sauces and seasonings are available ready-made; the following are the essential ones for preparing Japanese food.

13 Sauces & seasonings

塩 Shio [SALT]

Salt is the single most important seasoning ingredient in the world—it has no substitute. The history of salt in the Japanese kitchen is explained in detail at the beginning of the book (see pp.10–11).

How it is made There are no beds of rock salt in Japan, so all Japanese salt is obtained from seawater. Up until 1972, when Japan started using the modern and more economical electric ionization technique, it was common to see saltpans up and down the coast of the Seto Inland Sea.

Buying and storing Until 1997 all salt made and sold in Japan was controlled by a state monopoly. Today it is possible to buy many kinds of salt from all over the country. Salt keeps indefinitely if stored in cool, dry conditions.

Culinary uses In the Japanese kitchen, salt is the single most important ingredient, not only as a seasoning but also as a preservative and vital raw material for other products such as soy sauce and miso. It is used to draw out excess liquid and fasten color, and is a natural antiseptic.

Tai no shiogama-yaki
[SALT-BAKED PORGY]

I am unable to trace the origin of this curious method of cooking but I suspect it most probably came from China where cheap rock salt is widely available. Because the fish is wrapped in cheesecloth or Japanese paper, it does not taste too salty and remains succulent. The wasabi powder gives it extra flavor.

Serves 4
2 egg whites
1 lb. salt
4 tablespoons wasabi powder
1 whole porgy, about 1 lb., cleaned and gutted

In a dry clean bowl, whisk the egg whites until they reach the soft peak stage and add the salt and wasabi powder. Preheat the oven to 375°F.
 Wrap the fish in clean cheesecloth and line a baking sheet with aluminum foil. Spread one third of the egg mixture on the baking sheet and place the wrapped fish on it. Cover the fish with the rest of the egg mixture.
 Bake for 30–40 minutes, then crack open the baked salt, transfer the fish to a serving dish and serve.

▲ *A salt harvest.*

Nasu no shio-zuke

[SALT-PICKLED EGGPLANT]

Salt is widely used in pickling—it is, after all, the oldest preservative. One advantage of using salt is that it is a relatively quick process, taking 6 hours to 2 days; another advantage, in this recipe at least, is that the deep purple of the eggplant is perfectly preserved.

4 baby eggplant
1 tablespoon salt

Cut off the stems of the eggplant and cut them in 4, lengthways.

Rub salt all over them, especially over the skin, and lay them in a flat-bottomed plastic container. Pour in enough water to cover the eggplant and place a smaller lid over them.

Put a 2 lb. weight on top of the lid and leave for 6 hours. Pat the eggplant dry, chop roughly and serve.

醤油 Shoyu [SOY SAUCE]

Shoyu is arguably Japan's most famous seasoning ingredient. It goes back a long way and it is widely believed that the origin was an ancient fermented salt preserve called hishio. In 1254 a Zen Buddhist monk called Kakushin brought *Kinzanji-miso* from China and taught villagers in Yuasa in Kii prefecture how to make it. The villages soon discovered that the juice left at the bottom of the barrel was tasty and called it *tamari shoyu* (*tamari* means 'collected' and *shoyu* means literally 'oil of hishio'). By the mid sixteenth century the region had became a center for making soy sauce.

In 1587, the first light colored soy sauce, *usukuchi shoyu*, was made. It became widely used in Buddhist vegetarian cooking in Kyoto because it did not discolor other ingredients as dark soy sauce did. By the middle of the seventeenth century, the Tokugawa regime had established a powerful new federal government in Edo (present-day Tokyo) and many soy sauce brewers had moved to the Noda and Choshi areas, east of Tokyo, where they made a dark soy sauce called *koikuchi shoyu*. Today more than 80 percent of dark soy sauce, the most popular variety in Japan, is produced in Noda and Choshi.

There are five different varieties of soy sauce: the most popular *koikuchi shoyu* (dark soy sauce); the lighter colored *usukuchi shoyu* (popular in the Kansai region near Osaka and Kyoto); *tamari shoyu*. (the most familar in the West); *shiro shoyu* (a white soy sauce, rarely seen even in Japanese kitchens let alone in the West) and *saijikomi shoyu* (literally, second-time processed soy sauce).

How it is made The manufacturing process for the five different varieties is very similar. The main ingredients are soybeans, wheat, and salt (except that *tamari shoyu* contains no wheat). To make the darker variety, the soybeans are first washed, then steamed and mixed with crushed wheat. Malt bacteria are inserted and a moldy mixture called *shoyu koji* develops. Saltwater is added to the mixture and it is left to ferment—sometimes for more than a year—after which it is filtered and heated to stop further bacterial growth.

Appearance and taste The oxygen from the *koji* bacteria combines with the salt water to convert the protein from the soybeans into amino acids and the carbohydrate of the wheat into glucose. The remarkable workings of the *koji* bacteria determine the taste and flavor of each batch of soy sauce. Soy sauce comes in varying shades of brown and although it tastes quite salty to the unfamiliar palate, it is much less salty than it used be, as a result of increased awareness of heart disease. Shoyu has an appetizingly nutty aroma with a slightly sweet taste.

Buying and storing If you want to buy just one variety of shoyu, buy the all-purpose dark one. All commercial shoyu is pasteurized, so there is no need for refrigeration, but the flavor gradually deteriorates after the seal is broken and it is best to use it within a few months. Keep it in a cool, dry cupboard.

Health benefits The salt content of soy sauce varies according to the variety—*tamari* (the only one suitable for people on a wheat-free diet) is generally least salty, while the light colored variety is 18–19 percent salt. According to Japanese government guidelines, the maximum salt intake per day should be ½ oz., which is the equivalent of 4 tablespoons of soy sauce.

Culinary uses Soy sauce is the single most important ingredient in the Japanese kitchen and is used in almost every aspect of cooking, usually as a seasoning agent. Some recipes call for just a drop. This is known as *kakushi-aji* (hidden taste): the idea is not for the soy sauce to be discernable but to give the dish more depth. Soy sauce is also used as a natural deodorizer for fish and meat; as a marinade; and as a dipping sauce for raw fish or sushi. It makes an excellent base for salad dressing and sauces such as teriyaki.

◀ ◀ *Inspecting the fermentation process in a soy sauce factory.*

Sake no teriyaki

[SALMON TERIYAKI]

I always have a jar of homemade teriyaki sauce in the refrigerator, ready to turn chicken or oily fish into something more special. I also make different flavors of teriyaki by infusing it with garlic, chile, or ginger. Teriyaki sauce keeps for 2 weeks in the refrigerator.

Serves 4

4 salmon fillets, each weighing 4 oz.

½ teaspoon salt

For the teriyaki sauce

3 tablespoons soy sauce

3 tablespoons saké

3 tablespoons mirin

1 tablespoon granulated sugar (vary the amount to suit your taste)

Sprinkle the salt over the fish and refrigerate while you make the sauce. Put all the ingredients for the sauce in a shallow saucepan over a medium heat and stir to ensure that all the sugar dissolves. Bring to a boil, then reduce the heat to low and simmer until the sauce has been reduced by about a quarter. Let cool.

Pre-heat the oven to 350°F. Line a baking sheet with aluminum foil, put a rack on top and lay the fillets skin side down on the rack. Brush with the sauce, cook for 5 minutes, brush with more sauce and cook for another 3 minutes before brushing with sauce again. Repeat once or twice more until the fish is cooked. Transfer each fillet to a serving plate, drizzle over a small amount of teriyaki sauce and serve.

Buta rosu no yunan-zuke

[ROAST PORK FILLET IN YUNAN SAUCE]

Yunan sauce is soy sauce mixed with saké, mirin, and a citrus juice such as yuzu. I prefer to cook the meat first before marinating it in the sauce so that the juices from the cooked meat blend with the sauce, giving a delicious salad dressing. This is roast pork Japanese style—serve it with a generous quantity of salad leaves.

↘ *Roast pork fillet in yunan sauce.*

1 lb. pork fillet

1 garlic clove, finely shredded

Salt and pepper

For the yunan marinade

8 fl oz. (1 cup) soy sauce

3 fl oz. (5 tablespoons) saké

4 fl oz. (½ cup) mirin

2 tablespoons yuzu juice or 2 limes sliced into rings

7 oz. (6 cups) salad leaves of your choice

For the salad dressing

2 fl oz. (3½ tablespoons) yunan marinade

1 teaspoon shredded ginger root

4 tablespoons virgin olive oil

Rub the meat with the garlic, salt and pepper and leave to stand for 15 minutes. Meanwhile, preheat the oven to 425°F.

Line a roasting pan with aluminum foil and roast the meat for 15 minutes before reducing the oven temperature to 350°F and roast it for 20 minutes more. While the meat is cooking, mix all the ingredients for the marinade in a container big enough to hold the meat, then put the cooked meat straight into it to marinate overnight.

Just before eating, mix the salad dressing, take the meat out of the marinade and cut it into thin slices. Arrange the salad leaves on a large serving plate and lay the slices of pork on top. Dress and serve.

味噌 Miso [MISO]

Miso and soy sauce are the two most important seasoning ingredients in Japanese cuisine—they could be called the flavors of Japan—and they share the same origin although miso is the older of the two. Despite the Japanese way of life becoming more Western over the last 150 years, boiled rice, a small dish of pickles and a bowl of miso soup remains the archetypal Japanese meal. Millions of Japanese people still begin the day with miso soup.

History Miso is widely believed to be derived from an ancient salt preserve called *koku bishio,* a fermented mixture of salt and grains such as rice, soybeans and wheat. The technique for making miso was probably introduced from China at the same time as Buddhism; certainly by the eighth century miso was being made inside temple grounds and by farmers. Miso was an important field supply for warring samurai during the 150-year-long civil war which finally came to an end in the early seventeenth century.

How it is made Until recently, one would see straw ropes of *miso-dama* (miso balls) hanging under the eaves of rural farmhouses. Soybeans would be cooked, crushed and made into balls the size of ostrich eggs, then tied with straw ropes and hung up to grow a natural mold. The moldy balls would then be mixed with salt and water to make miso paste. Miso balls are a rare sight in Japan today.

There are four basic varieties of miso. The most popular variety, *kome miso* (rice miso), accounts for about 80 percent of total domestic production. It is made from boiled, crushed soybeans mixed with a culture called *koji,* made from rice. Salt is added and the moldy mixture is left to mature for 6 months to 3 years. *Mugi miso* is made with soybeans, wheat or barley, *koji* and salt, and is sometimes called *inaka miso,* meaning 'country miso,' as it is the variety often made by farmers in the countryside. A third variety is *mame miso,* so-called because it is made with soya beans, *koji,* and salt alone; the main producers of *mame miso* are concentrated in the area around Nagoya. The fourth variety is *chogo miso,* which is blended and seasoned with different flavorings.

Appearance and taste The color of miso ranges from light cream to almost black, taking in the golden brown of peanut butter and dark brown on the way. In general, the lighter the color the less salty the miso. All miso has a distinctive fermented-bean flavor and aroma.

Buying and storing In the West, miso is sold either in plastic packaging or in containers. If in doubt about which color miso to buy, choose the middle of the range, light brown one. Miso keeps for a long time if stored in an airtight container in the refrigerator.

Health benefits Miso is a very healthy food, packed as it is with vitamin E and various minerals. Easily digested —the protein of the soybeans has been converted into amino acid—miso is found to be effective in lowering high blood pressure and cholesterol. Some research suggests that miso wards off cancer; it certainly helps the liver cope with alcohol and nicotine. I find a bowl of miso soup is the best hangover cure!

Culinary uses Miso is a versatile seasoning ingredient. It can simply be dissolved with dashi broth to make soup or used in many simmering dishes and regional hot-pots. The light colored *shiro miso* (white miso) is sometimes called *saikyo miso.* A regional speciality of Kyoto, it makes an excellent marinade for tofu, fish, and meat. *Dengaku miso,* good for coating broiled tofu, is a delicious mixture of miso and a variety of seasonal ingredients. Miso is also used to make dressings.

Sake no miso yunan yaki

[SALMON MARINATED IN CITRUS MISO]

Here white miso is mixed with soy sauce, saké, and mirin and steeped with yuzu to give a wonderfully flavorsome sauce. The miso ensures that the marinated ingredient stays succulent even when cold.

Serves 4

4 salmon fillets, skin on, each weighing 4 oz.
½ teaspoon salt

For the miso yunan

8 fl oz. (1 cup) white miso paste
16 fl oz. (1¾ cups) saké
12 fl oz. (1⅛ cups) cup mirin
7 tablespoons soy sauce
7 tablespoons light soy sauce
2 tablespoons yuzu juice or 2 limes sliced into rings

First make the marinade. Put the miso paste in a large mixing bowl, add the saké and mirin little by little and mix well. Add both types of soy sauce and the yuzu juice and combine.

Sprinkle the salt over the salmon fillets and leave for 10 minutes before laying them in the miso mixture to marinate overnight.

Preheat the oven to 325°F. Take the fish out of the miso mixture and wipe it clean. Line a baking sheet with aluminum foil and lay the fillets on-a rack above it. Bake for 10 minutes, then turn over to cook the other side for another 10 minutes.

Tofu no miso-shiru

[MISO SOUP WITH TOFU]

This is the basic soup to which other ingredients can be added: spinach, green beans, snow peas, carrots, leeks, onions, eggplant, turnips, pumpkins, potatoes, mushrooms, bamboo shoots, cabbages, white-meat fish (such as sole, red snapper, sea bass), pork, and shellfish.

▸ *Making miso.*
▸ *Miso soup with tofu.*

Serves 4

1¾ pints (4 cups) konbu no tsuke dashi (see p.121)
2 oz. silken tofu (soft variety), diced
4 tablespoons light or medium colored miso paste
4 scallions, chopped diagonally

Heat the dashi broth in a saucepan over a medium heat. Do not let it boil as this will spoil the delicate flavor. Add the tofu, reduce the heat and simmer for 2 minutes.

To dissolve the miso paste, put it in a large ladle. Add a little hot broth to the ladle, and with a fork gently mix the broth with the miso to make a runny paste.

Submerge the ladle in the broth to wash away the paste and repeat the process until all the miso paste has dissolved. Add the chopped scallion and turn off the heat. Serve hot in individual bowls.

酢 Su [JAPANESE RICE VINEGAR]

The recent rise in the popularity of sushi in the West has turned the spotlight on Japanese rice vinegar. It is one of the oldest seasoning ingredients in the Japanese kitchen, introduced from China in the fourth century at the same time as the technique for brewing saké. According to a historic cookery book published in 1695, early rice vinegar was made with salted Japanese plums. The original rice vinegar was called *Izumi-su*, because it was first brewed in the region of Izumi (southern Osaka), or *kara-saké*, meaning 'bitter saké.' In 1649 a brewer in Nagoya first succeeded in manufacturing *kasu-su* (rice vinegar made from saké pulp). The invention of *kasu-su*, a much cheaper form of vinegar, revolutionized sushi, making it Japan's new fast food.

How it is made Unless labeled *yone-su* or *kome-su* (pure rice vinegar), most Japanese vinegars are called simply *su* or *kokumotsu-su* (grain vinegar) and contain other grains such as barley, wheat, and rice husks. The manufacturing process is a cross between that of saké and soy sauce. The rice is washed, soaked, and steamed, then yeast is added to form a rice culture called *koji*. This first fermentation produces alcohol and after fermenting for up to a year the alcohol becomes vinegar.

Appearance and taste Most rice vinegar is a light bronze color and has a beautiful aroma. It tastes pleasantly sweet and very mildly sour—not sharp like wine vinegar or distilled malt vinegar. A residue of sugar from the fermentation process remains, giving an average acidity of 4–5 percent.

Buying and storing Japanese vinegar is sold in bottles and will keep a very long time if stored in a cool, dark cupboard. Once the bottle is opened, the aroma soon deteriorates, so it is best to use it as soon as possible.

Health benefit Rice vinegar contains over 70 types of organic acid and 15 different types of amino acid, and this determines the taste and aroma. Many Japanese Buddhist monks live well into their nineties, a longevity which is attributed to extensive use of vinegar in their diet. Rice vinegar aids digestion. It is also, as I learnt from a friend who is a sushi chef, an excellent natural skin conditioner and I soak my hands in diluted vinegar.

Culinary uses Vinegar is one of the most widely used ingredients in the Japanese kitchen. It sterilizes, preserves, and acts as a natural antiseptic; it is also used to neutralize fishy odors, reduce saltiness, and tenderize meat. It brightens up the color of cooked vegetables and a small amount will highlight the flavor of almost any simmered or stewed dishes.

Sushi su

[SUSHI VINEGAR]

There are no fixed measurements when it comes to making sushi vinegar. The general rule is the stronger the filling or topping—meaty fish like tuna and mackerel count as 'strong'—the saltier and less sweet the vinegar mixture.

4 tablespoons rice vinegar
2 tablespoons granulated sugar
½ teaspoon salt

Mix all the ingredients in a non-metallic bowl and stir to dissolve all the sugar and salt. The above amount is for 10½ oz. (1½ cups) rice—dry weight. See below for how to prepare sushi rice.

Sushi meshi

[SUSHI RICE]

The importance of the rice is sometimes underestimated —too much attention is paid to the filling or topping. Good sushi begins with good quality rice and vinegar. Sushi rice can be prepared up to 3 hours in advance. Keep it covered to stop it hardening and do not refrigerate.

10½ oz. (1½ cups) Japanese-style short grain rice
1 piece dry konbu (kelp), postcard size
11 fl oz. (1⅓ cups) water
1 quantity sushi vinegar (see p.222)

Put the rice in a strainer and wash thoroughly until the water runs clear. Drain and leave to stand for 30 minutes before cooking. (This is to let each grain of rice absorb some water so that it needs less water for cooking, allowing for the addition of the sushi vinegar later.)

Make a few cuts in the konbu to help release its flavor. Put the washed rice and half pint of water in a heavy-based saucepan. Add the konbu and cover with a tight-fitting lid. Bring to a boil over a low to medium heat. Resist the temptation to lift the lid: just listen out for the sound of it bubbling. When it boils, turn the heat up to high and cook for 5 minutes more before turning off the heat and leaving it to steam for 10 minutes.

Meanwhile make up the sushi vinegar as described in the recipe.

Discard the konbu and transfer the cooked rice to a moistened shallow mixing tub. Pour a third of the vinegar over a spatula into the rice. Spread the rice evenly in the tub to make it cool more quickly. Add another third of the vinegar, using a slicing motion to coat the grains of rice and separate them. Fan the rice gently to help it cool.

Continue to fold the vinegar mixture into the rice with the spatula until it begins to look glossy and has cooled down to room temperature. Cover the rice with a clean damp dish towel until needed.

▸ Traditional rice vinegar barrels at Mitsukan vinegar museum.
▸ Asparagus with vinegar miso.

Asuparagasu to su-miso

[ASPARAGUS WITH VINEGAR MISO]

Su-miso is a traditional combination of two classic Japanese ingredients: rice vinegar and miso paste. This healthy sauce is simple to make and peps up any boiled vegetable.

Serves 4
1 bunch fresh asparagus, cleaned and trimmed
For the vinegar miso
7 oz. white miso paste
1 tablespoon granulated sugar
1 tablespoon saké
1 teaspoon rice vinegar
2 egg yolks

Steam the asparagus. In a mixing bowl, mix the miso, sugar, saké, and vinegar to a smooth paste. Add the egg yolks and stir well. Arrange the asparagus on 4 serving plates, spoon over the vinegar miso and serve.

味醂 Mirin [SWEET JAPANESE COOKING WINE]

Not surprisingly, the cooking wine most widely used in the Japanese kitchen is made of rice. There is no record of mirin, saké's younger brother, until 1593.

How it is made Mirin is made with steamed rice; *koji* (rice culture) and *shochu* (a Japanese spirit distilled from rice and other grains, such as barley, and starches such as sweet potatoes) are mixed, fermented, brewed, compressed and filtered.

Appearance and taste Mirin is an amber colored, syrupy liquid that has a mild aroma of saké. It tastes like very sweet saké. There are two varieties of mirin and a mirin-flavored synthetic saké. Mildly acidic *hon-mirin* is 45 percent sugar and 14 percent alcohol, while *hon-naoshi mirin* has a higher alcohol content of 22 percent. The mirin-flavored synthetic saké is a much cheaper alternative and is less than 1 percent alcohol.

Buying and storing All mirin is sold in bottles. Once opened, a sugary white substance will form around the cap: this is the residue from the evaporated alcohol and is harmless. The flavor and aroma of mirin deteriorate after the bottle is opened so it should be kept in the refrigerator.

Culinary uses Mirin not only brings sweetness and a faint aroma of saké, it also gives food an attractive shininess. It is used in many simmered dishes and in glazing sauces such as teriyaki. Although it is not intended to be used as a sweetener, 3 teaspoons of mirin will replace 1 teaspoon of sugar.

Nishime

[SIMMERED CHICKEN AND VEGETABLES]

A big dish of *nishime* always lifts my spirits: it's full of delicious vegetables all cut into pretty bite-size pieces and the many hours of gentle simmering fill the kitchen with a wonderful smell.

Serves 4
4 dried shiitake mushrooms, soaked in water
4 oz. skinless, boneless chicken thighs
2 tablespoons vegetable oil
12 snow peas, cut diagonally in half
½ carrot, peeled and cut into slices ½-inch thick
4 oz. (⅔ cup) renkon (lotus root), drained and quartered into chunks 1-inch thick
½ burdock, cut into 1-inch chunks
½ konnyaku (devil's tongue), cut into bite-size pieces
17 fl oz. (2 cups) dashi broth (see p.169)
4 fl oz. (½ cup) mirin
2 tablespoons granulated sugar
4 tablespoons light soy sauce

Start by reconstituting the dried shiitake mushrooms in a cup of hot water. Leave to soak for 10 minutes. When soft, discard the stalks, cut into quarters and reserve the juice.

Cut the chicken thighs into bite-size pieces. Heat a large shallow saucepan over a medium heat and add the oil. Cook the chicken, add the vegetables and sauté for 3 minutes. Add the dashi broth, mirin, sugar and soy sauce and reduce the heat to as low as it will go.

Cut out a circle of aluminum foil that is just smaller than the saucepan and sit it inside. Simmer for 1 hour or until almost all the liquid has disappeared. Serve hot or at room temperature.

Daikon to buta no nimono

[SIMMERED DAIKON WITH PORK]

A combination of fatty belly of pork and plain daikon makes this dish delicious and easy to digest.

Serves 4
10 oz. (1⅔–2 cups) daikon (Japanese radish), peeled
13 fl oz. (1½ cups) dashi broth (see p.169)
2 tablespoons mirin
2 tablespoons light soy sauce
4 oz. pork belly, thinly sliced
To garnish
2 scallion, finely chopped

Cut the daikon into slices ⅓ inch thick, then cut each slice into quarters. Put the dashi broth, mirin, and soy sauce in a saucepan and bring to a boil over a medium heat. As soon as the dashi mixture comes to a boil, reduce the heat to low and add the pork.

Cook for 20 minutes, then add the daikon slices and simmer until the cooking liquor has been reduced by half. Divide between 4 serving dishes, garnish with the chopped scallion and serve.

▲ *Simmered chicken and vegetables.*

This section is divided according to whether the drinks are alcoholic or non alcoholic. Japan's most traditional non alcoholic drink is, of course, green tea. Saké is Japan's most famous alcoholic drink and the term can be used to refer to other alcoholic drinks too. The growing popularity of Japanese cuisine seems to have resulted in a wider range of 'saké' being offered in restaurants and liquor stores.

Wagashi is a general term which covers all Japanese confectionery, not Western-style confectionery such as cakes and chocolates. Japanese confectionery is unique and quintessentially Japanese. All the ingredients—rice and other grains, pulses and sugar—are vegetarian; eggs and cooking oils are rarely used, and milk and other dairy products are completely absent. Most of all, wagashi are works of art—delicate creations which reflect the beauty of nature in an entirely Japanese way. Flowers, trees, wild birds, animals, and the transient nature of the seasons are all represented.

14 Drinks & confectionery

茶 Cha [TEA]

Japanese people have been drinking tea since ancient times. It was introduced from China in the sixth century at the same time as Buddhism, though initially the upper classes regarded it as medicinal. Tea did not become popular as a drink until the late twelfth century when Zen Buddhism spread through Japan (see p.16). Nowadays the daily tea drunk in Japan tends to be 'green' tea, rather than brown or red tea from China and India—Japan grows different varieties and has its own manufacturing methods.

How it is made Top quality teas such as maccha, gyokuro, and sen-cha are protected from direct sunlight for 1–3 weeks before being harvested in early May. This increases the level of amino acid in the young leaves and reduces bitterness. Freshly picked leaves are immediately steamed to prevent fermentation and discoloration, then are dried, firstly by a rolling and scrunching process and secondly by hot air.

Appearance and taste The appearance and taste of tea varies hugely. The color, shape and size of the leaves, and the color, clarity, aroma, and flavor of the brew, determine the quality of tea.

Maccha This is powdered tea, which is used mainly in formal tea ceremonies. A little macha is added to hot water in individual bowls and stirred with a small bamboo whisk. Made from freshly picked young leaves that are steamed, dried flat, and then powdered, maccha is bright green, with a distinctive aroma and a slightly sweet taste.

Gyokuro 'Dewdrop of a jewel' is, as its elegant name suggests, the best quality leaf tea and this quality is reflected in its price. Baby leaves are handpicked in early spring, then steamed, dried, and finely rolled. A glossy deep green, this tea has a delicate but refreshing aroma and should be brewed not in boiling water but in warm water about 120°F.

Sen-cha This literally means infused tea—it is middle-of-the-road, everyday tea. Brew this in the same way as gyokuro (see p.229) but use hotter water.

Ban-cha This is Japan's equivalent of strong tea. A coarse tea, it is served freely at Japanese restaurants as it is the most suitable tea to drink with a meal. There are varying grades of ban-cha: the lower the grade the larger the leaves and the more stems and twigs it has. Brew it with boiling hot water.

Hoji-cha Hoji-cha—roasted ban-cha—is a slightly bitter, smoky brown tea with character, sometimes served at the end of a meal. Brew it in the same way as ban-cha.

Genmai-cha This is a mixture of ban-cha and toasted grains of rice. Yellowish green, it has a pleasant nutty flavor. Brew it in the same way as ban-cha.

Mugi-cha This is not strictly tea at all, as it is made from roasted whole grains of barley and drunk chilled in summer. Nowadays mugi-cha is more often sold in large teabags that one infuses in cold water. Brown and nutty tasting, it makes a refreshing summer drink.

▾ *A rolling, deep green tea plantation.*

▾ *Maccha.*

▾ *Genmai-cha.*

A perfect cup of gyokuro tea

Serves 4

Fill a small teapot with boiling hot water and pour the water into 4 small teacups. Allow the teapot to cool down a little and add 4 teaspoons gyokuro tea leaves.

Let the water in the teacups reach a temperature of 120–140°F, then pour it back into the teapot. Leave to brew for 2 minutes. Swirl the teapot before half-filling each teacup. Top them up in reverse order so that the infused tea is shared out equally.

Maccha ice cream with adzuki bean paste

This is not strictly a drink recipe but I think you will like it. It is an extremely easy recipe that will give a sophisticated Japanese touch to the end of your dinner.

Serves 4

1 heaped tablespoon maccha powder
2 tablespoons tepid water
1 lb. high-quality vanilla ice cream

To serve

4 tablespoons ready-made, canned sweet adzuki paste

▲ *Sen-cha.*

Put the maccha powder in a large mixing bowl, add the water and mix well to dissolve. Add half the ice cream, mix thoroughly, then add the rest of the ice cream.

You can mix until the ice cream is uniformly pale green or stop while it is still streaky.

Freeze for 1 hour. Allow 2 scoops per person and serve with a tablespoon of the sweet adzuki paste on top.

Maccha

[MACCHA]

Maccha is not drunk as an everyday tea; a small amount is served in a bowl at formal tea ceremonies. A bowl of maccha is Japan's equivalent of a shot of espresso coffee —it is very strong and will keep you awake if you drink too much of it. To get the most out of the experience, eat a Japanese candy beforehand.

Serves 4

Warm a bowl (a deep soup bowl is ideal) with hot water and dip in the tip of a bamboo whisk (or a small metal one) to stop the tea staining it. Discard the water.

Put 1–2 teaspoons of maccha powder in the bowl and add 2 fl oz. (4 tablespoons) hot, but not boiling, water.

Using the bamboo whisk, first stir, then whisk vigorously, until all the tea powder is dissolved and the tea becomes frothy.

酒 Saké [JAPANESE RICE WINE]

Japan's most traditional alcoholic beverage is made from fermented rice. Although it has long since been overtaken by beer and, more recently, wine as a mealtime drink, its culinary and cultural significance cannot be overstated. The fact that more varieties of saké, of a better quality, are now available outside Japan has made it an internationally recognized drink.

How it is made The method for brewing saké is the most complex of any beverage on earth. Although it has undergone many technical refinements, the basic procedure has always remained the same. A special variety of rice is milled (or polished), washed, and steamed. Rice lacks the enzymes essential for converting rice starch into sugar, but a yeast called *koji* can produce these enzymes and those necessary to convert the sugar to alcohol. The *koji* is added to the steamed rice, which is fermented at a high temperature and humidity in a special room. Mixing *koji*, plain steamed rice, water, and pure yeast cells creates a yeast starter called *moto*. Over the next two weeks, a mixture of highly concentrated yeast cells is developed. After the mixture has been moved to a larger tank, more rice, *koji*, and water are added in three stages to make a mash called *moromi*, which is left to ferment for 18–32 days. This mash is then pressed, filtered and pasteurized before being left to age for about six months.

Appearance and taste Clear to look at, saké is said to have as many as 400 flavor components. There are five basic qualities, however—dryness, sweetness, bitterness, acidity, and astringency/ tartness—and each brand of saké has its own unique combination of these five qualities. Saké should have a subtle but not overpowering aroma.

Buying and storing The saké labeling system has improved greatly, making it more accessible for both Japanese and non Japanese. Some labels carry *nihonshu-do*, which gives the buyer some idea of the dryness or sweetness of the saké, based on the amount of residual sugar and alcohol. The scale ranges from very dry (+15) to very sweet (–15), with a neutral value typically being somewhere between –3 and +5. The *sanmi-do* refers to the acidity, which indicates the lightness or heaviness of the saké, ranging from 0.6 to 2.8—the higher the figure, the heavier the saké. Choosing saké is a matter of personal taste and to make it more confusing, price gives very little guidance. If neither of these figures is available or is written in Japanese and you can't read them, ask for *dai-ginjo*, *ginjo*, *junmai-shu* or *hon-jozo*.

Dai-ginjo is the highest quality saké available and is the most expensive. At the polishing stage, at least 50 percent of each grain of rice is removed, leaving a core of pure starch. To make the next highest-quality sake, *ginjo*, at least 40 per-cent of each grain must be polished off. *Junmai-shu* means 'pure rice saké' (no sugar or alcohol is added), while *honjozo* is made from rice that has had 30 percent of the grain removed and some alcohol added.

▲ *A couple enjoy their saké (a bottle each!) in a Japanese restaurant.*

Saké keeps a reasonably long time if stored in a cool, dark place. Drink it within a few weeks of opening, as the aroma and flavor will deteriorate.

Culinary uses In cooking, saké adds flavor and depth to many dishes. It is also used in marinades and to neutralize the strong smell of fish and meat.

Shochu Literally translated, this means 'fiery spirits.' It is a spirit distilled from rice and other grains and pulses, as well as sweet potatoes. Once considered the poor man's saké, it has recently become fashionable, especially among young people, who drink it as a cocktail. It has a high alcohol content of 20–25 percent, reaching as high as 45 percent in some varieties. It is normally drunk diluted with hot or cold water or other mixers such as soda water, depending on the season.

Tori no sake mushi

[CHICKEN STEAMED IN SAKÉ]

Steaming is a very gentle way of cooking—because the chicken or fish or whatever you are steaming does not come in direct contact with water or cooking liquid, the taste is enhanced and the flavor of the saké comes through.

Serves 4
14 oz. skinless, boneless chicken thighs
½ teaspoon salt
4 fl oz. (½ cup) saké
To serve
4 teaspoons wasabi power, mixed with the same
    amount of water
Soy sauce

Prick the chicken all over with a fork and lay it flat in a shallow dish. Sprinkle over the salt, add the saké and set aside for at least 3 hours or overnight.

Place the chicken in its dish in a steamer and steam for 20–30 minutes or until the chicken is cooked. Let the chicken cool down inside the steamer.

Cut the chicken into slices and arrange on 4 serving plates. Serve with a small mound of wasabi paste on the side and drizzle with soy sauce.

Madam Butterfly

[JAPANESE BLOODY MARY]

I invented this cocktail—and have since become rather fond of it!

Serves 4
14 fl oz. (1¾ cups) tomato juice
4 fl oz. (½ cup) shochu
4 teaspoons yuzu (or lime) juice
To serve
½ teaspoon sansho pepper

Mix the tomato juice, shochu, and yuzu juice together. Divide between 4 chilled glasses and serve with a sprinkling of sansho pepper.

▾ *Japanese bloody mary.*

和菓子 Wagashi [JAPANESE CONFECTIONERY]

The advent of Buddhism in the middle of the sixth century brought with it a wide range of items from China, including *Togashi* (literally 'fruits from China'). Before the sixth century the only snacks available to the Japanese were fruit and nuts, but by the eighth century 20 types of *Togashi* were being eaten at imperial court banquets and religious ceremonies. *Senbei* (rice biscuits) were among the earliest Togashi and they are eaten to this day.

With Zen Buddhism in the twelfth century came the reintroduction of tea drinking and the practice of eating light snacks between meals. This period produced *yokan* and *manju wagashi*, both of which have survived to this day. The mid sixteenth century, when Portuguese traders arrived in Japan, saw another important change in Japanese confectionery: Western confectionery, such as kasutera (sponge cakes) and *konpeito* (star-shaped sugar lumps), made with sugar, eggs, and oil, dazzled the Japanese with its richness and sweetness. Wagashi developed and flourished, becoming an established part of the country's diet, and by the early Edo period (1603–1868)—a formative time for modern Japanese cuisine—a confectionery shop in the center of Edo (later Tokyo) was selling 172 different varieties of wagashi.

Wagashi are not eaten as desserts at the end of a meal, but more as an accompaniment to tea. Today there are countless kinds of Japanese confectionery made and sold all over the country, and each town and village has its own local specialities. They can be divided into three basic groups: *higashi* (dry confectionery), made from rice flour or the flour of other grains and cooked until dry and often hard; *nama-gashi* (raw confectionery), made of raw or semi-cooked ingredients, which contain a lot of liquid, so are often very soft and do not keep for more that a few days; and *han-nama-gashi* (half-raw confectionery), which covers everything in between. *Han-nama-gashi* are often made from fresh ingredients, but because they are cooked and contain less water, they are slightly harder and keep longer than *nama-gashi*. The following are the wagashi most likely to be found in the West.

Senbei (Rice biscuits) Senbei are made mainly from rice flour mixed with water; the dough is then steamed, kneaded, shaped, and dried before finally being toasted or deep-fried in oil and seasoned. One of the oldest forms of wagashi, they were first introduced from China sometime between the sixth and eighth centuries.

Rakugan This is a good example of dry confectionery. Rakugan means literally 'fallen wild goose'—there are stories about how it acquired its curious name. It is made from rice flour, wheat flour, and powdered soybean or other powdered grains and pulses mixed with sugar and pressed into various shaped molds. It appears regularly at tea ceremonies.

Yokan The ingredient most commonly used to make *han-nama-gashi* is sweet adzuki bean paste, though sometimes sweet potatoes or sweet chestnuts are used. Sweet adzuki bean paste comes semi-cooked in a firm, rectangular block about the size of a pencil case and keeps for several weeks. Taste and appearance vary, since ingredients such as nuts, citrus fruits, beans, and even green tea powder are used to flavor and color it.

Manju Another popular form of semi-cooked confectionery, manju is a sort of filled bun, made from wheat or rice flour and steamed or sometimes toasted. In China, where manju originated, the fillings are normally meat, while the Japanese have always preferred beans and other sweet fillings such as fruit. In Japan, practically every natural beauty spot, temple, and shrine has its own manju of different shapes, colors and flavors.

Daifuku-mochi This is a simple, semi-cooked cake, made of sticky glutinous rice paste stuffed with sweet adzuki bean paste. Steaming the rice flour gives an elastic dough that is smooth and opaque. It is one of the most popular varieties of confectionery in Japan and is sold all year round.

Ohagi/Bota-mochi Ohagi is another very popular wagashi. It delights both young and old at seasonal festivals such as the cherry blossom viewing in April, the spring and autumn equinoxes, and the moon viewing evenings in autumn. I must confess that I have a complete weakness for this sweet and sticky dumpling. One of my fondest childhood memories is of watching my grandmother steaming a mixture of normal eating rice and sticky glutinous rice, forming egg-size balls and then covering them with sweet adzuki bean paste, sesame seeds or the aromatic, roasted soybean powder that is known as *kinako*.

Azuki mizu yokan

[SWEET ADZUKI AND KANTEN CAKE]

Yokan (hard-set sweet adzuki bean paste) is a very popular Japanese confectionary. Mizu yokan is a much softer and lighter version that is eaten chilled in the summer.

Serves 4
½ stick kanten (see p.128), dry weight of ¼ oz.,
   soaked in water for 1 hour
8 fl oz. (1 cup) water
4 oz. (½ cup) granulated sugar
5 oz. ready-made, canned sweet adzuki bean paste

Drain the kanten and squeeze dry with your hands. Put in a saucepan, add the water, bring to a boil and gently simmer for 15 minutes until the kanten has completely dissolved. Add the sugar, stir to dissolve and remove from the heat. Pour through a fine strainer into a bowl.

Add the adzuki paste to the sweetened kanten mixture and stir well until the paste is dissolved. Put the mixing bowl over cold water, stirring gently to prevent the bean paste from settling at the bottom.

When the mixture has begun to set, transfer to a metal or plastic container measuring about 8 x 6 inches, which you have first lined with clingfilm. Leave to set at room temperature. Take it out of the mold by lifting the plastic wrap, cut into 4 equal portions and serve.

Shiratama manju

[SWEET DUMPLINGS]

I try not to make these too often as I end up eating them all. They are soft and very comforting.

Makes 12 dumplings (6 plain, 6 with sesame seeds)
5 oz. ready-made, canned sweet adzuki bean paste
7 oz. shiratama-ko (rice drops, see p.33)
4 fl oz. (½ cup) water
3 tablespoons toasted white sesame seeds

Divide the adzuki bean paste into 12 equal portions and roll each portion into a small ball.

In a bowl, add a little water at a time to the shiratama-ko and mix well to make a dryish mixture. Divide into 12 dumplings, the size of a golf ball, and put an adzuki paste ball in the center of each one.

Roll 6 of the dumplings in sesame seeds and leave six plain. Put 4 of the dumplings into a large mixing bowl lined with waxed paper, cover the bowl with plastic wrap, and microwave for 1½ minutes. Repeat the process twice to cook the remaining 8 dumplings. Serve at room temperature.

▲ *Sweet dumplings.*

Resources

useful addresses

UK & Ireland

Akaneya
81 Northumberland Avenue,
Reading RG2 7PW
T: 00 44 (0)118 931 0448

Arigato Japanese Supermarket
48–50 Brewer Street, London W1
T: 00 44 (0)20 7287 1722

Asia Market
18 Drury Street, Dublin 2, Ireland

Asta 1
22–26 Broad Street Place, Eldon
Street, London EC2M 7JY
T: 00 44 (0)20 7638 2404

Atari-Ya
7 Station Parade, Noel Road,
London W3
T: 00 44 (0)20 8896 1552

JA Centre
Unit B, Eley Industrial Estate,
Eley Road, London N18
T: 00 44 (0)20 8803 8942

Marimo
350–356 Regent's Park Road,
Finchley, London N3
T: 00 44 (0)20 8346 1042

Midori
19 Marlborough Place, Brighton,
East Sussex BN1 1UB
T: 00 44 (0)1273 601 460

Muji (Soho)
26 Great Marlborough Street,
London W1V 1HL
T: 00 44 (0)20 7494 1197

Natural House
Japan Centre, 212 Piccadilly,
London W1V
T: 00 44 (0)20 7434 4218

Oriental City
399 Edgware Road, London NW9
T: 00 44 (0)20 8346 1042

Setsu Japan
196A Heaton Road, Newcastle-
Upon-Tyne NE6
T: 00 44 (0)191 265 9970

Wing Yip
395 Edgware Road, London NW2
T: 00 44 (0)20 8450 0422

544 Purley Way, Croydon CRO
T: 00 44 (0)20 8688 4880

375 Nechells Park Road,
Nechells, Birmingham B7 5NT
T: 00 44 (0)121 327 6618

Oldham Road, Ancoats,
Manchester M4 5HU
T: 00 44 (0)161 832 3215

Holland

Toko Dun Yong
Stormsteeg 9, 1012 BD
Amsterdam
T: 00 31 (0)20 622 1763

Australia

Daimaru
211 Latrobe Street, Melbourne,
VIC 3000
T: 00 61 (0)3 9660 6666

David Jones
86–108 Castlereagh Street,
Sydney, NSW 2000
T: 00 61 (2) 9266 5544

Germany

Trieu Asia Food Versand GMBH
Theodor-Heuss-Strasse 30–32,
70806 Kornwestheim
T: 00 49 (0)71 54 80 26 88

USA & Canada

Fujiya Fish & Japanese Foods
3524 Shelbourne, Victoria,
Vancouver, Canada
T: 00 1 250 598 3711

Hamakko
88 Lincoln Highway, Rahway,
New Jersey, USA
T: 00 1 732 382 5628

Maruwa
1746 Post Street, San Francisco,
CA 94115, USA
T: 00 1 415 771 2583

Midori Mart
2104 Chestnut Street,
Philadelphia, PA 19103, USA
T: 00 1 215 569 3381

Miyamoto
382 Victoria, Westmount,
Montreal, Quebec, Canada
T: 00 1 514 481 1952

Saga Mini Mart
122 East 42nd Street,
New York, USA
T: 00 1 212 661 3299

useful websites

www.asia-online-shop.de
www.japanweb.co.uk
www.mountfuji.co.uk
www.japanesefood.about.com

Index

photographic acknowledgements

Key: GI – Getty Images; C – Corbis; LP – Lonely Planet; I – Impact Photo Library; RH – Robert Harding; PPS – Pacific Press Service; TI – Travel Ink;
(t) – top; (m) – middle; (b) – bottom; (l) – left; (r) – right

2 Jun Miki/GI; 6 (t) Dimitri Kessel/GI; 6 (b) Photowood Inc./C; 7 (t l) Antony Giblin/LP; 7 (t r) Christopher Rennie/RH; 7 (b l) Martin Moos/LP; 7 (b r) Jun Miki/GI; 9 (l) Asian Art & Archaeology, Inc./C; 9 (r) Carl Mydans/GI; 10 (l) Frank Carter/LP; 10 (r) James Marshall/C; 11 Takao Nishida/PPS; 12 (l) Simon Rowe/LP; 12 (r) P. Van Riel/RH; 13 (l) Chris Stock/TI; 13 (r) Shunji Kamemura/PPS; 14 Tadashi Kajiyama/I; 15 Tadashi Kajiyama/I; 16 Steve Vidler/PPS; 17 (t) Yo Nagata/PPS; 17 (b) Akira Kaede/GI; 18 Toshitaka Morita/PPS; 19 Bettmann/C; 20 (l) Michael Gover/I; 20 (r) Michael Freeman/C; 21 Tom Wagner/C SABA; 22 Asian Art & Archaeology, Inc./C; 22 (t) J. Greenberg/RH; 22 (b) Christie's Images/C; 24 Horace Bristol/C; 27 (t) Michael S. Yamashita/C; 27 (b) Shuzo Mitsui/PPS; 28 Horace Bristol/C; 30 (l) Junko Kimura/GI; 30 (r) Oliver Strewe/LP; 35 Robert B. George/PPS; 36 Oliver Strewe/LP; 38 Liz Thompson/LP; 40 Peter Guttman/C; 42 Masaaki Horimachi/PPS; 46 Bettman/C; 48 Yashiaki Nagashima/PPS; 50 Bettman/C; 56 Michael S. Yamashita/C; 58 Tadashi Shinohara/PPS; 64 Michael S. Yamashita/C; 68 Royalty-Free/C; 70 Michael S. Yamashita/C; 72 Shigenobu Hayashi/PPS; 74 Noritoshi Yamaguchi/PPS; 76 Hiroshi Fujita/PPS; 80 Image Eye/PPS; 84 (l) Kelly-Mooney Photography/C; 84 (r) G. Hellier/RH; 86 Shigenobu Hayashi/PPS; 88 Michael S. Yamashita/C; 92 (l) Noritoshi Yamaguchi/PPS; 92 (r) Oliver Strewe/LP; 94 Ric Ergenbr/C; 96 Horace Bristol/C; 98 Michael S. Yamashita/C; 100 Michael S. Yamashita/C; 104 Shigenobu Hayashi/PPS; 108 Michael S. Yamashita/C; 112 Takao Nishida/PPS; 118 Takanori Yamakawa/PPS; 120 Michael S. Yamashita/C; 123 James Marshall/C; 124 Michael S. Yamashita/C; 126 Horace Bristol/C; 128 Shigenobu Hayashi/PPS; 130 Dave Bartruff/C; 132 Ben Simmons/PPS; 134 Katsuji Iwao/PPS; 136 Natalie Fobes/C; 142 Michael S. Yamashita/C; 144 Michael S. Yamashita/C; 146 Michael Freeman/C; 148 Jeffrey L. Rotman/C; 156 Michael S. Yamashita/C; 158 Christie's Images/C; 160 Michael S. Yamashita/C; 162 Takeo Shimizu/Photo Bank/PPS; 164 Takeo Shimizu/Photo Bank/PPS; 166 Joel W. Rogers/C; 169 Tadashi Shinohara/PPS; 172 Martin Moos/LP; 174 Martin Moos/LP; 178 Takashi Yamaguchi/PPS; 180 Gideon Mendel/C; 186 Kinji Kanai/PPS; 187 Oliver Strewe/LP; 190 Gary Braasch/C; 193 Noritoshi Yamaguchi/PPS; 198 Kinji Kanai/PPS; 200 Archivo Iconografico, S.A./C; 206 (l) Shuzo Mitsui/PPS; 206 (r) Kazuo Matsukura/PPS; 210 Michael S. Yamashita/C; 212 Michael Busselle/C; 214 Michael S. Yamashita/C; 216 James Marshall/C; 218 B.S.P.I/C; 220 Katsuji Iwao/PPS; 222 Kimiko Barber; 226 Shigenobu Hayashi/PPS; 228 Satoshi Onuki/PPS; 230 Michael S. Yamashita/C